LexisNexis
Questions and Answers

Property Law
2nd edition

LexisNexis
Questions and Answers

Property Law

2nd edition

Laura-Leigh Cameron-Dow

LLB (Hons) (Bond), Grad Dip Legal Prac, (College of
Law), LeTTOl (Sheffield), PhD Cand (Bond)
Adjunct Teaching Fellow, School of Law, Bond University

LexisNexis Butterworths
Australia
2012

LexisNexis

AUSTRALIA	LexisNexis Butterworths
	475–495 Victoria Avenue, Chatswood NSW 2067
	On the internet at: www.lexisnexis.com.au
ARGENTINA	LexisNexis Argentina, BUENOS AIRES
AUSTRIA	LexisNexis Verlag ARD Orac GmbH & Co KG, VIENNA
BRAZIL	LexisNexis Latin America, SAO PAULO
CANADA	LexisNexis Canada, Markham, ONTARIO
CHILE	LexisNexis Chile, SANTIAGO
CHINA	LexisNexis China, BEIJING, SHANGHAI
CZECH REPUBLIC	Nakladatelství Orac sro, PRAGUE
FRANCE	LexisNexis SA, PARIS
GERMANY	LexisNexis Germany, FRANKFURT
HONG KONG	LexisNexis Hong Kong, HONG KONG
HUNGARY	HVG-Orac, BUDAPEST
INDIA	LexisNexis, NEW DELHI
ITALY	Dott A Giuffrè Editore SpA, MILAN
JAPAN	LexisNexis Japan KK, TOKYO
KOREA	LexisNexis, SEOUL
MALAYSIA	LexisNexis Malaysia Sdn Bhd, PETALING JAYA, SELANGOR
NEW ZEALAND	LexisNexis, WELLINGTON
POLAND	Wydawnictwo Prawnicze LexisNexis, WARSAW
SINGAPORE	LexisNexis, SINGAPORE
SOUTH AFRICA	LexisNexis Butterworths, DURBAN
SWITZERLAND	Staempfli Verlag AG, BERNE
TAIWAN	LexisNexis, TAIWAN
UNITED KINGDOM	LexisNexis UK, LONDON, EDINBURGH
USA	LexisNexis Group, New York, NEW YORK
	LexisNexis, Miamisburg, OHIO

National Library of Australia Cataloguing-in-Publication entry

Author:	Cameron-Dow, L-L.
Title:	Property law.
Edition:	2nd edition.
ISBN:	9780409326468 (pbk).
	9780409331790 (ebook).
Series:	LexisNexis Questions and Answers.
Notes:	Includes index.
Subjects:	Property law — Australia.
Dewey Number:	346.9404

Typeset in Sabon and Optima.

Printed in China.

Visit LexisNexis Butterworths at www.lexisnexis.com.au

Contents

Contents

Preface

The purpose of this text is to provide students of property law with an accessible reference point for tutorial and exam questions. The text is divided into sections which match the breakdown of topics in most tertiary institutions' curricula. There is no right or wrong order; the subject has too many different approaches to try and determine one as better than another. It is hoped that the breakdown here follows a certain logic, in that some topics build on the previous, but in many ways a number of property law topics are discrete, and any order is therefore, unsurprisingly, discretionary.

The questions and answers which comprise the backbone of this text are meant to be typical of the kinds of problems which confront property law students in tutorials and exams. Suggested timeframes for completion of answers are included, but with the caveat that this will always be a matter for the individual examiner. Naturally, there is a great difference between what might be expected from a student who is given weeks of investigation to devote to an answer submitted as a research task, and a student who must complete an answer in a short period during a closed-book exam. Some of the questions call for a rather traditional 'essay-style' approach, while others require a more practically oriented 'problem-style' technique to be employed. Many questions may necessitate a synthesis of each of these strategies.

The model answers provided here do not purport to be 'model' in the sense of 'perfect' or 'flawless'. First, there is no such thing as a 'perfect answer' in the study of law. As a discipline, we devote time and skill to being able to identify the opposing view to an issue, and so every answer will have multiple perspectives — some more readily justifiable and generally accepted than others. Every case, every circumstance and situation, is unique. Legal work, like the human behaviour which is its object, is not an objective science. It would be fair to say that many of the answers provided here are deficient or incomplete in some way — there is always one more argument, one more reference and one more perspective that could be included. However, these answers still serve a purpose — they underscore some of the subjective and idiosyncratic aspects of legal problem-solving.

On the other hand, there are certainly some important problem-solving techniques which should be employed by any legal student. A meticulous reading of the hypothetical facts is always important, and often overlooked, particularly under the stress of exam conditions. An extra five minutes reading is well worth it, when compared with 45 minutes spent on addressing the wrong issue! An ability to identify and separate legal issues and problems from unconnected material is fundamental to all types of legal problem-solving. Similarly, it is always vital to set out an answer in a coherent and logical configuration. Presentation and style should be tailored to maximise the reader's comprehension. Throughout the text students should endeavour to compare the 'model' answers with some of the pointers included under the heading 'Examiner's Comments', which follows each answer which might give insight to other avenues that could have been explored in the answer.

In addition to these technical tips, the 'Examiner's Comments' section often provides further references to relevant materials. Along with the section entitled 'Keep in Mind', the notes should assist students in identifying extra material, and also make them aware of the pitfalls associated with that particular type of question.

It is hoped that this text shall be of some use to students of property law in developing some of the technical skills, as well as the detailed and specific knowledge, which are the dual requisites of every competent property lawyer. While the subject sometimes seems tough, the concepts have multiple applications and form a core part of any lawyer's legal knowledge.

I would like to thank my own past teachers, Professor Michael Weir and Assistant Professor Winnie Ma, for instilling in me such an appreciation of property law which has led to my enjoyment in teaching it, and my recognition of how widely applicable are its concepts and rules. I would also like to thank Dr Tina Hunter for her assistance in writing Chapter 6 for this book.

Do not doubt that mastery of the subject is absolutely achievable, and I hope this text assists you in reaching that goal.

Laura-Leigh Cameron-Dow

Table of Cases

References are to paragraphs

Table of Cases

Table of Statutes

References are to paragraphs

Chapter 1

Concepts of Property and the Doctrines of Tenure and Estates

Key Issues

1-1 All property law courses taught at Australian tertiary institutions attempt some analysis of the conceptual and theoretical bases of property law. No two do it in quite the same way. Some lecturers begin the subject with a broad theoretical background to property law, providing a theoretical backdrop against which the later practical constructs can be overlaid. Others focus on the concrete practical applications of property law, and leave the theory to the end, as a concluding overview of what lies behind the application the students have already learned. Both of these educational models naturally include attempts to combine 'black letter' law with conceptual material, either by looking back upon theories, or by building towards a theory-based finale. A third model interweaves practical application and theory throughout the course, without separating concepts into a distinct topic. All approaches are equally valid. In this text some of the more theoretical concepts have been included here at the beginning. Later chapters also include reference to the theoretical foundations underpinning each specific topic, weaving them in with the more practical approaches to problem-based questions.

A theoretical approach to property law encompasses almost too broad a range of issues to give any meaningful description. Beyond the more pure philosophical questions such as 'what is property?', there lie questions which call for ethical, historical or economic inputs. These questions often focus upon justifications for, or objections to, the idea of property — either in specific contexts or more universally. They frequently come to the fore when a court or other institution is asked to recognise or protect 'rights' of a novel kind, or when long established rules are challenged as unjust or impractical, which occurred during the recognition of native title rights. For example, we all understand and value (at least to some degree) the idea of privacy but is privacy a thing which is capable of ownership? And how does privacy for an individual differ from the commercial concept of confidential information which is so valued by corporations? Should these rights be considered personal property rights or are they more appropriately founded in contracts or torts law? There are many other instances where novel 'rights' are asserted. Do we own our own bodies? If we do then we should be able to sell parts of them — a practice which that has led to incalculable misery and exploitation in many economically disadvantaged countries. The term 'rights' can also be used to discriminate and differentiate and create inequality, and we should constantly question the continued maintenance of time-honoured assumptions and practices. In Australia, as in many other common law countries such as New Zealand and Canada, the question of native title or 'land rights' has provided the *sine qua non* of property-centred conceptual, theoretical and philosophical debate. All of the cultural, historical, economic and personal issues referred to above can be seen in the struggle of indigenous peoples for the recognition of their unique relationship to the land.

This chapter also covers two ancient common law doctrines of property law — the doctrines of tenure and estates. Long thought to be little more than historical driftwood, in recent years (and largely as a result of the partial recognition of Aboriginal land rights by common law courts), these doctrines have re-emerged as significant to our understanding of the basic theoretical underpinnings of the law of property.

1-2   Before attempting the following questions, please ensure you are familiar with the following:

✓ philosophical and theoretical treatments of private property as they have developed in western society and culture;

✓ recent developments in the legal recognition of native title rights in Australia, as well as in comparable jurisdictions such as Canada and New Zealand;

✓ the role of the state in regulating and modifying private property rights, particularly with respect to the rights of women;

✓ statutory provisions which empower the courts to vary private property rights on the basis of 'marriage-like' relationships, for example, de facto relationships legislation.

Question 1

1-3   What arguments have been made for and against the institution of private property?

Time allowed: 45 mins

Answer Plan

1-4 This question calls for a fairly straightforward approach. The basic task is descriptive in nature, although a better answer will adopt a critical approach and commentary. There are probably many ways to tackle this question, and thus many ways to set out an answer plan; a simple strategy is mapped out below. If this question was attempted as a 'tutorial' essay, then it would be advisable to expand on the plan. Remember that under exam conditions even a simple plan, such as the one below, will help you keep within the permitted time constraints. Preparing a plan under exam conditions is never a waste of time and will keep you structured and on track in your answer:

- Introduction;
- Arguments for ...
    - ♦ the 'first occupation' theory;
    - ♦ the 'labour' theory;
    - ♦ the 'economic efficiency' theory;
    - ♦ the 'idealist' theory,
- Arguments against ...
    - ♦ property is theft or slavery;
    - ♦ property leads to, or entrenches, inequality;
    - ♦ property as a power relationship — Marxist analyses,
- Conclusion.

Answer

1-5 As a cultural institution, private property is virtually universal throughout human societies. By contrast, although traces of communal ownership still exist in the legal systems of most states, it is essentially only within a few indigenous societies that the concept of communal property can be said to dominate. Private property concepts otherwise govern the lives of most people. The numerous theoretical foundations for the institution of private property can be grouped under four broad headings: the 'first occupation' theory; the 'labour' theory; the 'economic efficiency' theory; and the 'idealist' theory. Some of the arguments against the institution of private property are inherent within the theoretical justifications. There have, over centuries, also been objections to the conventional justifications on more general bases. Similarly, in order of increasing sophistication, arguments against the institution of private property may be conveniently grouped as follows: property is theft or slavery; property leads to or entrenches inequality; and property as a power relationship, including Marxist analyses of private property.

'First occupation' theory

1-6 The 'first occupation' (or 'earliest possession') theory accords legal protection to the claims of the first or earliest possessor of land or a thing. It is encapsulated in the saying that possession is nine-tenths of the law. The theory is most appropriate where there is an abundance of the thing which is being claimed, normally a rarity. In reality the 'first occupation' theory is of limited application, being evident mainly in disputes over abandoned chattels and land. The theory does not provide a general justification for private property rights; it merely accounts for why a superior right is accorded to an earlier possessor (as against subsequent possessors). With regards to goods, the expedience of rules based upon possession is clear. However, with regards to land where the right claimed may be virtually perpetual, arguments based upon expedience are harder to sustain. For this reason, at least in international law (which long supported the claims of colonising states on the basis of the 'first possession' theory), the theory has been criticised.

'Labour' theory

1-7 The 'labour' theory is generally accredited to John Locke. It is embodied in the aphorism 'as the sower sows, so shall he reap'. The theory is based on the idea that the expenditure of energy by a person in creating or adapting a thing justifies private ownership. The theory is easy to understand in the context of a society where a person is individually engaged in the production of individual material items, such as a farmer producing his or her own crop or a carpenter producing furniture. It is more difficult to recognise the relevance of this theory in complex economies where service industries account for the labours of many, or in a society where many goods are mass produced requiring multiple production processes and hundreds of people. Intellectual property rights are probably the most common modern example of the application of the theory.

Several objections have been offered to this justification of private property. The theory, to a degree, attempts to carry over the energy of the producer to the new item: in a sense that energy is never lost, merely transformed into mass. It might equally be said that this energy, once expended, is 'lost' forever. Another repudiation of the theory is based on the recognition that, especially in complex economies, all labour occurs in a social context — a context of mutually supportive labours, all aspects of which contribute in some way towards productive pursuits. In other words, no person's labour is truly original and completely self-sustained — no one person can produce everything they need and ultimately each individual relies on the labour of others to provide at least some of what is needed to exist. Lastly, there is no real reason why the distribution of the outcomes of labour should determined with sole reference to the maker of the item. One might just as easily determine the question of distribution by asking 'who needs this?'

'Economic efficiency' theory

1-8 The 'economic efficiency' theory, propounded by Posner and others, is that legal protection should be extended to property rights because such protection provides a stimulus for the resourceful use of land and other things. It emanates from the observation that people tend to be more careful with things in which they have a personal stake. As such, its aim is the elimination of wasteful activity and the promotion of efficient enterprise. It is dependent upon an economic model of an objective 'market', which rewards the efficient and punishes the wasteful. It argues that if production creates profit, then the best way to promote maximum profit is to promote maximum production, and under this theory people will produce as much as possible in order to increase their own gains. In reality, the apparent sophistication of the 'economic efficiency' theory fades when extraneous factors which tie up the free market, such as cartels and price-shifting, are taken into consideration. It may be argued, on the basis of such observable market distortions, that this model may in fact be more likely to generate inefficiency and waste. It is also arguable that the destruction of the economically inefficient may be a loss to society in other (non-economic) terms. The reality is that mass production often results in less profit, and there is more profit per item, and often overall, to be gained in restricting the availability of items, which is diametrically opposed to this theory.

'Idealist' theory

1-9 The legal protection of private property has also been argued for on the basis that it is necessary for the articulation of human personality and dreams. Few of us are immune from a feeling of satisfaction or contentment with the acquisition of a new thing, or the retention of a thing passed to us from our ancestors. This theory, known as the 'idealist' theory, stresses the social utility of widespread happiness among the population. It is an offshoot of libertarian and utilitarian political theory. The theory would appear to be most applicable to personal chattels, and might also encompass dwelling houses. For reasons similar to those which undermine the efficacy of the 'economic efficiency' theory, namely the concentration of most productive property in the hands of a few, the 'idealist' theory fails to justify the ownership of extensive productive resources.

Theoretical arguments against private property

1-10 Independent of the criticisms of particular arguments for the existence of private property, theoretical objections to private property may be put into four general categories. They range from a crude 'property is theft' argument to more sophisticated analyses of the effects of private property as an expression of power within society. All such objections ultimately proceed from a touchstone of 'fairness'.

Writers like Proudhon regarded private property as a form of theft. A similar criticism was also made by Blatchford, who said:

> The earth belongs to the people ... So that he who possesses land possesses that to which he has no right, and he who invests his savings in land becomes the purchaser of stolen property.

In the same vein, Tawney was critical of 'passive' property such as ground rents. An extension of this argument, noted by Henry George, is that where workers are compelled by economic necessity to work the land of another, the other is thereby enabled to 'reap what he has not sown', while the worker is reduced to a form of slavery. The argument is somewhat circular because without a concept of private property the notion of 'robbery' is comparatively meaningless.

A second fundamental argument against private property is that the institution tends to promote inequality. Where inequality, in terms of the advantages which private property brings in terms of education, health care and wealth, becomes exaggerated it can be observed to result in social dislocation. Most theorists would recognise that a certain degree of inequality is inevitable, and perhaps even desirable. Exponents of the 'economic efficiency' theory, for example, would argue that a certain degree of inequality provides the incentive for enterprise. Exponents of the 'idealist' theory might argue that inequality can mean diversity and differentiation — both desirable conditions for social harmony. Both of these theories nevertheless assume a level playing field, or that each individual begins the race from the same starting position. This is usually not the case: where people are permitted to confer, upon their death, property on their descendants this can, as Becker has noted:

> ... lock members of succeeding generations into positions of undeserved advantage and disadvantage.

The inequality argument is, therefore, not necessarily an argument against the institution of private property. It is, however, a strong argument about the rules for the distribution of property within a private property system. The manifest unpopularity of death duties, all the same, demonstrates how firmly entrenched are our concepts of private ownership.

Some writers have analysed private property as a manifestation of power. For writers such as Renner, Laski and Gray, private property represents a power structure. It is valued more for the personal power it invests in the property owner rather than for its use per se. Ownership of resources, particularly large-scale ownership of productive and industrial commodities and facilities, affords a high degree of control over those people who are dependent upon only their individual labour to generate an income. A propertied 'class' of employers and landlords can then be said to hold power over those who are dependent upon them for wages and shelter. This is also the basic tenet of Marxist theory. Marxists object to private property in the so-called means of production, the seat (as they see it) of social power. According to more refined Marxist analysis, private property 'alienates' people from their true personalities. The institution of private property has, in this sense, led to a repudiation of humankind's social and communal character. It is seen as necessarily destructive of human potential and the capacity for decency.

Murphy J in *Dorman v Rodgers* (1982) 148 CLR 365 at 372 stated:

> Property is an extremely wide concept with a long history ... Throughout the history of the common law the concept of property has been used to recognise the legitimacy of claims and to secure them by bringing them within the scope of legal remedies ... They might first be formulated as social claims with no legal recognition. As they become accepted by reason of social or political changes they are tentatively and then more surely recognised as property. The limits of property are the interfaces between accepted and unaccepted social claims.

As a social institution, private property is nearly omnipresent in human civilisations. The arguments for the institution of private property offer only limited vindication for the retention of the institution. Indeed many of the arguments against the institution of private property are internal to the theoretical justifications themselves. There has also been a tradition of questioning the conventional rationalisations. Arguments against the institution of private property proceed from varied moral, ethical or metaphysical bases, but each stresses the unfairness of private as opposed to more communally focused concepts of ownership.

Examiner's Comments

1-11 For all its accomplishments, this answer lacks a real 'thesis statement'. Even in 'descriptive' questions it is imperative to identify for the reader, at the outset, what will be demonstrated. Otherwise any answer will lack direction and purpose. As the answer goes on to show, there is an idea, or 'touchstone' of 'fairness' which could have been incorporated into the introductory paragraph, and then artfully developed throughout the body of the answer. It needs to be stated clearly at the beginning.

Other than this, the sample answer provides a balanced overview of the major arguments for and against the institution of private property. It may have been enhanced by referring in appropriate places to other theorists: for example, in the early paragraph on 'first occupation' it may have been helpful to cite C Rose, 'Possession as the Origin of Property' (1985) *UChiLR* 73. Similarly, in the next paragraph, on the 'labour' theory, it might have been noted that the energy spoken of, once expended, is 'lost' forever to the actor, and there acknowledged R Nozick, *Anarchy, State And Utopia*, Blackwell, Oxford, 1975. With this type of topic such a task could justifiably be seen as boundless. It will depend very much upon the conditions, that is examination or tutorial preparation, under which the answer is written, whether it is possible to be as comprehensive as one might wish! On the other hand, the use of concrete examples to illustrate theoretical points is very nicely done indeed.

Keep in Mind

1-12 Students should keep in mind the following:

- Always introduce any answer with a 'thesis' — a statement of the aims of the argument. Ensure that the thesis gives direction to the answer, and that each successive paragraph goes some way, in the plan, to proving or disproving the veracity of the thesis.
- While a descriptive essay requires something of a 'broad brush' approach, do not be afraid to utilise specific examples or writers to illustrate a point. Students should explain theoretical points with concrete examples, and refer to authorities where they are germane.
- Although in recent years, all around the world, communist governments have yielded to the 'free market', do not discount Marxist interpretations of property. As *theory*, Marxism remains a potent intellectual tool, and it is to be ignored only at the students' peril.

 Question 2

> **1-13** How has our understanding of private property shaped our understanding of the rights of citizenship of the modern state?
>
> **Time allowed: 45 mins**

 Answer Plan

1-14 There are many ways to approach an open-ended, and possibly somewhat inflammatory question such as the one broached here; therefore, the following is but a suggestion.

This question calls for an examination of the relationship between our ideas about private property and our concepts of citizenship. The relationship between these ideas is not new, nor indeed even a product of just the last few centuries. However, the question specifies 'the modern state' and therefore an answer should attempt to confine its discussion to more recent developments rather than attempting a long-term historical project. For similar reasons the answer might well also confine itself to what is broadly known as 'western civilisation', however generalised that term might now be.

Key liberal theorists such as John Locke and Jeremy Bentham should be considered, as well as the political and economic circumstances which comprised the background to the formulation of their ideas. Critiques of liberal models of property and citizenship, such as feminism and Marxism, can assist in providing the type of counter-legal analysis which the question calls for. Attendant upon these theoretical models are some concrete examples: by focusing on the position of those whom the results of the legal articulation of liberal concepts of property and citizenship tend to disadvantage, this theoretical critique can be grounded in real experience.

 # Answer

1-15 The concept of private property is enshrined in most western countries. The right to hold property and to protect it has historically been central to the development of a 'rights'-based discourse in western civilisation. The desire to demarcate what is personal property and the protection of this property was of primary concern to the early rights theorists. The arguments of the early theorists reflect certain social mores of their time and clearly reflect the divisions of society. The essay will also look at the position of conflict theorists in response to liberal traditional thought on the issues of property and citizenship. The premise of the 'rights discourse', and its translation into material concerns shall be considered, looking specifically at women and indigenous Australians.

Rights and property theories

1-16 One of the most notable theorists on the concept of rights and property was John Locke (1632–1704). John Locke argued that the government's fundamental purpose was to defend 'life, liberty and estate'. Locke's arguments are typical of the eighteenth and nineteenth century liberal rationale. While Locke was in support of a government which supported private property rights, he was more sceptical about government interference in this sphere. Thus there became a division between public and private domains in his ideas. Possession of property was nominated by Locke as a 'natural right' which was god-given, and distribution of property was understood by Locke to be related to the amount of labour individuals were prepared to undertake. Locke proposed that there existed a 'state of perfect freedom' in which individuals had the right to dispose of their possessions and persons as they wished.

Theories explaining property rights changed with time. There was less reference to 'natural rights' and instead a shift to a more 'capitalist model'. Bentham argued that the ability to accumulate property gave individuals the incentive to work and to promote industry. Critics of this theory of property include, most notably, Karl Marx. In simple terms, Marx thought that the political and economic conflict between individuals was created by a system of privilege based upon false notions of 'tradition'. Marx argued that a small elite controlled the majority of property and that this 'propertied class' was able to exploit those without such means in order to reap the profit without having to labour themselves for it. Marxists would argue that the legal institutions and systems are a creation of the 'propertied class' used to reinforce and maintain their position as the elite. Therefore, citizenship is merely a definition which carries certain privileges with it. To the Marxists the elements of citizenship are an integral part of the maintenance of a class-based system. They operate by extending privileges to certain 'members', while those who pose a threat to the established order are excluded.

One of the most glaring examples of property and citizenship as inclusive and exclusive paradigms is the case of the indigenous people of Australia. When the English 'settled' Australia they brought with them, and installed English law. Having decided that there were no legal systems which attributed ownership of property, as they understood it, it was declared that the land was 'terra nullius' or land belonging to no one. Australian land was appropriated to the English according to English property law. Apart from not recognising the indigenous people's relationship with the land, the settlers also deprived them of citizenship. Indigenous people were not truly recognised as citizens in their own land. Many were massacred and many were made to work in labour camps without pay, essentially as slaves. Indigenous Australians were deprived of voting rights until the 1960s and it was also frequently necessary for indigenous people to carry papers in order to leave the missions and camps where they lived and worked. Indigenous children were taken from their families, and many were made to work in 'white' family households. This history of the 'citizenship' of indigenous Australians supports the Marxist view that the structures of law and government do not necessarily support an egalitarian society but can be, and in Australia have been, an instrument of oppression used against Aboriginal Australians.

Feminist viewpoint

1-17 A feminist analysis of the relationship between property and citizenship is provided by Carole Pateman whose analysis focuses upon the concept of 'property' as being that which each individual has in his or her own person. She refers to the marriage contract, which like the general 'social contract' involves a contractual relationship between the exploiter and the exploited. Through the marriage contract, the system of patriarchy ensured that men kept women in a subordinate position. While the marriage contract carries certain symbolic social and political power relationships, the marriage contract has also carried with it, for women, a loss of legally recognised rights. This was shown in a concrete manner through women's lack of property and legal rights prior to the Married Women's Property Acts in Australia. Prior to the Acts, women who married lost their legal rights, which were subsumed by their husbands. Blackstone states that:

> By marriage, the husband and wife are one person in law; that is, the very being or legal existence of the woman is suspended during the marriage, or at least is incorporated and consolidated into that of the husband; under whose wing, protection and cover she performs everything ...

Therefore, women ceased to be citizens as soon as they opted for marriage. The only possessions which women were permitted to entrust in a will were clothing and personal items, unless they had permission to dispose of other property from the husband, who could later revoke it. In Australia, the last of the states to enact the Married Women's Property Act was Tasmania in 1935.

Private property is integral in the debate about citizenship. Citizenship brings with it certain rights and privileges, private property being one of these. Our understanding of private property and its distribution says a great deal about the values and structure of our society. In western societies, the rationale behind property ownership is based upon a concept of reward and industry, but historically has also been selective about whose industry is able to receive such rewards. This rationale, while seemingly fair and merit-based, is quickly revealed to be based upon patriarchal, elitist, sexist and racial assumptions. Citizenship qualifications and private property form a complex structure of demarcation where certain classes of people are entitled to maintain ownership of property with its associated rights, while those who do not qualify are denied membership.

Examiner's Comments

1-18 On the whole this is a good answer to a difficult question. The answer does not shy away from controversial views, and expresses a firm thesis which is well argued and strongly supported. It adopts a critical approach and contains a good 'mix' of theory and practical examples. Another strength is a clearly discernible structure which permits the reader to follow the argument with comparative ease. The value of these strengths can never be underestimated.

It is a very good idea for an answer to a question of this kind to illustrate its thesis with some examples. In this instance the answer refers, at some length, to the experiences of citizenship of women and Aboriginal people and situates those experiences within a property-based context. The utilisation of secondary materials and commentaries, particularly those of philosophers and political scientists, has been effectively worked into the structure of the answer. It is well done, as far as it goes, but may have been further enhanced by reference to various materials such as reports of royal commissions and parliamentary inquiries.

Keep in Mind

1-19 Students should keep in mind the following:

- An answer to a question such as this must be approached with some discretion. By no means does the question call for a detailed exposition of the legislative arrangements for national citizenship. Nor indeed will there necessarily be much profit in scanning cases about property matters for instances where citizenship might have been mentioned. Neither of these standard legal approaches will be capable of producing an answer to the question posed.

- To a very large degree this kind of question provokes an 'anti-legal' approach — a method which requires the student to read the law 'against the grain' and adopt a critical position. In this kind of inquiry, it is often what remains unsaid in the legal materials, the assumptions and premises based on the social values and attitudes of the time, which frequently go unchallenged in the law, and which need to be exposed and analysed.
- Students who, in other studies, have read philosophy, sociology, history or political science may feel themselves to have a natural advantage with questions of this kind. Do not make assumptions of this kind. A good answer will need to draw upon non-legal knowledge in order to develop the critique which is appropriate. But this is not to say that legal knowledge is irrelevant here, or that students who have no such background should be deterred from attempting an answer to questions of this order. It is one of the tests of property law to be able to confront the limitations of strict legalism. Legal and non-legal materials need to be blended, balanced, compared and contrasted in a graceful and incisive way. It is usually a great challenge to get the 'mix' just right.

 # Question 3

> **1-20** Until the decision by the High Court of Australia in *Mabo v Queensland (No 2)* (1992) 175 CLR 1 (*Mabo*) it had always been understood that Australian land law was fixed firmly in the feudal mould comprised of the doctrines of tenures and estates. This 'understanding' has now been questioned and to a certain degree redefined. The reappearance of the feudal notion in *Mabo* exposes an opportunity to contemplate how an historical attitude towards the law in fact shapes its contemporary unfolding. (M Stuckey, 'Feudalism and Australian Land Laws: A Shadowy Ghostlike Survival?', *University of Tasmania Law Review* 13, 1994, 102–15).
>
> Discuss.
>
> **Time allowed: 45 mins**

 # Answer Plan

1-21 This essay should be introduced with a reference to the history of the doctrine of tenure, the feudal system and *Quia Emptores*. From there the reception of the doctrine in Australia, and its first application in *Attorney-General v Brown* (1847) 1 Legge 312 (supporting the feudal principles of tenure), should be covered briefly. Other relevant cases in this lineage include:

- *Cooper v Stuart* (1889) 14 App Cas 286;
- *Attorney-General v Williams* (1913) 16 CLR 404; and
- *Randwick v Rutledge* (1959) 102 CLR 54.

It should be made clear that all of these cases, although not necessarily dealing with Aboriginal land rights, rest on the concept of 'terra nullius'.

The main thrust of the essay needs to focus upon more recent treatments of Aboriginal land rights cases, particularly:

- *Milirrpum v Nabalco Pty Ltd and Commonwealth* [1971] ALR; and
- *Mabo v Queensland (No 2)* (1992) 175 CLR 1 (*Mabo*).

Detailed discussion of *Mabo* is integral to a good answer. It should be noted that *Mabo* rejected the doctrine of terra nullius, and modified the doctrine of tenure to fit contemporary Australian land use management and to reflect the basic human rights of indigenous Australians. Detailed consideration of the judgments of each of the members of the High Court is required.

Other developments, such as the Native Title Act 1993 (Cth) and *Wik Peoples v Queensland* (1996) 187 CLR 1, may also demonstrate the significance of feudal law and its review in land law cases.

The answer should conclude by explaining how the High Court in *Mabo* utilised historical perspectives in its analysis of the doctrine of tenure.

 # Answer

1-22 The doctrine of tenure had its origins in English feudal law. It was part of the law received into Australia upon settlement. The doctrine has been regarded as so fundamental that 'it could not be overturned without fracturing the skeleton which gives our land law its shape and consistency': Brennan J in *Mabo v Queensland (No 2)* (1992) 175 CLR 1.

When William, Duke of Normandy, conquered England in 1066 AD all land fell to him as an owner by right of conquest. This was the genesis of the doctrine of tenure. The doctrine expressed the lines of communication through which power in the era was expressed and underpinned, consolidating Norman rule in England. In theory, all land was granted by the king to his principal followers as 'tenants in chief'. In turn, they granted land to their followers, and so on down through the feudal hierarchy. This process was known as 'subinfeudation'. In exchange for holding land, a tenant provided services of various kinds to their lord. When a tenant died, his or her land reverted, via what was known as an 'escheat', to the lord, who might then re-grant the land to the heir of the deceased tenant upon the payment of 'relief', a form of tax. At the top of the feudal pyramid was the king who, in legal theory, remained the ultimate owner of all land, in much the same way as the Commonwealth today retains ultimate ownership of all land rights in Australia, the only exception being where the Crown's rights are burdened by native title. Allodial land, that is land without a lord and therefore outside of this system, was held not to exist in England.

Subinfeudation

1-23 The system of subinfeudation was essentially a mechanism for ensuring the maintenance of the feudal social, economic and military order. It was, as such, inherently rigid and unable to cope with changes in social conditions. Not long after the establishment of Norman rule, the system began to fragment. In 1290, the statute *Quia Emptores* put an end to this system of subinfeudation and permitted land to be traded freely, without the necessity of obtaining the permission of the immediate lord.

Doctrine of tenure in Australia

1-24 This doctrine was 'received', in the sense described by Blackstone, into Australia, as part of those laws which were fundamental to the operation of the English legal system. The first application of the doctrine of tenure in Australia was by the Supreme Court of New South Wales in 1847. In *Attorney-General v Brown* (1847) 1 Legge 312 Stephen CJ held that the feudal system was applicable to land ownership in Australia, and said that the Crown's rights were not merely political but were therefore of a proprietary nature. Since then, the doctrine has been applied by the High Court of Australia in a number of cases. In *Cooper v Stuart* (1889) 14 App Cas 286, the High Court indicated that prior to settlement Australia did not have any land law or tenures, but that these concepts were received upon settlement, confirming the position that the Crown obtained its right to impose its legal system because the land was terra nullius.

In *Attorney-General v Williams* (1913) 16 CLR 404, the High Court said that the feudal principles of the doctrine of tenure had overall application in Australia. In *Randwick v Rutledge* (1959) 102 CLR 54, the court cited and approved *Attorney-General v Brown* (1847) 1 Legge 312. All of these cases could be said to rest on the proposition that indigenous people had no legally enforceable rights to land, continuing the endorsement of the doctrine of terra nullius. *Milirrpum v Nabalco Pty Ltd and Commonwealth* [1971] ALR 65 (*Milirrpum*) was a more modern case, where the Supreme Court of the Northern Territory indicated that the High Court cases mentioned above confirmed the principle that all land was owned by the Crown. Blackburn J held that the most that any individual could do would be to hold land of the Crown. His Honour also held that land could not be owned allodially.

In *Mabo*, the High Court distinguished the decision in *Milirrpum*, rejected the doctrine of terra nullius, and modified the doctrine of tenure to fit Australian conditions more appropriately. The doctrine was refined in order to cope with contemporary land use management and to better reflect the recognition of basic human rights for indigenous Australians. Deane and Gaudron JJ discussed the feudal principle of medieval times and indicated that its only application in 1788 was limited to the Crown's rights in escheat and also to ownership of shorelines and headlands. Their

Honours' underlying thesis was that a 'radical title' was vested in the Crown and that the most an individual could own would be an estate in fee simple. Deane and Gaudron JJ distinguished those earlier High Court decisions which indicated that an absolute title vested in the Crown, on the basis that those cases were not about Aboriginal land rights and that those decisions demonstrated a collective paucity of reasoning.

Toohey J held that the distinction between sovereignty (or political rights) and land title was important, but his Honour failed to elaborate on the matter. Toohey J said that the doctrine of tenure was based on a legal fiction which should not be given any wider application than its essential operation required. Accordingly, for Toohey J, this meant that indigenous Australians were possibly entitled to a fictitious lost Crown grant upon which their land rights could be given foundation. Brennan J, with whom Mason CJ and McHugh J agreed, also considered the feudal basis for the proposition of absolute Crown ownership and concluded that it was too late in the day to apply the allodial argument in Australia. His Honour said that the doctrine of tenure did exist and had ubiquitous application in Australia. Brennan J held that radical title was adapted from feudal theory which made the Crown the owner of all unalienated land. However, his Honour also held that the doctrine of tenure did not apply to land which had not been granted by the Crown to Europeans. Brennan J cited the old English cases of *The Tanistry* (1608) Davis 28 and *Witrong v Blany* (1674) 3 Keb 401 as authority for the common law recognition of existing native title rights, and held that such a recognition could be discerned from a failure on the part of the Crown to expressly extinguish such rights. Dawson J, the only dissenting judge, held that although a radical title vested in the Crown upon conquest, survival of native title rights depended upon the express recognition of those rights by the Crown. His Honour said that the matter was better suited for legislative resolution.

In summary, all of the judges utilised an historical perspective in their analysis of the doctrine of tenure and its applicability to contemporary Australia. Deane and Gaudron JJ distinguished earlier cases and said that the doctrine of tenure, in the strict sense, did not apply in modern Australia. Toohey J utilised a traditional concept of the common law, the fictitious Crown grant, to extend the operation of the doctrine to Aboriginal land rights. Brennan J refused to overturn the doctrine but said that it could only apply to land titles which were created by the Crown. Dawson J, in dissent, adopted the most conventional common law approach to the doctrine of tenure.

Following the decision of the High Court in *Mabo*, the Commonwealth Parliament enacted the Native Title Act 1993. This Act recognises the existence of native title to land which stands outside the doctrine of tenure. It is complemented by reciprocal legislation in all states and territories. The question of whether pastoral leases issued under various legislative regimes of the states effectively extinguished native title was considered by the High Court in *Wik Peoples v Queensland* (1996) 187 CLR 1 (*Wik*). The argument that extinguishment had been effected was rejected by the court, by a majority of four out of seven justices. This judgment was followed by the enactment of the Native Title Amendment Act 1998 (Cth), which was the legislative response to the issues raised by *Wik*.

The principles of feudal land law have therefore been received in and recognised as applicable to Australia. They have been applied in a number of High Court cases and subjected to a significant degree of redefinition in *Mabo*. They have also been embodied in comprehensive legislation. However, while the principles of the doctrine of tenure have been modified as necessary, their contemporary application has its basis in the historical foundations of feudal law.

 ## Examiner's Comments

1-25 In the sample answer above, a competent focus is maintained on the question, and a very decent attempt made to come to terms with its implications. However, there is also some evidence of skirting the issue.

This is a challenging question, and although the cases and many of the issues encompassed here are quite well-known, the question asks that they be approached from a certain perspective. This sample answer makes a convincing attempt to address the historiographical issues raised, and for this it must be commended. Nonetheless there is a quite noticeable drift into historical description, which is not really imperative to a good answer. Some elements of straightforward historical narrative are called for, but they should not be allowed to detract from the more discursive project envisioned in the quote rendered for comment. The question asks for more than a description of the history of native title in Australia — it asks for commentary upon the identified judicial methodology of historicism, or perhaps pseudo-historicism. Accordingly, when the answer reaches its conclusion, its task is not really completed.

The answer may have been further enhanced by reference to the decision of the High Court in *Fejo v Northern Territory* (1998) 156 ALR 721.

 ## Keep in Mind

1-26 Students should keep in mind the following:

- Possibly the single most common error in tutorial essays and examination answers is where a student, who is familiar with the background to the law in a certain area, simply tells the examiner all that the student knows about the area, without really attempting to come to grips with the question posed. It is clearly not sufficient to 'talk around' the topic and thus evade answering the actual question. Never think that near enough is good enough: confront the question squarely.

Chapter 2

The Creation, Transfer and Enforceability of Proprietary Rights: An Introduction

Key Issues

2-1 The key concept in property law is that property is a 'bundle of rights'. The focus of the course is on how those rights can be created, broken up, and transferred to and from, or exercised against others. An often used analogy is that of a bundle of sticks representing property rights in an item. The transferring and handling of those property rights is much like breaking up the sticks in the bundle and giving sticks or pieces of sticks to different people while retaining others, and then getting some sticks back: *leases, licences, profits a prendre, easements, doctrine of estates;* and sometimes going to court to see who has the greater rights, or 'bigger stick': *competing equities, adverse possession.* If students can grasp the analogy then the concepts of property can become much simpler to understand.

Thus proprietary rights may be created 'originally', when the item in which rights are held is first created, such as an invention; or they may be acquired or transferred from another, as above. The acquisition of rights may be consensual, as in a sale and purchase of land, or they may be non-consensual, as in bankruptcy. All of these rights only exist because they are recognised, either at common law and/or in equity, which can recognise rights beyond those recognised under common law, such as rights arising from the doctrine of estoppel.

The multiplicity of types of proprietary interests, and the fact that such interests typically exist simultaneously in regard to a single physical item of property, means that conflicts and competitions often arise between the holders of interests, resulting in the 'who has the bigger stick' question. The rules as to how proprietary rights are created, transferred and enforced, form the subject matter of this chapter.

Because of the evident breadth of this topic, and also because of the limited scope of a tutorial-focused 'question and answer' work such as this text?, it is not possible to give a comprehensive treatment of all of the issues a student will meet in the study of the creation, transfer and enforceability of proprietary interests.

This chapter, which is intended as an introduction only, attempts to feature some of the more involved themes, to give an overview of the topic and acquaint students with some keynote concerns. The chapter begins with an exploration of the distinctions between the various means of acquiring proprietary rights, whether 'originally' or by transfer from another, and in the latter case the differentiations which exist between voluntary and involuntary transfers. From this point, there is a specific focus upon the acquisition of proprietary rights by transfer, starting with an examination of the vexed questions of rights arising from gifts or purported gifts of Torrens land, followed by a very broad question encompassing most of the ways title in land can be transferred. The chapter concludes with a look at the law of priorities.

2-2 Before attempting the following questions, please ensure you are familiar with the following:

✓	the distinction between proprietary rights, which may be created 'originally', and proprietary rights acquired or transferred from another;
✓	the distinctions between proprietary rights recognised by the common law and proprietary rights recognised in equity;
✓	the rules which govern transfers of proprietary rights for valuable consideration, and the rules which govern the voluntary acquisition of proprietary rights (gifts);
✓	the rules governing transfer of title for old system land and land under Torrens title;
✓	the system of prioritising conflicting claims to property.

Question 1

2-3 What is the distinction between property acquired by transfer and the original acquisition of property? By what means or in what circumstances may one acquire property by 'original acquisition'?

Time allowed: 30 mins

Answer Plan

2-4 When addressing a question that asks 'what is the distinction between' two things, the answer must start by identifying and explaining each of the two things in the question, and then continue to explain the differences between them.

Here the answer needs to identify and define the different ways in which property may be originally acquired, then identify and define the different ways in which property may be acquired by transfer, and then finally examine the differences between the two. A number of categorising systems can be used; below is merely one option.

By *transfer* (from another):

- by consensual transactions:
  - sale;
  - gifts *inter vivos*;
  - declarations of trust;
  - gifts in wills,
- by non-consensual transactions:
  - bankruptcy and judgment execution;
  - compulsory acquisitions;
  - non-testamentary succession (intestacy and family provisions schemes).

By *original acquisition*:
- creation or manufacture;
- assuming possession;
- fixtures;
- under the doctrines of accession, intermixture and accretion;
- via the application of equitable principles —
  - the constructive trust;
  - estoppel.

The question asks that this hierarchy (or whichever is chosen) be explained. The primary goal here is to identify the differences between the two essential modes of acquisition and then to consider (briefly) acquisition by transfer. The second part of the question requires a more detailed focus upon the various means by which property may be secured by 'original acquisition', and so each of the identified modes must be described and explained.

 # Answer

2-5 The procurement of property by 'original acquisition' covers circumstances where the proprietary interest acquired by a person is entirely novel in its nature, even if at face value it might appear to have been in some way derived from the rights or interests of some other person. Some instances of original acquisition are easily recognisable, for example, when a hunter captures a wild animal or an author writes a book. Other instances of original acquisition are apt to be confused with transfers of interests, especially where those transfers occur without the consent of the original owner. This essay will initially describe, albeit briefly, the various forms of acquisition by transfer. It will be shown that in all such cases the interest acquired is the same as that which is disposed of or surrendered. Then this essay will discuss the diverse modes of original acquisition pointing out, where appropriate, some of the difficulties associated with such a categorising project.

2-6 The most familiar forms of consensual transactions, sale and gifts *inter vivos,* are easily recognised as modes of proprietary acquisition where an interest is transferred from and by one party (respectively, the vendor or the donor) to another (again respectively, the purchaser or the donee). Declarations of express trust, where a party divests himself or herself of the beneficial ownership of property and vests that interest in another, is also a clear example of transfer. It does not matter whether the declaration was for valuable consideration, nor does it matter if the original party remains the legal owner, or if he or she at the same time (or later) vests the legal ownership of the property in a third party as the trustee. It may be thought that in the cases of gifts and declarations of trust that the transfer is not necessarily consensual, because the donee and the beneficiary do not have to accept or even be aware of the transfer. However, here the person doing the giving is willingly giving up their entitlement, as opposed to a non-consensual transfer such as bankruptcy where a person loses their entitlement without any consent being sought. Similarly, gifts in wills are an example of consensual transfers, with the testator freely choosing to make the gift and the beneficiary remaining free to disclaim it. In all of these examples an initial owner freely and willingly conveys a particular interest to a new owner who agrees (at least impliedly) to accept that same interest.

2-7 Transfers by non-consensual transactions occur in circumstances where the law operates to consign a person's proprietary interest in land or goods without their consent. In bankruptcy and the execution of judgments, the property of debtors may be acquired to satisfy their proven debts. The Commonwealth and all the states and territories also have legislative powers to compulsorily acquire a person's property. In the case of the Commonwealth this is subject to a constitutional obligation to pay compensation, although the states may resume property without the payment of any compensation. A final example of non-consensual transfer is in relation to non-testamentary succession involving the rules of intestacy and family provisions schemes. In these cases, statutory regimes exist to distribute a deceased's property, either according to a strict design (in the case of simple intestacy), or according to the discretion of the court (where there has been a successful application under a Family Provisions Act). In all of these examples the interest transferred, although it was assigned without the consent of its initial owner, remains the same interest in the hands of its recipient.

2-8 Putting aside these consensual and non-consensual transfers as a means of acquiring property, the various means by which the acquisition of property may be appropriately described as 'original', all exhibit a feature which is lacking in consensual and non-consensual transfers of property: the acquisition of a right which is not identical or referable to the right or interest of a previous owner. The most obvious means by which property may be 'originally' acquired is by creation or manufacture. Where a person invests their labour and time in a creative process and in so doing makes a new thing, for example, writes a book, then that new thing is theirs.

The raw materials (in the above example, the blank papers and the ink), have lost their identity and substance and have been converted into something entirely new and different. The law is virtually a direct expression of Locke's labour theory of property. It is important to note that the common law provides only a very basic kind of protection for the acquisition of property rights by creation. On the other hand, there is quite extensive protection for creative acquisition under statute. The Commonwealth Parliament, under its powers in s 51(xviii) of the Constitution, has provided for statutory codes covering patents, designs, copyrights and trademarks. In either case, however, the interest of the creator is not referable to the rights or interests of any prior person.

2-9 One may also acquire property by assuming possession. The law of possession does not require the rights be transferred from another. The rules which govern possession are dependent upon whether the property in question is land or goods. As far as land is concerned, any person in possession of land, whether lawfully or wrongfully, has a title to that land which derives solely from their possession. Any other person who seeks to displace or usurp that possession must be able to show a better title than that of the possessor. This may be done by proving a documentary title or a prior possession (without abandonment) within the relevant statutory period for bringing an action (which is generally 12 years from the date upon which an action arose) for trespass or the recovery of land.

Similarly, the possession of goods carries with it a title to the goods. Again, any person seeking to displace that possession must be able to show a better title than that of the possessor. This may be done by proving a documentary title or a prior possession (without abandonment), within the relevant statutory period for bringing an action (which is generally six years from the date upon which an action arose) for trespass, conversion or detinue. In either case, the rights of the possessor derive from their own acts of possession coupled with their intention to possess. Where land is truly deserted and has never been possessed then its first settlement will be good against the whole world. This is extremely rare, but may perhaps apply to islands newly formed by volcanic action. Where the goods are wild animals, having no prior possessor, capture is normally considered to be possession, although there are numerous cases which have introduced some fairly complicated rules and fine distinctions in this area, particularly where there is a dispute between the hunter and the owner of land where the animal is captured or felled. There is also extensive legislation of the Commonwealth and the states and territories which regulates and protects native fauna.

2-10   Under the doctrine of fixtures, property may be acquired without any formal or informal transfer. Where a chattel is physically attached to land it may lose its independent character and become subsumed within the real property. There is no apparent transfer by the chattel owner — merely a recognition at law that the thing, by virtue of its affixation, has ceased to exist as a separate entity and that the realty has acquired a new feature. This expression of the doctrine is not free from debate and courts continue to endeavour, although without much success, to express in clear and unambiguous terms why this is so. There may be sound policy reasons for such a rule, particularly where a court is concerned about the potentially wasteful effects of dismantling structures, but such policies do not account for the categorisation of the law of fixtures as a kind of original acquisition. Whether, in truth, it is best to consider the doctrine of fixtures as a mode of 'original' acquisition, or whether it is better to understand the operation of the doctrine as an example of a non-consensual transfer remains open to question.

2-11   Other means by which property may be 'originally' acquired can be found under the doctrines of accession, intermixture and accretion. The doctrine of accession deals with circumstances where goods are annexed or joined together. The doctrine is sometimes invoked in relation to spare parts for motor vehicles in attempts to extinguish the title of the part owner in favour of the vehicle owner.

In *Rendell v Associated Finance Pty Ltd* [1975] VR 604, O'Bryan J of the Supreme Court of Victoria held that the doctrine of accession was limited to circumstances where the annexed spare part had become unidentifiable, or where it could not be removed without damage to the vehicle. The test expressed by his Honour therefore is redolent of the simple 'degree of annexation' test under the doctrine of fixtures, and for this reason the categorisation of the doctrine of accession as a mode of original acquisition may be open to criticism. The doctrine of intermixture applies to situations where goods become so mixed as to become indistinguishable as separate entities. The classic example is where discrete shipments of grain are mixed within a single silo. The rule is that the owners of the ingredients then own the mixture as tenants in common.

The doctrine of accretion applies where land borders water. Sometimes, owing to the deposit of silt, sand or other substances, additional land may be 'created' which an owner of adjoining land may claim as his or her own. Where the land borders inland waters, the doctrine may also apply where the high watermark of a lake recedes or where a river changes its course. Where the doctrine applies to newly surfaced land, it is clear that it is a means of original acquisition, as the new land had no previous owner. Where the doctrine applies to changes in river courses then it is possible to say, conjecturally, that it is a kind of non-consensual transfer.

2-12   Original acquisition of proprietary rights may also occur via the application of equitable principles. The courts have been very active in recognising the rights of parties who have been subjected to various forms of unconscionable conduct, and giving expression to those rights by the application of constructive trusts and of equities arising from the doctrine of estoppel. Although such rights arise from litigation and have a remedial function, they are ultimately proprietary in their nature and bear all the usual features of an 'interest' in some material or intangible thing. It may be disputed, for the reasons already stated in relation to the doctrines of fixtures and accession, that these rights are more properly understood as non-consensual transfers, but the objection here is more difficult to maintain. The right recognised in the successful claimant need not, and frequently does not, correspond with interest held by the defendant, and in this sense it is true to say that the application of equitable principles is an example of acquisition by 'original' means.

2-13   The distinction between property acquired by transfer and the original acquisition of property assists in an understanding of the law. By categorising the acquisition of property in this way, it is possible to rationalise why sometimes diverse legal rules apply to apparently similar circumstances. The appropriation of property by 'original acquisition' involves circumstances where the proprietary interest acquired by a person is entirely novel in its nature, and does not spring from the rights or interests of some other person. As such, it is more difficult to describe with precision the full compass of such rights than it is to define derived rights which, by their nature, must be susceptible to accurate demarcation. There is significant latitude for judicial creativity, and hence sometimes greater uncertainty, with regard to proprietary rights acquired by 'original acquisition' than other modes of proprietary acquisition.

Examiner's Comments

2-14   This answer is highly structured and contains innumerable terse generalisations about the state of the law. Both of these features are to be commended in an essay-style approach such as this. The introduction contains a strong and clear thesis statement which is slowly, but surely worked through in each successive paragraph. The reader is at no stage left in any doubt about what the writer has set about accomplishing, where in the scheme of the answer each piece fits, or how each part of the argument relates to its neighbours. An enormous span of property law is confidently and concisely laid out, without ado. Stylistically, the treatment is clinical yet accessible.

There is also much to be commended in the fault-finding technique which is embraced in relation to those aspects of the argument which are more tenuous. This is effected in an honest and open way, and the answer is the hardier for not attempting to gloss over these aspects. Instead, the answer is bolstered by its ready acceptance of the weaker facets of its strategy and its attempts to deal with them without undue sophistry.

What this answer lacks are reference points to the actual law. In numerous instances, 'cases' and 'legislation' are referred to, but almost entirely without specific citation. Where specific legislation has an impact upon a certain aspect of the answer, it must be cited. Similarly, important cases which express legal rules, or perhaps controversial cases which depart from accepted positions, must not be glossed over. To a certain degree, the detail which can be expected of a student in this regard is very much dependent upon the conditions under which the answer is presented. Certainly, an examiner of a closed-book examination will expect less in these terms than the examiner of a essay where the student has had the opportunity to consult texts, reports and compilations of legislative provisions. All the same, even for a closed-book examination, the above answer is deficient in this regard.

 ## Keep in Mind

2-15 Students should keep in mind the following:

- In answer to an essay-style question such as this, it is frequently tempting for students to oversimplify the state of law in order to present a logical framework upon which to comment. The law, in most instances anyway, is much less organised or coherent than we would like it to be. Even if the general thrust of the law in any particular area can be summarised without too much difficulty, it is simply a fact of life that, being a practical thing, the law contains inconsistencies which make its totally systematic representation almost impossible.
- Always be aware of the unconventional decision or provision which proves the exception to the general rule. Any answer which is able to adopt a systematising approach, but which also takes account of the anomalous departure from the norm, is to be preferred to a deceptively straightforward representation of that which is (in the end) a description of the imperfections of human experience.

 ## Question 2

> **2-16** Does Australian law still support the view of Dixon J in *Brunker v Perpetual Trustee Co (Ltd)* (1937) 57 CLR 555 that a donee of Torrens land can only acquire a statutory right to obtain registration?
>
> **Time allowed: 45 mins**

 ## Answer Plan

2-17 The essential argument here should be that Dixon J's view in *Brunker v Perpetual Trustee Co (Ltd)* (1937) 57 CLR 555 is no longer supported in Australian law. In *Corin v Patton* (1990) 169 CLR 540, the decision by the majority of the High Court supported Griffith CJ's view in *Anning v Anning* (1907) 4 CLR 1049, that a donee of Torrens land may be entitled to an equitable interest. Dixon J's reasoning in the *Brunker* case, and the support for his view in *Travica v Travica* [1955] VLR 261 and *Corin v Patton* (per Brennan J) must form the basis of this answer. The problems with the Dixon and Brennan JJ approach all need to be considered. They include:

- the lack of specific explanation of what the special statutory right to registration involves;
- that the approach is out of step with remedies such as constructive trusts; and
- the restrictions inherent in this approach.

The (current) orthodox approach, where the recognition of an equitable interest remains open to the court, should be detailed. Cases which need to be addressed here include:

- *Corin v Patton* (1990) 169 CLR 540 (per Mason CJ, McHugh and Deane JJ);
- *Anning v Anning* (1907) 4 CLR 1049 (per Griffith CJ);
- *Milroy v Lord* (1862) 4 De GF & J 264; 45 ER 1185;
- *Barry v Heider* (1914) 19 CLR 197.

A third approach, rejecting the existence of any interest (either legal or equitable) from Isaacs J in *Anning v Anning* should be noted.

In conclusion, it needs to be firmly stated that Dixon J's approach was discredited by the majority of the High Court of Australia in *Corin v Patton*.

Answer

2-18 The view of Dixon J in *Brunker v Perpetual Trustee Co (Ltd)* (1937) 57 CLR 555, that a donee of Torrens land can only acquire a statutory right to obtain registration, is no longer supported in Australian law. The High Court, in *Corin v Patton* (1990) 169 CLR 540, by a majority, supported the approach taken by Griffith CJ in *Anning v Anning* (1907) 4 CLR 1049, which held that a donee of Torrens land does gain an equitable interest in the land prior to registration, so long as the donor has done everything 'necessary' to transfer the land. However, Brennan J in *Corin v Patton* dissented from this position and declined to disregard the view of Dixon J in *Brunker v Perpetual Trustee*. There are two lines of Australian judicial authority dealing with the question of whether a gift of Torrens land is enforceable against the donor without registration. The major policy issue is this: to allow an unregistered donee enforceable rights in relation to the land in question will necessarily create an exception to the principle of indefeasibility of title enshrined in the Torrens legislation.

2-19 The approach of Dixon J in *Brunker v Perpetual Trustee* was described by Brennan J (in *Corin v Patton*) as the 'conventional' position. The view of Dixon J was that a donee of Torrens land, prior to registration, obviously held no legal interest in the land in question and nor did such a donee acquire an equitable interest in the land. Dixon J thus emphasised the importance of the principle of indefeasibility in holding the transfer to be ineffective. However, his Honour did say that a donee in this situation did acquire a 'novel right', under the legislation, to obtain registration. The approach of Dixon J was given further support by the Supreme Court of Victoria in *Travica v Travica* [1955] VLR 261. More significantly, this approach was also endorsed by Brennan J of the High Court of Australia in *Corin v Patton*. Brennan J held that a donee in these circumstances may acquire such a 'statutory right' to obtain registration. His Honour argued that to allow the donee an equitable interest in the land would be to extend equity beyond its proper bounds. Brennan J indicated that to permit an equity to exist in this situation would be to overturn, and not merely circumvent, the law. His Honour concluded that equity should not be allowed to overturn the indefeasibility of title provisions of the Torrens legislation.

All the same, there are difficulties with this approach. First, neither Dixon J nor Brennan J has ever expressly explained exactly what this special statutory right to registration involves. Second, the approach is out of step with equitable doctrines such as the availability of a constructive trust as a remedial device. Third, as a matter of policy, it may be argued that restricting the operation of equity in these circumstances might disappoint community expectations of the law.

2-20 The approach which gained the support of the majority of the members of the High Court, namely Mason CJ, McHugh and Deane JJ, in *Corin v Patton* was essentially that laid down by Griffith CJ in *Anning v Anning*. Griffith CJ held, applying the test in *Milroy v Lord* (1862) 4 De GF & J 264; 45 ER 1185, that when a donor of Torrens land had done all that he or she could do to equip a donee with all necessary means to obtain registration, the donee acquired an equitable proprietary interest in the land in question. This approach was also endorsed by the High Court in *Barry v Heider* (1914) 19 CLR 197. The majority of the court in *Corin* refused to follow the approach of Dixon J in *Brunker v Perpetual Trustee,* indicating that that view no longer represented the law in Australia. Their Honours argued that the Griffith approach assisted parties in meeting their expectations and had more support from other principles of equity and law than did Dixon J's approach. Accordingly, it was reasonable to make this exception to the doctrine of indefeasibility of title because, in such circumstances, the transactions between the parties were capable of proving that a gift was intended.

2-21 It is important to note that a third and much stricter approach to this question was articulated by Isaacs J in *Anning v Anning*. In his opinion, a donee of Torrens land prior to registration obtained no enforceable rights, either at law or in equity. The divergence of approaches taken by Griffith and Isaacs JJ in *Anning v Anning* led to one of the longest standing debates in the history of the High Court of Australia. The controversy was exacerbated by the judgment of Dixon J in *Brunker v Perpetual Trustee.*

In conclusion, the view of Dixon J in *Brunker v Perpetual Trustee* has now been discredited by a majority of the High Court of Australia in *Corin v Patton.* In the latter case, it was held that a donee of Torrens land may acquire an equitable interest in the land prior to registration rather than some statutory right to registration of the kind described by Dixon J in *Brunker v Perpetual Trustee.*

Examiner's Comments

2-22 On the whole, this is rather a good answer. It has a number of strengths and comparatively few weaknesses. As a general comment, one of the most significant features of this answer is its relative simplicity. This directness, in an area of the law which has been (to say the least) in confusion for decades, is indeed refreshing. Sometimes, in controversial areas, it can be a great advantage to be able to set out the problems and distinguish between the differing approaches with uncomplicated language. On the other hand, the answer might be criticised for lacking a certain degree of sophistication. More might have been said about some of the other cases in which the issues raised by the question have been canvassed by the High Court, and the discussion of policy issues might have been more detailed.

Some further cases in which the views of Dixon J have been discussed include:

- *Norman v FCT* (1963) 109 CLR 9;
- *Cope v Keene* (1968) 118 CLR 1;
- *Olsson v Dyson* (1969) 120 CLR 365;
- *Noonan v Martin* (1987) 10 NSWLR 402.

In relation to policy concerns, it may have been helpful to have further explained just which 'community expectations' are relevant to this area of the law. How, for example, do lay people understand legal forms and requirements, and what are the important considerations which courts need to bear in mind when determining disputes about imperfect gifts of land?

Keep in Mind

2-23 Students should keep in mind the following:

- As an essay question it is absolutely necessary that students answer the question which has been asked, rather than fall into the trap of attempting to state all that is known about this controversial area of the law.
- The question asks whether Australian law still supports Justice Dixon's view in *Brunker v Perpetual Trustee.* As such, some discussion of the judgments of the High Court in cases such as *Brunker* itself,

Anning and *Corin* is necessary. It is not, however, necessary for much (if any) detailed recitation of the facts in any of these cases. A good answer will avoid becoming bogged down in the particular fact scenarios of the cases in which Dixon J's approach was relevant to the decision.

- Similarly, this question does not require an itemised account of the steps, from the formation of the relevant intention to the actual procurement of registration, which need to be taken by donors (and possibly donees) in order to effect a valid gift. This sort of approach may be useful when attempting a problem-style question, but it is inappropriate for an essay.

Question 3

2-24 In 1942, Jennifer is the owner of a plot in North Queensland. She is offered a movie deal in Los Angeles and leaves instructions with her solicitor, Evinrude, to continue paying the rates and tending the land, as she wants to open a commune when she gets back. Evinrude falls in love with a Russian pen pal, forges Jennifer's signature on sale documents, and sells Jennifer's fee simple interest to Angelina.

Angelina turns the land into a high-end retreat for alcoholic executives and Evinrude sends the money to Russia to pay for his pen pal to come and be his bride. She never arrives and, until his dying day, Evinrude wanders Brisbane airport eagerly checking the passengers of every arrival from Russia, looking for her.

In 1952 Angelina marries one of the alcoholic executives and sells the retreat to Brad, who buys the land with a mortgage from Trustee Bank:

(a) The land is 'old system land', ie, land that has not been converted to the Torrens system, and is therefore not subject to the Land Title Act 1994 (Qld). Advise Jennifer.

(b) How would you change your answer if the land had been converted to Torrens system land, and if all the transactions had occurred since 1995 and were registered under the Land Title Act 1994 (Qld)?

(c) Instead of selling Jennifer's fee simple to Angelina, Evinrude transferred and registered the fee simple under Florence Finnigan, the name of his dead grandmother. Then Evinrude sold the land under Florence's title to Brad, who obtained a mortgage from Trustee Bank for the purchase. All the transactions have been registered under the Land Title Act 1994 (Qld). Advise Jennifer.

(d) What would happen if Joe Bloggs purchased the property from Brad and registered title?

Time allowed: 1 hour, 30 mins

Answer Plan

2-25 This question requires working through the scenarios supplied and first applying the old system rules to the transactions, and then applying the rules under the Torrens system. After that the question varies the scenario by first including a transfer to a fictitious person, and then by adding a transfer to an innocent purchaser after the registration to a fictitious person:

(a) This needs an explanation of registration of title, *nemo dat*, and how mortgages worked under the old system, to explain whether title has been transferred successfully.

(b) This needs application of the Torrens system of title by registration with a comparison against the old system scenario to see how they are different.

(c) The inclusion of transfer of title to a fictitious person necessitates examining the *Gibbs v Messer* [1891] AC 248 exception and its effect on transfer of title.

(d) The last variant simply requires assessing the impact on title transfer of adding an innocent purchaser after the *Gibbs v Messer* transaction.

Answer

(a) Old system land

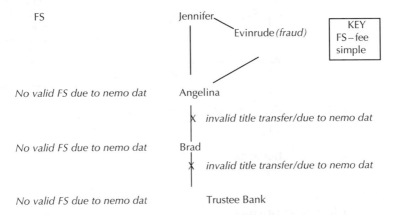

2-26 Under the old system, registration does not grant title. If title is to be passed successfully to each successive purchaser, then each previous title holder must have valid title to pass on, or the rules of *nemo dat* will apply. Under the *nemo dat quod non habet* principle, the grantor cannot grant an estate which they do not have.

Jennifer has a fee simple interest. Angelina gained her title through Evinrude's fraudulent dealings but because Evinrude does not have title, Angelina cannot get title, as per *nemo dat*. Therefore under the old system, even though Angelina is registered, she has registered invalid title and the registration is meaningless. As Angelina has no title she cannot pass on title, so Brad cannot get title from her either, without infringing the *nemo dat* principle. The current registered fee simple holder is the Trustee Bank, as under the old system a mortgage was a conveyance and not a charge, and the bank would hold fee simple until the mortgage was paid off, at which point the title would then be transferred to the mortgagee. Jennifer has to sue Trustee Bank to get her title back, and she is likely to succeed as all the transactions beneath her are tainted by Evinrude's fraud and thus invalid. Trustee Bank would have difficulty justifying their position as they obtained title through Brad, who had none to give; therefore, Trustee Bank suffers equally from the *nemo dat* principle.

The Trustee Bank will pursue a personal action against Brad for defective title (eg breach of contract), and Brad will then pursue personal action against Angelina, and Angelina against Evinrude. A chain of defective transfers of real property leads to a corresponding reversed chain of personal actions, and is a complicated, unwieldy system in which no one is likely to win, except Jennifer, who will get her house back.

 *Answer*

(b) Torrens title

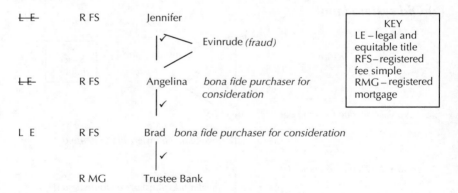

Conclusion

- Jennifer has no entitlement;
- Angelina has no entitlement;
- Brad has legal and equitable fee simple;
- Trustee Bank has registered mortgage.

2-27 Jennifer has legal and equitable fee simple because she is registered, and the Torrens system is a system of title by registration, not registration of title (Berwick CJ in *Breskvar v Wall* (1971) 126 CLR 376).

Once Angelina registers she gains legal title and is entitled to immediate indefeasibility upon registration (s 37 Land Title Act (Qld) 1994 (LTA);

Breskvar v Wall), free from all unregistered interests (s 184(1) LTA). In the diagram above, legal fee simple (L FS) moves from Jennifer to Angelina's registration, as only one person can be registered title holder at a time. Then it becomes a question of whether she has good title, in which case she will be entitled to equitable fee simple and will remain indefeasible, or whether she has bad title, in which case equitable fee simple will remain with Jennifer and Angelina's legal title will be defeasible by Jennifer. Under the Torrens's rules, Evinrude's fraud is irrelevant unless it can be imputed or attributed to someone on the central chain of title. However, there is no link between Evinrude and Angelina so his fraud cannot be imputed to her, which means she gains equitable fee simple and remains indefeasible, and Jennifer loses all entitlements and is left only with the remedy of seeking compensation from the Torrens system.

Lastly, has Angelina done anything to suggest she should not be entitled to good title? No, she appears to have displayed only good behaviour and she is a bona fide purchaser for consideration so the transfer of title is a valid transaction as represented by ✓ in the diagram. The issue in Torrens comes down to whether the purchasers' behaviour has been detrimental to their ability to retain title due to some form of unconscionable behaviour.

The same scenario can be repeated for the transaction between Angelina and Brad. Once Brad is registered, Angelina loses legal title because upon registration Brad gets immediate indefeasibility (s 37 LTA; *Breskvar v Wall*), free from all unregistered interests (s 184(1) LTA), so legal fee simple passes to Brad (L FS), leaving Angelina with potentially equitable fee simple (E FS).

There is no fraud by Angelina to be imputed or attributed to Brad, so it is now a question of whether Brad has done anything to suggest he should not be entitled to good title. Do any exceptions to indefeasibility appear to apply?

No, it appears Brad has demonstrated only good behaviour and is also a bona fide purchaser for consideration so the transfer of title is a valid transaction ✓. Brad obtains equitable fee simple as well, and Angelina retains no entitlement. Brad now has both equitable fee simple (E FS) and legal fee simple (L FS) in the diagram above, while Angelina has no fee simple entitlement.

The Trustee Bank has taken out a mortgage but unlike the old system, the mortgagor does not retain fee simple under Torrens, merely a charge over the property which is held as a security against the debt: s 74 LTA. This means the registration of the bank's mortgage entitles the bank to priority against the others, but does not affect Brad's indefeasibility of title. So this is also a valid transaction ✓, but Brad retains legal and equitable fee simple while the bank holds the registered mortgage, and the two registered interests co-exist simultaneously. Brad is bound by the registered mortgage as he is bound by all registered interests under s 184(1) LTA.

All the parties have obtained prima facie indefeasible title immediately upon registration (s 37 LTA; *Breskvar v Wall*), free from any unregistered interests: s 184(1) LTA. Their registered interests will remain indefeasible unless and until an exception to indefeasibility applies; none of the exceptions apply here.

The key differences between the old system and Torrens are:

- Mortgage: under the old system a mortgage was a conveyance and the bank held title until the debt was paid. Under Torrens a mortgage is a statutory charge over the land, ie an encumbrance on fee simple title, and the borrower retains fee simple.
- Effect of forgery: under the old system, forgery by anyone involved in the chain of transactions would invalidate any present, and subsequent transactions due to the *nemo dat quod habet* principle. Under Torrens, fraud does not affect the transfer of title to registered transactions unless one of the exceptions to indefeasibility applies, such as the fraud, personal equity or *Gibbs v Messer* [1891] AC 248 exceptions.

Jennifer's remedies: under the old system Jennifer is entitled to recover her fee simple title free of any mortgage, but under Torrens she loses fee simple and must claim compensation from the Torrens system under the insurance principle.

(c) Fictitious person exception

Conclusion

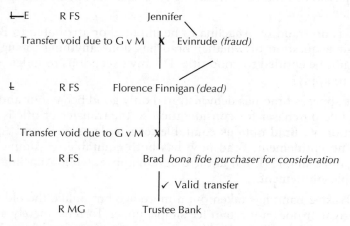

- Jennifer has equitable fee simple (E FS);
- Florence Finnigan has no entitlement;
- Brad has legal fee simple (L FS) but his title is void;
- Trustee Bank has a registered mortgage.

2-28 Jennifer has legal and equitable fee simple (L E FS) because she is registered, and the Torrens system is a system of title by registration, not registration of title (Berwick CJ in *Breskvar v Wall*).

Evinrude's fraudulent actions are irrelevant unless his actions can be attributed or imputed to the purchaser in the chain of title when the fraud exception would apply, but his fraudulent actions cannot be attributed to a dead person, so another exception must be used.

Once Florence Finnigan is registered, Jennifer loses her legal title because upon registration Florence Finnigan gets immediate indefeasibility (s 37 LTA; *Breskvar v Wall*), free from all unregistered interests: s 184(1) LTA (L FS moves from Jennifer to Florence when Florence gains legal title at registration).

The issue is whether Florence's title is indefeasible or whether an exception applies, giving her defeasible title. Yes: Florence Finnigan is dead so the *Gibbs v Messer* exception applies and the transfer of title is invalid as demonstrated by **X** in the diagram. However, simply making the transaction invalid would still leave a dead person as the holder of registered defeasible title. The court has rejected that option as being nonsensical on the certificate of title, so instead of being an invalid transaction, the transaction is deemed void. Although title is still in Florence Finnigan's name — legal fee simple has moved from Jennifer to Florence Finnigan who will have to be taken off the register using the appropriate remedies — the entire transaction is void, and Jennifer retains her equitable title (E FS) until she can get back her legal title(L FS). The general rule in *Gibbs v Messer* is that if any party to the transaction is dead or fictitious, then the transaction is void.

The same principles apply for the transfer of title from Florence Finnigan to Brad. Once Brad is registered, Florence loses legal title as upon registration Brad gets immediate indefeasibility (s 37 LTA; *Breskvar v Wall*), free from all unregistered interests: s 184(1) LTA. The issue is whether Brad retains indefeasible title and can take equitable entitlement from Jennifer, or whether one of the exceptions applies and his title is then also defeasible.

Brad has not done anything untoward to trigger a fraud or personal equity exception, and he is a bone fide purchaser for consideration, so the transfer of title is a valid transaction ✓. However, under the *Gibbs v Messer* rules, if any party to a transaction is dead or fictitious, then the transaction is void. Florence is a party to this transfer and therefore the transfer between Florence and Brad is void. Brad's registered legal title is therefore defeasible and Jennifer retains her equitable entitlement, and at this point would still be able to restore her legal title through application to the courts or the registrar.

Trustee Bank has registered its mortgage, and under Torrens this stands as a charge (s 74 LTA), and does not remove or replace any legal or equitable titles. The registration of the mortgage is a valid transaction ✓, no exceptions apply, and the indefeasible title holder will be bound by this mortgage: s 184(1) LTA.

Conclusion

As summarised beneath the diagram above, Jennifer has retained her equitable title and will be able to restore her legal title to regain her position as indefeasible holder of fee simple, as the transactions either side of Florence Finnigan's registration are void under the *Gibbs v Messer* rules. However, Jennifer will be bound by Trustee Bank's mortgage and will have to seek compensation.

(d) Joe Bloggs registers title

Conclusion

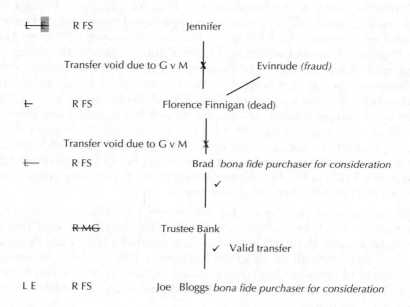

- Jennifer has nothing;
- Florence Finnigan has nothing;
- Brad has nothing;
- Trustee Bank has nothing;
- Joe Bloggs has legal and equitable fee simple: true indefeasible title.

2-29 All the transactions here are identical to those in answer (c). However, the purchase and registration of title by Joe Bloggs, bona fide purchaser for consideration, completely changes Jennifer's position. None of the exceptions apply to the transfer to Joe Bloggs and it is a valid transaction ✓. He will retain the immediate indefeasibility he received upon registration (s 37 LTA; *Breskvar v Wall*), free from any unregistered interests: s 184(1) LTA. This means Jennifer now loses her equitable fee simple entitlement to Joe Bloggs, leaving Jennifer with no entitlement at all, unable to regain her fee simple, and forced to seek compensation through the Torrens insurance principle.

Note: if the point at which Jennifer lost her entitlement to fee simple had to be determined to assess compensation, it would only be in this transfer, where Jennifer lost her equitable fee simple (E FS).

Examiner's Comments

2-30 One of the strengths of this answer is its careful step-by-step analysis of each of the transactions in each scenario. This is a very comprehensive question, covering all the basic options of transfer of title.

The use of diagrams is not ideal in a legal essay, but to answer a problem question, particularly under exam conditions, this would be a useful and clear way for a student to track and display the different transactions. The student has been very thorough and correctly grasped the concepts of indefeasibility and the differences between the old system land and Torrens. However, the student has failed to comment on and discuss the deferred indefeasibility demonstrated in the last scenario, due to *Gibbs v Messer*.

More information should have been provided about the remedies available by discussing how Jennifer could have regained her legal title. The student should have discussed the registrar's power to correct the Register, applications for compensation to Torrens, and when compensation can be calculated: for example, *Spencer v Registrar of Titles* (1909) 9 CLR 641; *Registrar General v Behn* [1980] 1 NSWLR 589; and *Keddell v Regarose* (1995) 1 Qd R 172.

This is the greatest weakness of this answer: the student has correctly identified the transactional outcomes but has failed to identify how to correct anything for their client. Overall a good effort was made on the transactional side, but the answer sorely lacks in the conclusion and remedies.

Keep in Mind

2-31 Students should keep in mind the following:

- One of the single greatest errors in a Torrens title question is to skip steps in the transfer chain, thereby giving title to the wrong party, claiming indefeasibility where there is none, or incorrectly applying deferred indefeasibility too early. These errors make the conclusion incorrect leading to incorrect remedies, incorrect compensation calculations, and anything dependent upon identifying the correct title holder will also be incorrect. This can turn into a downward spiral and write off an entire question for a student. Although diagrams should not be included in an essay answer, they can help avoid this issue, and if the answer is written out in full as well, there should be no reason to discourage any tools that assists students to clarify their thought processes.

- Forgetting remedies is another common error. Whenever students deal with Torrens issues, they should never end a question without doublechecking:
  a) Does the register need correcting?; and
  b) Does anyone deserve compensation?

Question 4

2-32 To celebrate their 10th wedding anniversary, Hector and Molly asked Angus (Hector's brother) and Rachel (Molly's identical twin sister) to look after their Rainforest Retreat while they toured Australia. They also left the certificate of title to their property with their trusted siblings.

On 22 November 2011 Rachel forged Hector and Molly's names on a contract to sell the property for $1.5 million to her friend, Tim. The contract is subject to Tim obtaining finance approval by December 14. The contract also specifies December 21 as the settlement date. Tim has paid a deposit of $150,000 and lodged a settlement notice on December 1.

On 23 November 2011 Angus forged Hector and Molly's names in an unconditional contract to sell the same property for $1.2 million to his wealthy colleague, Sally. Neither Sally nor Angus was aware of the earlier contract between Rachel and Tim. Despite her solicitor's advice, Sally decided against conducting any searches as she trusted Angus.

Answer Part A and Part B SEPARATELY (as these are alternative scenarios).

Part A: The sale to Sally was settled on December 8 after Sally duly paid the purchase price of $1.2 million to Angus. Sally is yet to lodge the transfer document for registration. Tim is yet to obtain his finance approval, and he has just found out about Sally's settlement. Angus and Rachel have absconded overseas. Hector and Molly are yet to return from their Australian tour. Advise Sally and Tim as to their legal position with respect to the property.

Part B: The sale to Sally was registered on December 11, a day after Hector and Molly returned from their Australian tour. Due to persisting storms and flooding since late November, the property is now worth only $900,000. Advise Hector and Molly on their rights in relation to the property.

Time allowed: 60 mins

Answer Plan

2-33 General view of the transactions:

- 22 Nov — conditional contract to Tim;
- 23 Nov — unconditional contract to Sally;
- 14 Dec — financial approval deadline for Tim to go unconditional;
- 21 Dec — Tim settlement date.

Part A

RO = registered owner; FS = fee simple

- 22 Nov — conditional contract to Tim;
- 23 Nov — unconditional contract to Sally;
- 8 Dec — Sally contract settled — unconditional — Sally gains equitable fee simple only, not registered;
- 14 Dec — financial approval deadline for Tim to go unconditional;
- 21 Dec — Tim settlement date.

Issue: There are competing equitable fee simple interests, Sally versus Tim, so it's necessary to compare parties' status: *Heid v Reliance Finance Corp Pty Ltd* (1983) 154 CLR 326.

It's necessary to highlight differences in equitable status, particularly as Sally has completely paid her purchase price, akin to *Osmanowski v Rose* [1974] VR 523.

1. Identify prior equity and later equity holders.
2. Do they have the same types of equitable interests, eg equitable interests in land or mere equities? If yes, then prior equity may prevail over later equity: *Rice v Rice* (1853) 61 ER 646.
3. Look at both parties' conduct and identify any merits, demerits or justifications, to determine who has the better equity: *Heid v Reliance* (Mason and Deane JJ):
   - Prior equity holder's demerits may postpone his or her priority: *Abigail v Lapin* [1934] AC 491.
   - Later equity holder's demerits may justify retention of prior equity holder's priority.

Part B

- 22 Nov — conditional contract to Tim;
- 23 Nov — unconditional contract to Sally;
- 8 Dec — Sally contract settled; it is unconditional but she only has equitable fee simple as she has not registered.

- Tim's contract is conditional, granting him equitable fee simple, as not registered;
- 11 Dec — Sally registered and she now has legal and equitable fee simple, while Tim only has equitable fee simple;
- 14 Dec — financial approval deadline for Tim to go unconditional;
- 21 Dec — Tim settlement date.

They are no longer competing equities as Sally is registered and has indefeasible title. Here the issue is whether Hector and Molly can get their house back, or are only entitled to compensation.

 ## Answer

2-34   Part A involves competing equities between Sally and Tim. As both Tim and Sally have equitable interests in land, Tim's prior equity would have priority on the basis of time (*Rice v Rice* (1853) 61 ER 646), subject to postponement of Tim's interest due to any unreasonable conduct (*Abigail v Lapin* [1934] AC 491), or if Sally can be determined to have the better equity in light of all the circumstances (Mason and Deane JJ in *Heid v Reliance Finance Corp Pty Ltd* (1983) 154 CLR 326).

Part A: Tim (prior equity holder)

Tim has paid a deposit (10% of purchase price), so he has handed over financial consideration. He has lodged his settlement notice promptly, as purchaser under s 138 Land Title Act 1994 (Qld) (LTA), giving notice to Sally and others of his interest in the property. It is not necessary for Tim to lodge a caveat: a settlement notice is equally effective at preventing registration of other interests, such as Sally's, under s 141(1) LTA. A settlement notice has fewer requirements than a caveat (s 139 LTA), and has the benefit of retaining Tim's priority over other instruments lodged. Under s 150 LTA Sally's transfer would be deemed to be lodged after Tim's transfer. There is also some debate as to whether Tim could lodge a caveat over a conditional contract.

He could try lodging a caveat before his settlement notice lapses. He is entitled to caveat in addition to lodging a settlement notice under s 151 LTA. Arguably, he has a caveatable interest pursuant to s 122(1)(a) LTA even if his contract remains conditional. This is because *Re Bosca Land Pty Ltd's Caveat* [1967] Qd R 119, which concluded a conditional contract is not caveatable on the basis that an equitable interest arises only when a purchaser is entitled to specific performance of contract, when a contract becomes unconditional, was not followed by later cases such as *Kuper v Keywest Constructions Pty Ltd* (1990) 3 WAR 419 or *Re Henderson's Caveat* [1998] 1 Qd R 632: 'With an expanded view of what can constitute an equitable interest in land, a correspondingly wider view of a caveatable interest ... can apply'. In *GPT Re Ltd v Lend Lease Real Estate Investments Pty Ltd* [2005] NSWSC 964 White J held: 'A purchaser under a conditional contract, where the vendor's obligation to convey is subject to an unfulfilled condition, has an equitable interest in the property which is sufficient to support a caveat'.

Tim has shown no postponing conduct, unlike *Abigail v Lapin* and *Breskvar v Wall*. His only significant demerit is that he is yet to obtain finance approval. Tim needs to satisfy this contractual condition.

Part A: Sally (later equity holder)

Sally has already completed settlement which is strong evidence of the potential detriment she would suffer, were she to lose priority, akin to *Osmanowski v Rose*. She does not have actual notice, but would have had constructive notice of Tim's prior equity if she had searched the register. It is possible this could lose her priority, as occurred in *Platzer v Commonwealth Bank of Australia* [1997] 1 Qd R 266 or *Moffet v Dillon* [1999] 2 VR 480. Had there been nothing to find on the register, her failure to search would not have damaged her priority (*Abigail v Lapin*), but given that Tim had lodged a settlement notice which would have put her on notice, the courts may deem she had constructive notice by deeming her position to be as if she had searched the register: *Bank of Credit and Commerce International (Overseas) Ltd v Akindele* [2001] Ch 437. It should also be noted she had not been misled or induced by Tim to act to her detriment.

Sally's decision to place her trust in Angus and go against her solicitor's advice is unjustifiable, and can be distinguished from *Jacobs v Platt Nominees Pty Ltd* [1990] VR 146 where the relationship in question was that of father and daughter, whereas the relationship between Sally and Tim is only that of colleagues. We are not told when Sally is lodging her title for registration, but any delay in lodging would further weaken her position.

In conclusion, it would seem that Tim's equitable interest would have priority over Sally's, on the basis of his being first in time, and that he has no postponing conduct in contrast to her constructive notice of his prior interest which is usually fatal to a claim. However, the fact that Tim has only paid a 10% deposit compared with her full purchase price does mean she will clearly suffer the greater hardship, and the courts may weigh that factor more heavily and give priority to Sally.

Part B: Hector and Molly versus Sally

2-35 Sally would obtain a prima facie indefeasible title immediately upon registration (*Breskvar v Wall*), which is free from Hector and Molly's unregistered interest: s 184(1) LTA.

Angus's fraud is irrelevant unless it can be imputed to Sally under a fraud exception to indefeasibility: s 184(3)(b) LTA. In the absence of any further information, there would appear to be no fraud by Sally as there is nothing to suggest she had any knowledge of Angus's forgery. None of the other exceptions to indefeasibility seems applicable. Thus the remedies under s 187 LTA to reclaim their title are unavailable to Hector and Molly.

Hector and Molly could be advised to caveat under s 122(1)(a) LTA against Sally's future dealings with the property while this issue is determined. In support of the couple's caveatable interest one could look to Barwick CJ and Gibbs J in *Breskvar v Wall* who were prepared to accept that previous registered owners, such as Breskvar or here, Hector and Molly, do retain an equitable interest in the land and not just mere equity, which would not be caveatable. Even if it were determined the couple only has mere equity, such mere equity can be a right in relation to land within the definition of 'interest' under the Acts Interpretation Act (Qld) 1954 s 36(b), and is therefore caveatable: *Mijo Developments Pty Ltd v Royal Agnes Waters Pty Ltd* [2007] NSWSC 199.

Hector and Molly may claim compensation under s 188(1)(a) LTA as they have been deprived of their fee simple because of the fraud of another person (Angus). Potentially s 189(1)(b) LTA could preclude the couple's compensation claim. Under *Registrar of Titles v Fairless* [1997] 1 VR 404 neglect by the claimant needs to be more than a contributing factor: if not the sole cause it needs to be considerable, a big or large contribution, before entitlement to compensation would be lost. The extent of the claimant's neglect is determined by considering the claimant's knowledge at the time.

Hector and Molly's neglect was in giving their certificate of title to their siblings. However, it could be argued that trusting their siblings is not neglect (*Jacobs v Platt Nominees*), and that they were justified in assuming their siblings would protect their interests.

The issue was phrased by Phillips and Tadgell JJA in *Registrar of Titles v Fairless*: even if their actions did constitute neglect, did their neglect substantially contribute to their deprivation, or was Angus's fraud the main cause of their loss? It is more likely the court would view Angus's fraud as the main contributing factor behind their loss, but while behaviour could still be deemed a large contributory factor (*Abigail v Lapin*), it is likely the courts will view the sibling relationship as providing a reasonable excuse for their conduct (Calloway J in *Registrar of Titles v Fairless*).

The other consideration is whether Angus committed the fraud or willful default while acting as Hector and Molly's agent. It is highly unlikely Angus was acting as their agent as determined by Callaway JA, or at least not acting within the scope of agency, as outlined by Phillips and Tadgell JJA in *Registrar of Titles v Fairless*.

Assuming that the couple remains entitled to compensation, then the measure of compensation would range from $900,000 (the property value at the date of court judgment under *Registrar General v Behn* (1981) 148 CLR 562) to $1.2 million (the property value at the date of claimant's deprivation: *Registrar of Titles (Q) v Crowle* (1947) 75 CLR 191).

The lower amount is likely and arguably sufficient to restore the couple to their pre-deprivation position, pursuant to *Registrar of Titles v Spencer*:

> Plainly the intention of the legislature is that a successful plaintiff can recover damages commensurate with the loss he has sustained in consequence of the wrongful deprivation — damages that will put him in the same position, so far as money can do it, as if the deprivation had not occurred. (*Registrar General v Behn*)

The court may award a slightly higher amount to cover related costs by analogy with *Keddell's* case, but some judges, as occurred in *Young v Hoger* [2002] QSC 013, may confine application of *Keddell's* case to mortgage transactions affected by fraud only, which would not assist Hector and Molly.

Examiner's Comments

2-36 The answer leans towards the stance expressed in *Rice v Rice*, which is perfectly acceptable, but does give recognition to some of the High Court of Australia decisions which have considered the evidential advantage which this 'prima facie' position may give a plaintiff who can show earlier possession. In cases such as *Lapin v Abigail* (1930) 44 CLR 166 and *Heid v Reliance*, there are suggestions by some of their Honours that the 'prima facie' temporal prioritising rule should not in any way fetter the court's consideration of the merits of the parties' claims. This kind of embellishment may not, ultimately, have any bearing on the advice given. There is probably no difference to the outcome of the priority dispute which depends upon the order in which one considers either the time of creation or the 'merits' of the claims rules. What is finally determinative is some imbalance in the merits of the claims.

Most of the cases could possibly have done with a little more discussion on their rulings and application thereof. In discussing *Fairless,* for example, more could have been made of the criteria that apply when neglect is the contributing factor, and the debate on whether conditional contracts are caveatable, or whether prior registered owners are entitled to caveat. They have all had much written about them and could have been discussed in more depth.

The answer arrives at the correct legal position, and accurately establishes the legal rules for determining the priority dispute. To its credit, the answer does examine with sufficient detail the general assessment of the merits of each party, something often missed by students. Overall, it is a well-constructed, detailed answer that clearly and correctly addresses the issues in the question.

Keep in Mind

2-37 Students should keep in mind the following:

- Do not mix and match the priority rules. Each rule concerns a particular and unique type of competition. Adopt a strict approach, by classifying interests and then applying rules. If there is doubt about the nature of the interest, it may be necessary to go through the exercise more than once in order to cover all the options. A different characterisation may lead to the application of a different rule, and may result in a different ranking of the interests. Alternative analyses are not uncommon where the 'interest' in doubt is equitable in nature, and therefore less easily characterised.

- Do not forget that notice (actual, constructive or imputed) of the interest of the prior interest holder will normally be fatal to the claim of a later interest holder. Examine the later holder's conduct and omissions for evidence of constructive notice.

- When examining the conduct of a prior interest holder (for postponing conduct), do not try to impugn any aspect of conduct merely on the basis of it being less than absolutely pure. Relevant misconduct will be such as is reasonably foreseeable to affect the interests of other parties who may be interested in the property concerned: see *FAI Insurances Ltd v Pioneer Concrete Services Ltd* (1987) 15 NSWLR 552.

Chapter 3

Torrens System

Key Issues

3-1 Legislation providing for the registration of documents in a deeds registry had a number of benefits. First, the prioritising of documents according to the date of registration encouraged persons to register documents. Second, persons taking interests in land could search and ascertain what interests affected that land. Third, there was security against loss and destruction: the registry provided a repository for documents.

However, despite the advantages, there were also defects in the system. Any title was derivative. It was dependent on the chain of title supporting it. Any defects in the chain of title were not cured by registration. Registration did not perfect instruments; it merely gave them priority. In addition, there was always the need to investigate the title by examining prior documents to ensure title was securely based. Further, such investigation required specialised skill, especially where the title became more complex through subdivision, creating divergent chains of title. And even though the title might be thoroughly investigated, it could still be set aside through fraud, or where some defect escaped the investigator.

The Torrens system was established to address the problems arising out of a registration of documents system. In essence, it achieved this by the act of registration in itself, establishing title in the applicant for registration. The applicant might come before the registrar based on some documentary evidence (eg a transfer or a mortgage), but the title flowed not from that documentary evidence, but by the act of registration. When it came to an investigation of title, there was no need for the investigator to look any further than the registry to establish the title. If there were any defects in the manner in which the applicant for registration became registered, these defects were cured by registration. The result was that the applicant's title became indefeasible, subject to some limited exceptions (those set out in s 42 of the Real Property Act 1900 (NSW) or ss 184(3)(b) and 185 of the Land Title Act 1994 (Qld) (LTA), and rights *in personam*). As Barwick CJ stated in *Breskvar v Wall* (1972) 126 CLR 376 at 385:

> The Torrens system of registered title of which the Act is a form is not a system of registration of title but a system of title by registration. That which the certificate of title describes is not the title which the registered proprietor formerly had, or which but for registration would have had. The

title it certifies is not historical or derivative. It is the title which registration itself has vested in the proprietor. Consequently, a registration which results from a void instrument is effective according to terms of the registration. It matters not what the cause or reason for which the instrument is void.

The questions that follow deal with the subject of fraud as an exception to an indefeasible title, the position of the potential registered proprietor between settlement and registration, caveats and equitable interests under the Real Property Act 1900 (NSW) and the Land Title Act 1994 (Qld). The material consists of one essay-type question and four problem-type questions. Each successive problem question raises issues dealt with in the essay answer and in previous questions. Therefore some of the detail in the earlier questions might not be evident in the later answers in order to avoid repetition. The questions cover the different varieties of fraud under Torrens: fraud by the registered owner, fraud by a third party, fraud by the registered proprietor, mortgage fraud, the *in personam* or personal equity exception, and compensation due to complete or partial deprivation of an interest by the actions of a third party.

3-2 Before answering the questions, students should have an understanding of the following matters:

✓ sections 42, 43, 43A of the Real Property Act 1900 (NSW);

✓ section 164 of the Conveyancing Act 1919 (NSW);

✓ sections 11A, 184, 185, 187, 188, 189 of the Land Title Act 1994 (Qld);

✓ the concept of fraud under the Real Property Act 1900 (NSW) and under the Land Title Act 1994 (Qld), as discussed in:

  – *Abigail v Lapin* [1934] AC 491;

  – *Assets Co Ltd v Mere Roihi* [1905] AC 176;

  – *Australian Guarantee Corp Ltd v De Jaeger* [1984] VR 483;

  – *Bahr v Nicolay (No 2)* (1988) 164 CLR 604;

  – *Bank of South Australia Ltd v Ferguson* (1998) 151 ALR 729;

  – *Bourseguin v Stannard Bros Holdings Pty Ltd* [1994] 1 Qd R 231;

  – *Breskvar v Wall* (1972) 126 CLR 376;

  – *Fraser v Walker* [1967] 1 AC 569;

  – *Grgic v Australian and New Zealand Banking Group Ltd* (1994) 31 NSWLR 202;

  – *Heron v Broadbent* (1919) 20 SR (NSW) 101;

  – *Hilton v Gray* [2007] QSC 401;

- *Latec Investments v Hotel Terrigal Pty Ltd* (1965) 113 CLR 265;

- *Loke Yew v Port Swettenham Rubber Co Ltd* [1913] AC 491;

- *Mills v Stokman* (1967) 116 CLR 61;

- *Munro v Stuart* (1924) 41 SR (NSW) 203;

- *Presbyterian Church (NSW) Property Trust v Scots Church Development Ltd* [2007] NSWSC 676;

- *Pyramid Building Society (in liq) v Scorpion Hotels Pty Ltd* [1998] 1 VR 188;

- *Registrar General v Behn* (1980) 1 NSWLR 589;

- *Registrar of Titles v Fairless* [1997] 1 VR 404;

- *Registrar of Titles v Keddell* (1993) QCR 54;

- *Schultz v Corwill Properties Pty Ltd* (1969) 90 WN (Pt 1) (NSW) 529;

- *Spencer v Registrar of Titles* (1909) 9 CLR 641;

- *Valbirn Pty Ltd v Powprop Pty Ltd* [1991] 1 Qd R 295;

- *Waimiha Sawmilling Co v Waione Timber Co* [1926] AC 101 at 106;

- *White v Tomasel* [2004] 2 Qd R 438;

- *Young v Hoger* [2002] QSC 013,

✓ the concept of a 'dealing registrable';

✓ the principle in *Wilkes v Spooner* [1911] 2 KB 473;

✓ equitable interests under the Torrens system as discussed in:

- *Barry v Heider* (1914) 19 CLR 197;

- *Abigail v Lapin* [1934] AC 491;

- *Leros Pty Ltd v Terara Pty Ltd* (1992) 174 CLR 407.

Question 1

3-3 Discuss the concept of fraud in relation to s 42 of the Real Property Act 1900 (NSW). Your answer should refer to relevant case law and the effect of notice.

Time allowed: 2 hours

Answer Plan

3-4 This is a general essay type question calling for an overall view of the manner in which fraud is viewed in the Torrens system. In explaining the concept of fraud it is essential to refer to the various authorities that have reviewed and commented on the concept. A suggested answer outline is as follows:

- General introduction of fraud as dishonesty, moral turpitude as seen in *Wicks v Bennett* (1921) 30 CLR 80.
- Registration by virtue of another's fraud will not affect the registered proprietor in the absence of notice of that fraud: *Fraser v Walker* [1966] AC 569; *Breskvar v Wall* (1972) 126 CLR 376.
- Fraud must be brought home to the registered proprietor: *Assets Co Ltd v Mere Roihi* [1905] AC 176; *Loke Yew v Port Swettenham Rubber Co Ltd* [1913] AC 491.
- Fraud is not constituted by mere notice: *Munro v Stuart* (1924) 41 SR (NSW) 203.
- Fraud may be constituted by the dishonest repudiation of an agreement to recognise an outstanding interest: *Bahr v Nicolay (No 2)* (1988) 164 CLR 604.
- Fraud may be constituted by an agent's fraud: *Schultz v Corwill Properties Pty Ltd* (1969) 90 WN (Pt 1) (NSW) 529.
- Fraud may be constituted by false attestation of an instrument: *Australian Guarantee Corp Ltd v De Jager* [1984] VR 483; *Grgic v Australian and New Zealand Banking Group Ltd* (1994) 31 NSWLR 202.
- Fraud must operate on the mind of the 'defrauded person': *Bank of South Australia v Ferguson* (1998) 151 ALR 729.

Answer

3-5 Section 42 of the Real Property Act 1900 (NSW) provides that the title of the registered proprietor is paramount (often stated as 'indefeasible') subject to the exceptions provided for in the section. Upon registration the title of the registered proprietor becomes 'immune from adverse claims, other than those specifically excepted': *Fraser v Walker* [1967] 1 AC 569 at 585. One of those exceptions which deprives the registered proprietor from immunity is fraud. The fraud required to deprive a person of an indefeasible title is generally more than a mere disregard of rights of which the person seeking registration had notice. That is, more is required in order to lose immunity than what might be described as equitable fraud:

> Not all species of fraud which attract equitable remedies will amount to fraud in the statutory sense. The distinction may be illustrated as follows. In some circumstances, equity subjects the interest of a purchaser of unregistered land to an antecedent interest of which the purchaser has notice. However, in respect of land to which the Act applies, registration

of a transfer is not fraudulent in the statutory sense required to qualify the operation of the doctrine of indefeasibility, merely because the transferee knows that registration will defeat an antecedent unregistered interest of which the transferee has notice. *(Bank of South Australia Ltd v Ferguson* (1998) 151 ALR 729 at 732)

That is not to say that equitable fraud might not fall into the statutory concept of fraud in s 42 of the Real Property Act 1900 (NSW). Where the equitable fraud is a 'dishonest course' resulting from 'pretence and collusion in the conscious misuse of a power' *(Latec Investments Ltd v Hotel Terrigal Pty Ltd (in liq)* (1965) 113 CLR 265 at 273–4) then it will fall within the statutory concept, in other words, where the equitable fraud is dishonest. This is consistent with the traditional definition of fraud under the statute, stated by Lord Lindley in *Assets Co Ltd v Mere Roihi* [1905] AC 176 at 210:

Fraud ... means actual fraud, dishonesty of some sort, not what is called constructive or equitable fraud.

In *Wicks v Bennett* (1912) 30 CLR 80 at 91 fraud meant:

... something more than mere disregard of rights of which the person sought to be affected had notice. It imports something in the nature of "personal dishonesty or moral turpitude".

Assets Co Ltd v Mere Roihi

3-6 In *Assets Co Ltd v Mere Roihi* certain Maori land had been registered in the appellant's name. It had been claimed the appellant had obtained its title by fraud. The evidence showed that there had been no fraud by the company. In speaking of the registration of a registered proprietor, Lord Lindley stated at 210:

The mere fact that he might have found out fraud if he had been more vigilant, and had made further inquiries which he omitted to make, does not of itself prove fraud on his part. But if it be shown that his suspicions were aroused, and that he abstained from making inquiries for fear of learning the truth, the case is very different, and fraud may be properly ascribed to him.

In *Assets Co* the Privy Council further pointed out that fraud (at 210):

... must be brought home to the person whose registered title is impeached or to his agents. Fraud by persons from whom he claims does not affect him unless knowledge of it is brought home to him or to his agents.

In *Assets Co* the evidence of fraud broke down because no fraud could be attributable to the company or its agents.

Fraser v Walker

3-7 Again, in *Fraser v Walker* [1966] AC 569, Mrs Fraser, a tenant in common with her husband, executed a mortgage in her own right forging her husband's signature in addition. The mortgagee exercised the power of sale when the Frasers became in default under the mortgage.

The Frasers argued that the forged mortgage had no entitlement to registration and the rights flowing from registration for the mortgagee were void (which of course included the power of sale and subsequent vesting of title in the purchaser from the mortgagee).

The Privy Council stated that this argument would be destructive to the registration system. It referred to titles derived from void instruments and stated that the registration of those instruments was 'effective to vest and to divest title and to protect the registered proprietor against adverse claims': at 584. The Privy Council referred to the decision in *Assets Co Ltd v Mere Roihi* with approval adopting the view of 'fraud' taken in that case. A registered proprietor who took from a forged instrument was protected under the indefeasible provision, provided that registered proprietor was not a party to the forgery or did not know the instrument was forged.

Breskvar v Wall

3-8 The decision of the Privy Council in *Fraser v Walker* was adopted by the High Court in *Breskvar v Wall* (1972) 126 CLR 376.

The Breskvars executed a transfer by way of mortgage leaving the name of the transferee on the form blank. Their loan moneys came from Petrie. Petrie fraudulently entered Wall's name (Wall was Petrie's grandson) as transferee and registered the transfer. Wall later sold the land to Alban Pty Ltd, executing a transfer in the company's favour. Before registration of the transfer, the Breskvars lodged a caveat. Alban Pty Ltd argued that it was a bona fide purchaser for value, without notice of the interest of the Breskvars. Chief Justice Barwick, in his judgment, emphasised the validity of title under the Torrens system was not dependent on the title from which registration was derived. Registration vests the title. An instrument void by virtue of fraud will not affect the registered proprietor unless that fraud can be brought home to the registered proprietor (at 385):

> The Torrens system of registered title of which the Act is a form is not a system of title by registration. That which the certificate of title described is not the title which the registered proprietor formerly had, or which but for registration would have had. The title it certifies is not historical or derivative. It is the title which registration itself has vested in the proprietor. Consequently, a registration which results from a void instrument is effective according to the terms of the registration. It matters not what the cause or reason for which the instrument is void.

Loke Yew v Port Swettenham Rubber Co Ltd

3-9 Fraud was brought home to the registered proprietor in *Loke Yew v Port Swettenham Rubber Co Ltd* [1913] AC 491. The respondent company's agent (Glass) procured a sale and transfer of land by the registered proprietor on the basis of a fraudulent misrepresentation. Glass represented that the interests of the appellant, who was a tenant of the registered proprietor, would not be disturbed and signed a document to that effect. Following registration of the company's transfer, Glass (as the company's agent) brought proceedings to eject the appellant from the land. The Privy Council found the transfer was obtained by fraud and that there had been a deliberate attempt to deprive the appellant of his land. It was more than a case of proceeding to registration with notice of an outstanding interest. The respondent had gained registration only on the basis of a deceitful promise to recognise the outstanding interest.

Munro v Stuart

3-10 Mere notice of an outstanding interest will not deprive the registered proprietor of indefeasibility, on the basis of fraud, whether that notice is received before the contract for purchase of the registered interest or after contract, during investigation of title: *Munro v Stuart* (1924) 41 SR (NSW) 203.

In *Munro v Stuart,* the registered proprietor, prior to contract, had notice of various leases of less than three years duration in respect of the property he was acquiring. There was no definite agreement made between the purchasing registered proprietor and vendor of the property that, on registration, the registered proprietor would preserve or recognise the leases. On obtaining registration, the registered proprietor began ejectment proceedings against the tenants. The landlord under the leases (the vendor) began injunction proceedings against the registered proprietor.

Harvey J held the landlord/plaintiff's proceeding must fail, first, because if there was any fraud it was practised against the tenants and not the landlord, and the tenants were not the plaintiffs; and second, because merely having notice of an outstanding interest did not constitute fraud. It should be noted that at the time of the decision, notice of short-term tenancies was not specifically provided for as an exception under s 42 of the Real Property Act 1900 (NSW), as s 42(d) had not at that time been enacted.

Munro v Stuart is to be distinguished from *Loke Yew v Port Swettenham Rubber Co Ltd* in two respects. In the latter case, the respondent had made a fraudulent representation in order to induce the transfer of the property, and further, the respondent had agreed to recognise the unregistered interest of the appellant on acquisition of the property. Neither of these elements were present in *Munro v Stuart.* However, one of the elements, namely an agreement to recognise the unregistered interest or registration was present in *Bahr v Nicolay (No 2)* (1988) 164 CLR 604.

Bahr v Nicolay (No 2)

3-11 In *Bahr v Nicolay (No 2)*, Mr and Mrs Bahr sold their property to Nicolay, subject to Nicolay granting them a lease of the property and a right to repurchase. Nicolay then sold the property to the Thompsons. The sale agreement included a clause of acknowledgment by the Thompsons of the repurchase provision of the earlier contract. The Thompsons told the Bahrs that they 'recognised' the repurchase agreement, but later refused to sell the land when the Bahrs took up their right to purchase. The High Court found in favour of the Bahrs. Justices Wilson, Toohey and Brennan found that there was a constructive trust imposed on the registered proprietor (the Thompsons) to the extent of the interest held by the Bahrs. Mason CJ and Dawson J, however, found the conduct of the Thompsons fell within the statutory fraud exception. Their Honours endorsed the view (at 615) that the fraud section (in this case, the Transfer of Land Act 1893 (WA)):

> ... should be construed strictly "and the exception liberally". The section restricts, in the interests of indefeasibility of title, rights which would exist otherwise at law or in equity. And granted that an exception is to be made for fraud, why should the exception not embrace fraudulent conduct arising from the dishonest repudiation of a prior interest which the registered proprietor has acknowledged, or has agreed to recognise as a basis for obtaining title as well as fraudulent conduct which enables him to obtain title or registration.

Agent's fraud

3-12 It was said in *Assets Co Ltd v Mere Roihi* that knowledge of the fraud must be brought home to the registered proprietor 'or his agents' (at 210) to fall within the exception. A distinction is made where:

- the agent's fraudulent activity has resulted in the registration of the principal for the principal's benefit;
- the agent, although not involved in fraudulent activity from which the principal benefits, nevertheless has knowledge of the fraudulent activity which has resulted in the principal's registration;
- the agent acts fraudulently towards the principal for the agent's benefit thereby securing thereby the principal's registration.

In the first two cases, the agent's knowledge is imputed to the principal because there is a presumption the agent communicated knowledge in respect of the agency transaction to the principal. But can it be said that the principal is to be imputed with the knowledge of the agent's fraud against the principal? Street CJ thought not, in *Schultz v Corwill Properties Pty Ltd* (1969) 90 WN (Pt 1) (NSW) 529. In that case, a solicitor (Galea) forged a mortgage by the defendant company (for whom he purported to act) in favour of the plaintiff-mortgagee (Schultz), from whom he had instructions to act. The solicitor misappropriated the loan moneys. Later the plaintiff-mortgagee executed a discharge of the mortgage at the solicitor's behest, who advised that the 'amount repaid' would be invested.

In an attempt to regain security for the misappropriated loan moneys, the plaintiff argued that the registration of the mortgage should stand on the basis of *Fraser v Walker*. On the other hand, the plaintiff argued the discharge of mortgage should not stand. The basis for this argument was the tenuous assertion that indefeasibility was not attracted by the registration of a discharge of mortgage. In the absence of authority supporting the plaintiff's contention, Street CJ held that *Fraser v Walker* applied to the discharge of mortgage. To counter the plaintiff's argument, the defendant contended that the registration of the mortgage was obtained by the fraud of the plaintiff's principal, and that the fraud by the agent was brought home to the principal. (The plaintiff also used this argument against the defendant in respect of the discharge of mortgage.)

Street CJ rejected this imputation of agent's knowledge to the principal (at 541):

> ... the supposition that the agent [Clive Galea] communicated his own fraud to the principal [Mrs Schultz] is too improbable to be entertained even by a court of equity.

Fraud may also be brought home to the registered proprietor through a false certificate of attestation. If an instrument is lodged for registration with a certificate of attestation which is known to be false by the employees of the registered proprietor then it will amount to fraud. In *Australian Guarantee Corp Ltd v De Jaeger* [1984] VR 483, the employees of the mortgagee corporation (AGC) knew that the person who attested the signature of the mortgagors had not seen one of the mortgagors execute the mortgage. In fact, that mortgagor's signature had been forged. The court stated (at 498):

> ... when AGC presented the subject instrument of mortgage for registration, it was representing to the Registrar of Titles, as against the mortgagors, an honest belief that they, and each of them, had executed the instrument in the presence of a witness who, if it came to the point, could be relied on to prove the execution. To lodge an instrument for registration in the knowledge that the attesting witness had not been present at execution must deprive the lodging party of an honest belief that it is a genuine document on which the Registrar can properly act.

De Jaeger's case was also characterised by the fact that the employees of AGC failed to make further inquiries to ascertain the true position in relation to the execution of the mortgage. It is to be distinguished for this reason from the decision in *Grgic v Australian and New Zealand Banking Group Ltd* (1994) 31 NSWLR 202. In *Grgic*, the impersonator of the registered proprietor was introduced to the bank's employees by a customer whom the employees knew. In fact, the impersonator was introduced as the father of the male customer. The impersonator signed a mortgage in the presence of the employees, forging the signature of the registered proprietor. The signature compared favourably with the signature of the registered proprietor on an independent document. The court stated (at 222):

> In the circumstances, it being well established that a person who presents for registration a document which is forged or has been fraudulently or improperly obtained, is not guilty of "fraud" if he honestly believes it to be a genuine document which can be properly acted upon ... and that a less than meticulous practice as to the identification of persons purporting to

deal with land registered under the provisions of the Act does not constitute a course of conduct so reckless as to be tantamount to fraud.

The person defrauded

3-13 For the fraud exception to apply, the person claiming fraud must have the fraud committed against himself or herself. It is not sufficient that some fraudulent conduct be present in the transaction. The fraud:

> ... to be operative, must operate on the mind of the person said to have been defrauded and to have induced detrimental action by that person. (*Bank of South Australia Ltd v Ferguson* (1998) 151 ALR 729 at 734)

In *Ferguson's* case a branch manager had forged the respondent's signature to a 'statement of position' document setting out the respondent's financial position. Later, a valuation of the respondent's property had been altered by the replacement branch manager, having the effect of increasing the value of the respondent's property. The respondent was not aware of any of these matters. On the basis of these documents, the bank's regional office approved a loan to the respondent secured by mortgage over his property, a loan on which he later defaulted.

The respondent argued that the broad picture of the documents amounted to fraud within the exception under the Act and that fraud was brought home to the bank as registered proprietor of the mortgage. The High Court adopted the rationale of the judgment of the dissenting Matheson J in the Full Court. The 'statement of position' was not prepared or used for the purpose of harming or cheating the respondent, nor did it have that effect. Further, the valuation was not a mortgage term, nor was the respondent under a serious mistake about the mortgage contents in respect of any fundamental term.

The alleged fraud of forged signature and altered valuation had no operational effect on the decision of the respondent to grant a mortgage in favour of the bank.

Examiner's Comments

3-14 The essay covered the matters raised in the outline. One of the difficulties in an essay of this nature is how to order the various aspects of fraud under discussion. For example, in defining fraud, should the issue of notice be discussed in full at that stage or treated in full at some later stage as it was in this essay? Here, it was dealt with later because it flowed into the considerations raised in *Bahr v Nicolay (No 2)*. Further, it seemed preferable to deal with concepts such as bringing fraud home to the registered proprietor before dealing with *Bahr v Nicolay (No 2)*. However, the order of the essay is as much about personal choice as anything else. As long as the topics flow in a logical fashion it really does not matter in what order they are discussed. What is important is that all matters are covered.

The answer has been written at length to be instructive. In an exam situation the quotations from the cases might be excluded and the number of cases dealt with abbreviated and restricted.

Keep in Mind

3-15   Students should keep in mind the following:

- Sometimes students omit the issue of fraud arising from the attestation of an instrument: issues raised in such cases as *Grgic & De Jaeger*. It is important to deal with fraud on this level.
- Distinguishing that equitable fraud is not necessarily (if at all) fraud for the purpose of the statute requires mention. This is also important when raising the issue of notice.
- Mention of the various types of notice, constructive imputed and actual, and how notice is regulated by the Conveyancing Act 1919 (NSW) is often overlooked. The answer did not deal with this matter on the basis that it has been covered elsewhere: see **Question 1, Chapter 4**. However, under exam conditions, discussion of notice is required.
- The point made by the High Court in *Ferguson's* case (that the fraud must operate on the mind of the person claiming to be defrauded to that person's detriment) is an insight into the understanding of fraud that should be mentioned.

Question 2

3-16   Kate owns an apartment in Townsville. Before going to join her boyfriend on a commune in India she asks her brother, David, a lawyer, to look after all her property matters while she is away. Unbeknown to Kate, David has a gambling problem. At the time, the apartment is worth $550,000.

Two months after Kate leaves, David forges Kate's signature and registers Kate's apartment in his own name. David's secretary, Susie Siren, has just inherited some money so he sells it to her for $250,000, all she has available, then he heads to Las Vegas. An issue with subsidence is suspected in the building, and the property is now valued at only $350,000. Susie registers her title and puts the apartment on the market through Lucky Real Estate. The subsidence rumour has been proven unfounded, and Jack Jones makes an offer to buy the apartment at $350,000, well below the current market value of $450,000, but as he already has an approved mortgage and can settle quickly the estate agent persuades Susie to agree.

Jack gets his pre-approved mortgage funds from National Investment Fund (NIF) and settles the contract and Susie banks the funds. Then Jack registers his title but, before NIF has registered their mortgage, Susie and Jack put the house on auction, sell it to Larry Lizard for $500,000 cash, and head for the Bahamas together, very pleased with their clever con. Kate returns from India to find Larry in residence as the registered owner of her apartment, and David nowhere to be found:

(a) Advise all parties on their options.

(b) How much money do Jack and Susie take to the Bahamas?

(c) What might be Kate's compensation, if any?

Time allowed: 2 hours

 Answer Plan

3-17 This is a problem question dealing with Torrens fraud. Each transaction needs to be dealt with separately to ensure appropriate allocation of knowledge and liability.

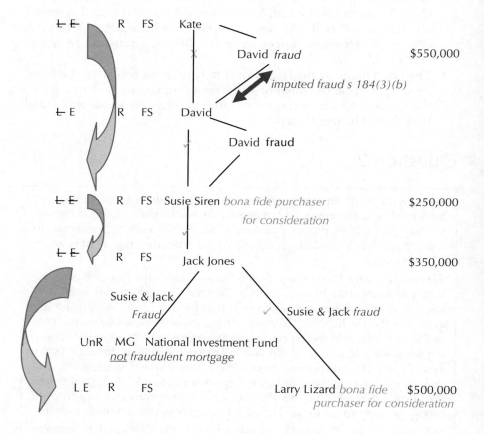

(Note: arrow shows transfers of equitable title from party to party; that is the 'E' representing the equitable entitlement to fee simple interest.)

Kate to David: no leaving of certificate of title and no negligence on her part (*Abigail v Lapin* [1934] AC 491): value $550,000.

David forges into own name: s 184(3)(b) Land Title Act (Qld) 1994 (LTA) fraud applies; therefore, Kate loses legal title (L) upon David's registration but retains equitable title (E) as David is not indefeasible.

David sells to Susie Siren $250,000 (value $350,000): no suggestion of impropriety on Susie's part (bona fide purchaser for consideration); Susie registers and gains legal title (L) from David; Kate loses equitable title (E) upon Susie gaining good defeasible title (arrow from E besides Kate to E besides Susie) and Susie now has indefeasible title.

Susie sells to Jack $350,000 (value $450,000): no impropriety here as Susie has indefeasible title and Jack is a bona fide purchaser for consideration; Jack registers so legal title (L) passes from Susie to Jack; he has good indefeasible title too so equitable title (E) transfers from Susie to Jack as well (arrow).

NIF: defeasible and not binding mortgage due to lack of registration; possible delay in registration but could be standard business delay, nothing to suggest negligence; *not* fraudulent mortgage.

Jack to Larry: fraudulent behaviour by Jack as he knows there should be a mortgage on the title, but he sells without disclosing and takes the money for himself; Susie involved in the con on a criminal basis but no longer has any title in the house; cannot impute Jack or Susie's fraud to Larry.

Larry: gains legal title (L) from Jack upon registration; bona fide purchaser for consideration so gains equitable title (E) from Jack as well (arrow).

Kate: lost equitable (E) and legal (L) title, so must apply for Torrens compensation.

Answer

3-18 This problem question deals with multiple property transfers with various fraudulent activities along the way. This answer will address each transfer individually to determine the status of the parties at each point.

(a) All parties' options

Title transfer from Kate to David

3-19 Upon registration David gets immediate indefeasibility (s 37 LTA; *Breskvar v Wall* (1972) 126 CLR 376), free from all unregistered interests: s 184(1) LTA. Under s 184(3)(b) LTA, David's fraudulent actions are imputed to his title and his title becomes defeasible and the transaction becomes invalid; therefore, David has legal title but no equitable entitlement. Were Kate to return at this point, she would still retain her equitable entitlement to her fee simple and would be able to get back her legal title through the courts due to David's fraud.

Title transfer from David to Susie

3-20 Upon registration Susie gets immediate indefeasibility (s 37 LTA; *Breskvar v Wall*), free from all unregistered interests (s 184(1) LTA), and she gains legal title from David. As Susie is a bona fide purchaser for consideration, she gains equitable fee simple as well, despite obtaining title through David's fraud, as *nemo dat* does not apply under Torrens.

Title transfer from Susie to Jack

3-21 Upon registration Jack gets immediate indefeasibility (s 37 LTA; *Breskvar v Wall*) free from all unregistered interests (s 184(1) LTA), so he gets legal fee simple from Susie. There is no fraud in Susie's passing of title to Jack, so Jack is a bona fide purchaser for consideration here and gains equitable title as well from Susie.

Jack and bank

3-22 This is a valid transaction, as there is no suggestion he fraudulently deceived the bank when taking the mortgage, nor is there any suggestion the bank was negligent in their processing of his mortgage application. The only issue here is the bank fails to register its mortgage prior to the next sale, and there is no information given suggesting this was caused by an improper delay. A delay by the bank in lodging would have argued against their mortgage being enforceable anyway, and the fact that it was not lodged prior to Larry's registration still makes it unenforceable, so either way Larry is not bound by their unregistered mortgage under s 184(1) LTA. The bank could still pursue Jack on a personal and contractual basis, and he has criminal charges to face, but lack of registration ensures there is no link between the land and the mortgage once title passes to Larry.

Title transfer from Jack to Larry

3-23 Upon registration Larry obtains immediate indefeasibility (s 37 LTA; *Breskvar v Wall*), free from all unregistered interests (s 184(1) LTA), so he gains legal fee simple from Jack. As the fraud by Susie and Jack cannot be imputed to Larry and there is no association between them, Larry is a bona fide purchaser for consideration and obtains equitable fee simple as well, giving him indefeasible title.

Conclusion

3-24 Kate has neither legal nor equitable entitlement and must sue for compensation under Torrens.

David — has no entitlements but is criminally liable for fraud.

Susie — has no entitlements, but may be liable for conspiring with Jack against NIF.

Jack – no entitlements but would be criminally liable for intentionally defrauding NIF.

NIF – because their mortgage is unregistered, they will be unable to enforce it against Larry, who is only bound by registered interests. NIF would have to pursue Jack or turn to their own insurance, unless they could prove the problem was attributable to the processes of the Torrens system, in which case they could try and claim insurance from Torrens. They are unlikely to get compensation as the fraud involved was not Torrens fraud; it seems they just did not register quickly enough so probably have to rely on their own insurance.

Larry – he is the final bona fide purchaser for consideration and as he has indefeasible title, he will be fully entitled to both legal and equitable fee simple for the property.

(b) Jack and Susie's funds to Bahamas

3-25 Jack and Susie took all the funds Susie received for her sale to Jack, that is $350,000 that Jack and NIF paid as the purchase price, and they took the entire proceeds that Larry paid in cash at the auction, $500,000 — a total of $850,000.

(c) Kate's compensation

3-26 Kate would be entitled to claim the value of her property under the Torrens insurance principle and s 188 LTA, as a person who has suffered loss or damage through deprivation of an interest in land. Kate has been deprived of her interest in land through the actions of David. It is unlikely Kate will lose any of her entitlement due to contributory negligence, as there is no suggestion she handed over documents to David, enabling him to carry out his fraud (*Abigail v Lapin* [1934] AC 491), and she had every reason to trust him as he was her lawyer: *Registrar of Titles v Fairless* [1997] 1 VR 404.

3-27 The amount Kate can claim will be either the value at the time of deprivation of her interest (*Spencer v Registrar of Titles* (1909) 9 CLR 641), or the value at time of trial (*Registrar General v Behn* (1980) 1 NSWLR 589), whichever is lower, while bearing in mind the aim of compensation is to put the claimant back to the same position she would have been in but for this event, or as near as possible: *Registrar-General v Behn* (1981) 148 CLR 562 at 568.

At the time of deprivation, that is when Kate lost her equitable entitlement to her fee simple, the house was valued at $350,000, while at the time of trial it appears to have gone up to $500,000, if one uses the purchase price paid by Larry as a gauge. Although the lower figure was $350,000 at the time of deprivation, the aim of compensation is to restore her position to where she would be currently had the loss not occurred, so presumably to enable her to buy an equivalent home, compensation would have to be $500,000. Kate does not appear to have contributed to her own loss, so it is possible the courts will give her the higher figure, given the lower figure was only briefly valid due to a suspected issue with the building, later proven to be unfounded.

Examiner's Comments

3-28 This is a fairly straightforward question on the surface and the student has approached it in a logical, well-thought out manner. The advantage of dealing with it this way, although it may seem unwieldy, is there is less likelihood of error through mistaken attribution of fraud, which is apt to occur in these types of questions.

There is not much legal analysis as such, but the question does not really call for it. This is a good example of a solid answer to a straightforward Torrens title transfer question.

Keep in Mind

3-29 Students should keep in mind the following:

- Students who fail to work through each transaction individually and in order are likely to make simple errors, such as assuming Jack's purchase from Susie contained fraud, which it did not, or that the mortgage was obtained fraudulently, which it was not.
- Students often incorrectly determine value at time of deprivation at the point where legal title was transferred at registration, that is where Kate lost legal fee simple upon David's registration into his own name. However, value at deprivation is determined at the point at which the claimant was deprived of their right to regain their title, which occurs when equitable entitlement (E) is lost. It is important to note that legal title and equitable title do not always transfer at the same time if the legal title is found to be defeasible, as occurred here. The diagrams, showing when legal title (L) was transferred as opposed to when equitable title (E) was transferred, can be a useful tool to keep track of which interests transfer when.

Question 3

3-30 Keith has been the tenant of Jeanette's small factory in Brisbane under an unregistered four-year lease since January 2009.

Jeanette decides to sell the factory and signs a standard commercial contract to transfer the fee simple to Anna in May 2011. The contract makes no mention of Keith's lease but has the following standard condition:

"The buyer has read and agreed to the lease documents provided by the seller."

While discussing the contract over coffee, Jeanette tells Anna that Keith's lease is still unregistered but she will try and get it done before the sale, and says 'Either way, please make sure you look after him; he's a great tenant.' Anna left the meeting and wrote to Jeanette and Keith, stating:

'Don't worry, I know my law. The lease is safe.'

Just before settlement Jeanette calls Anna to say she has not had a chance to register Keith's lease due to the rush to get things ready for the sale. Anna reassures Jeanette that she will 'look after things with Keith'.

Anna becomes the registered owner of the factory in May 2011. Three months after registration, Anna decides to demolish the property and notifies Keith to vacate the premises.

Advise Keith.

Time allowed: 1 hour, 30 mins

Answer Plan

3-31 This question deals with the *in personam* issue using a short lease scenario, so the following issues need to be discussed:

- Is there the possibility of a short lease exception? No.
- Will Anna become bound through having notice of the unregistered interest? No.
- When did the purchaser have the intention to deprive the unregistered interest holder of their interest?
  - ◆ Prior to registration: fraud exception;
  - ◆ After registration: *in personam* exception:
- *In personam* exception:
  - ◆ Is this a purchase on terms or an undertaking to acknowledge?
  - ◆ How strong is the wording in the contract?
  - ◆ What other information, besides the contract, did the seller give the purchaser about the unregistered interest?
  - ◆ What kind of undertaking did the purchaser make to the seller or the holder of the unregistered interest prior to registration?

Conclusion: is the new purchaser bound by the unregistered interest?

Answer

3-32 Anna obtained a prima facie indefeasible title immediately upon registration (s 37 Land Title ACT 1994 (Qld) (LTA); *Breskvar v Wall* (1972) 126 CLR 376), which is free from Keith's unregistered lease: s 184(1) LTA. In order to make his lease binding on Anna, Keith needs to invoke exceptions to indefeasibility, specifically the short lease, fraud or personal equity exceptions.

Short lease exception

3-33 This cannot apply here as Keith's lease is for four years, and the short lease exception only applies to unregistered leases of three years or less as defined in Sch 2 LTA under s 4 LTA.

Fraud and in personam exception

3-34 To determine if either of these apply, the following information from the facts will be assessed:

- Standard condition in contract: 'The buyer has read and agreed to the lease documents provided by the seller'.
- Pre-contract written statement to Jeanette and Keith: 'Don't worry, I know my law. The lease is safe'.
- Pre-settlement oral statement to Jeanette: 'Look after things with Keith'.

Section 184(3)(b) LTA: fraud by Anna

3-35 There was only a standard condition in the contract. If this represented mere notice of Keith's unregistered interest then it would be insufficient to bind Anna (s 184(2)(a) LTA; *Mills v Stokman* (1967) 116 CLR 61). *Assets Co Ltd v Mere Roihi* [1905] AC 176 says that dishonesty, designed cheating or moral turpitude is required in order to apply the fraud exception. The issue is whether Anna had an intention to deprive Keith of his lease, and if so, when did Anna have that intention?

If Anna had the intention to deprive him of his interest under his lease before registration, then her pre-contract written statement and pre-settlement oral statement would constitute fraudulent misrepresentations, akin to *Loke Yew v Port Swettenham Rubber Co Ltd* [1913] AC 491. If Anna only had the intention to deprive him of his interest after registration, that is she had a change of heart after registration in May 2011, then this would be supervening fraud, which may fall outside the fraud exception in light of the High Court's equal split in *Bahr v Nicolay (No 2)* (1988) CLR 604.

Wilson and Toohey JJ's exclusion of supervening fraud seems to have more judicial support than Mason CJ and Dawson J's inclusion of supervening fraud (*Bourseguin v Stannard Bros Holdings Pty Ltd* [1994] 1 Qd R 231), although Davies JA did dissent in *White v Tomasel* [2004] 2 Qd R 438.

Assuming Keith can successfully raise the fraud exception, he may ask the Supreme Court to direct the registrar to register his lease under s 187(2)(b) LTA. If Keith cannot raise the fraud exception, he will have to turn to the *in personam* or personal equity exception.

Section 185(1)(a) LTA: equity arising from Anna's act?

3-36 The issue is whether Anna 'purchased on terms' Keith's lease (Brennan J in *Bahr v Nicolay*) or gave an undertaking to acknowledge Keith's lease, akin to *Presbyterian Church (NSW) Property Trust v Scots Church Development Ltd* [2007] NSWSC 676. The former is more likely to suggest she signed the contract fully aware of the lease and its precise terms, representing a much stronger undertaking than the latter, which implies a general awareness of the existence of the lease, but not necessarily much more. There is no suggestion here that Anna has actually been given the full copy of the lease, and it is more likely to be an undertaking to acknowledge, rather than a purchase on terms. Neither is determinative on its own without further consideration of the issues, as discussed below.

An analysis is needed of all the communication passing from purchaser to seller and/or the holder of the unregistered interest, to determine if the undertakings given will give rise to personal equity in favour of Keith.

Is the phrase 'agreed to' in the standard condition in the contract more than mere notice, and if not, would Anna's pre-contract written statement 'The lease is safe', and her pre-settlement oral statement 'Look after things with Keith' give rise to personal equity in favour of Keith? This can be determined by comparing the strength of these statements with various cases which set the bar for this issue.

Valbirn Pty Ltd v Powprop Pty Ltd [1991] 1 Qd R 295

3-37 This case had a much stronger contractual clause than in this instance. There the sale was subject to 'acceptance of the leases', and the purchaser gave written and formal acceptance of the leases. Clearly under this standard Anna's actions would not give rise to personal equity in favour of Keith.

Bahr v Nicolay

3-38 In this case the purchaser also gave a stronger and more specific acknowledgement of the relevant interest, followed by written confirmation of such acknowledgement. Again, under this standard Anna's actions would not give rise to personal equity in favour of Keith.

Bourseguin v Stannard Brothers

3-39 This case had the strongest contractual clause, 'their being totally satisfied with the terms of such leases', but it was deemed insufficient to raise personal equity. It was held, however, in the obiter dicta that silence may amount to patent cheating and thereby raise both fraud and personal equity exceptions.

Although Anna's written and oral responses to Jeanette's statements about the need to register Keith's lease are ambiguous, they are more than silence and arguably constitute Anna's acknowledgement of Keith's lease. Thus it would be inequitable or unconscionable for Anna to depart from such acknowledgement. Unlike the fraud exception, the personal equity exception definitely extends to Anna's act after her registration: *Grgic v ANZ* (1994) 33 NSWLR 202.

The question does not state whether Anna collected any rent from Keith, which could strengthen Keith's case and could serve as acknowledgement and recognition of Keith's status by Anna.

Assuming Keith can successfully raise the personal equity exception, the court would require Anna to honour Keith's lease (which may include registering Keith's lease). In light of *Bahr v Nicolay*, the court may:

- declare that an express trust exists between Anna and Keith to reflect the parties' intention (Mason CJ and Dawson J); or
- impose a constructive trust on Anna on the basis of unconscionability (Brennan, Wilson and Toohey JJ).

Examiner's Comments

3-40 This answer works through the different strands of a personal equity exception quite well. The analysis could have been presented in a more flowing, argumentative style, but the basics of the issues and argument are there. The gist of the fraud argument is also there, but perhaps could have been explained more clearly, as it seems a bit muddled. All of the arguments raised could have been done so with more depth, but it does successfully touch on and explore all the relevant points.

Keep in Mind

3-41 Students should keep in mind the following:

- The nature of the personal equity exception requires a comparison of the strength of the contractual provisions and any statements made by the seller and holder of the unregistered interest, with any acknowledgments or undertakings made by the purchaser. Often students do not pull all the instances of those communications out of the question and thus fail to include them in their analysis. It is a good idea to identify all communication both ways early on in the answer.
- Students often neglect to address all the options, as was done here: short lease, fraud and personal equity exceptions. Students should remember you seldom assess supervening fraud without checking for actual fraud first, and an unregistered lease should always raise the short lease exception, even if only to be discarded.

Question 4

3-42 Giuseppe Verdi, an Italian immigrant with poor English skills, is the registered owner of a waterfront house at Varsity Lakes. He married Edith when he arrived in Australia. Edith and her daughter, Harriet, then moved into the house with him.

In February 2010 Harriet stole Giuseppe's passport and driver's licence. She also obtained a replacement certificate of title for the Varsity Lakes house. She forged Giuseppe's signatures on various documents in order to mortgage the house to Happy Lenders Bank in return for a loan. Then she made an appointment with William, the senior bank officer of Happy Lenders Bank.

William had met Harriet before when she had come in with Giuseppe and translated for her stepfather. William had found Giuseppe's strong Italian accent difficult to understand, and Harriet was much easier to deal with than the old-fashioned and stubborn Giuseppe. William was relieved when Harriet came to the meeting without Giuseppe on 25 February 2010. Harriet told William that Giuseppe could not attend due to illness, so she was attending the meeting and submitting the mortgage documents on Giuseppe's behalf. She also told William that she had taken Giuseppe to a Justice of the Peace (JP) in a shopping centre earlier in the day to have his signatures witnessed. She then told William that Giuseppe had incurred a lot of medical expenses recently, so she sweet-talked William into extending the mortgage value to $500,000, even though the last valuation of the Varsity Lakes house dated February 2010 was only $475,000.

After Happy Lenders Bank's mortgage was registered over the Varsity Lakes house on Monday 1 March 2010, William gave all the mortgage documents to Zane, a junior bank officer responsible for filing documents. As Zane went through the documents he became concerned that the JP on the documents was not on the Bank's internal list of recognised JPs. Zane also noticed that Giuseppe's signatures on these documents did not match the signatures on the previous documents in the file, and that the property valuation was lower than the mortgage value.

Zane sent William an email on Wednesday 3 March 2010:

> Please provide the contact details of the JP on Giuseppe Verdi's mortgage documents and a copy of your request to him to verify the signatures and his reply, as per Internal Policy SV02, so that I can add them to the file. Please also provide justification for the high mortgage value.

William emailed his reply to Zane that Wednesday afternoon:

> Are you querying whether I followed procedure? I have been with Happy Lenders Bank for 15 years and never been questioned like this! I shall get the documents to you on Monday and I will be discussing this with your manager!

William then advised the human resources manager that he needed to take urgent leave. He has been unreachable since the evening of 3 March 2010.

Meanwhile, Harriet has gone to the United States with the loan money, and the value of the Varsity Lakes house dropped to $440,000 in April 2010 due to an interest rate increase. Mario (Giuseppe's friend) urges Giuseppe to approach the Registrar of Titles to see what they can do.

Advise Giuseppe with respect to Happy Lenders Bank's registered mortgage over his Varsity Lakes house.

Time allowed: 45 mins

Answer Plan

3-43 This is a fraud question and covers three different kinds of fraud. Each should be addressed individually.

Straight fraud: imputing or attributing of fraudulent actions to title holder: not applicable as Harriet's actions cannot be attributed to Giuseppe.

Section 184(3)(b) Land Title Act 1994 (Qld) (LTA), fraud by the registered proprietor (bank): has William, as the bank's agent, committed fraud? This is very hard to prove as precedent provides a very high standard of test so unlikely.

Section 11A fraud: fraudulent mortgage where the bank fails to verify the ID of the mortgage applicant — likely.

Remedies and consequences: will Giuseppe be bound by the mortgage and if so can he get compensation?

Answer

3-44 This answer will advise Giuseppe on his position concerning the registered mortgage over his property. Prima facie Giuseppe is bound as his indefeasible title (s 37 LTA; *Breskvar v Wall* (1972) 126 CLR 376) is free from all unregistered interests but bound by registered interests (s 184(1) LTA), and the mortgage is registered.

Fraud exceptions

3-45 The only way Giuseppe can avoid being bound by the mortgage is if he can make one of the exceptions to indefeasibility apply.

Fraud by the registered owner

3-46 If Harriet's fraud can be imputed or attributed to Giuseppe, then the mortgage would be fraudulent. Such an eventuality would make Giuseppe liable for other issues, but is irrelevant as he had no part in Harriet's fraud, and nothing can be imputed to him.

Fraud by the bank

3-47 Section 184(3)(b) LTA: fraud by the registered proprietor or its agent. (Here this would be fraud by William acting on behalf of the bank.)

William's actions need to be examined to determine if he has acted so negligently, or with such unconscionable disregard, that his actions could be deemed fraudulent. There are many precedents showing that the courts have set a high standard.

It is necessary to identify what actions William has taken that could be deemed negligent to the point of fraudulent. William has accepted at face value that Harriet is authorised to act as Giuseppe's agent, and he failed to check with Giuseppe or request some verification of authority.

William has failed to verify that Giuseppe actually signed the documents by checking with the Justice of the Peace in question, or by checking with Giuseppe himself, or by matching his signatures to past signatures held on file. William also failed to follow internal procedures about checking whether the JP was on the bank's approved list, contacting the JP directly to verify signatures, and checking the mortgage figure was below the valuation figure. Despite all this, William does not appear to have demonstrated any actual dishonesty, although his sudden disappearance suggests he may have been aware that his actions were less than correct. However, that alone is not enough to prove any involvement in Harriet's plans or any intention to defraud.

The test is whether William was dishonest, willfully blind, recklessly indifferent or voluntarily ignorant: *Assets Co Ltd v Mere Roihi* [1905] AC 176; *Waimiha Sawmilling Co v Waione Timber Co* [1926] AC 101 at 106). Although his behaviour might appear to fit the description, under *Grgic v ANZ Banking Group Ltd* (1994) 33 NSWLR 202 it could be argued that he was careless, or as Powell JA put it 'less than meticulous in seeking to establish that' Harriet was authorised to act as Giuseppe's agent, and that Giuseppe had actually signed the documents.

Under *Hilton v Gray* [2007] QSC 401 William's failure to follow internal procedures would not be deemed sufficient to make the mortgage defeasible. William's failure to make further inquiries is also not deemed fraud as he displayed no actual dishonesty: *Pyramid Building Society (in liq) v Scorpion Hotels Pty Ltd* [1998] 1 VR 188.

The courts have deemed there must be proof of dishonesty by the person who registered the title (*Vassos v State Bank of South Australia* (1993) 2 VR 316), and William's actions do not meet that criterion. Fraud may take various forms, such as 'pretence and collusion in the conscious misuse of a power' or a 'dishonest course' as defined by Kitto J in *Latec Investments v Hotel Terrigal Pty Ltd* (1965) 113 CLR 265, or registering an instrument which the registrant knows to be forged: *Australian Guarantee Corp Ltd v De Jager* [1984] VR 483 and *Beatty v Australia and New Zealand Banking Group Ltd* [1995] 2 VR 301. William's behaviour is very similar to that in *Young v Hoger* [2002] QSC 013 but there again the behaviour was not deemed sufficient to make the mortgage defeasible.

Lending more than the value of the property is not a breach of the bank's duties, although it can be a breach of internal procedures. As above, this will also not reach the standard of fraud, or make the mortgage defeasible.

Section 11 fraud

3-48 Giuseppe's last option is to make the mortgage defeasible under a s 11A LTA breach.

Under ss 11A and 11A(2) LTA, the bank is under a duty to verify a borrower's identification. Under s 185(1A)(a)(i) LTA, if there has been a failure to satisfy the s 11A LTA criteria and the mortgage is forged (as defined under s 185(1A)(b) LTA), then according to s 185(5) LTA, the bank will lose its protection under s 184(1) LTA and the mortgage will then become defeasible. Mere negligence is sufficient and the onus of proof is on the bank to show that reasonable steps were taken. William has failed to take reasonable steps to verify the identification of the borrower and has breached s 11A LTA, and the mortgage is forged, as Harriet and not Giuseppe signed it. Therefore, it is likely the mortgage would be deemed defeasible.

3-49   A last option for Giuseppe would be to prove supervening fraud by demonstrating an intention on the part of the bank, or its agent William, to defraud Giuseppe post contract.

Here we are not given contractual terms or pre-settlement behaviour to examine and contrast with *Valbirn Pty Ltd v Powprop Pty Ltd* [1991] 1 Qd R 295 or *Bahr v Nicolay (No 2)* (1988) CLR 604. However, it is possible that William's post contract behaviour and disappearance could be deemed evidence of unconscionability and qualify as supervening fraud, which would make the mortgage defeasible, but this is probably a stretch. This would be an alternative way for Giuseppe to make the mortgage defeasible if he did not succeed under s 11 LTA. If William's act created equity, it would be an exception to indefeasibility: s 185(1)(a) LTA.

Remedies

3-50   If Giuseppe could make a case under s 184(3)(b) LTA or s 185(1A) LTA, he could bring a Supreme Court application to order the registrar to cancel the mortgage under s 187 LTA. Under s 185(1)(a) LTA, the Supreme Court could also declare the mortgage void. If Giuseppe had to apply for compensation, he would be granted the lower of the market value or mortgage value of the house. The mortgage is $500,000, which is greater than the value of the house. It is at the court's discretion whether they grant him more than the value of the house which is $440,000: *Registrar of Titles v Keddell* (1993) QCR 54. The goal of compensation is to restore the applicant to the position they would have been in had the loss not occurred: *Registrar General v Behn* (1980) 1 NSWLR 589. Here, if that goal is to be achieved, Giuseppe would really need $500,000 to clear the entire mortgage.

 # Examiner's Comments

3-51   This question covers multiple versions of fraud and is reasonably thorough in its analysis of each. It could be more cohesive in structure and this answer is more exemplary of an exam answer than a researched and prepared tutorial or assignment. The s 11A LTA breach could have done with more explanation, but the basic application of statute is there. A reasonable attempt.

Keep in Mind

3-52   Students should keep in mind the following:

- Students tend to focus on the category of fraud that they think will get over the line and fail to address all the alternatives. A thorough answer should attempt all possible solutions, no matter how unlikely.
- Given the difficulty of overcoming fraud by the registered proprietor, students often dismiss it or skimp in this area. Despite the very high bar set by the courts, it should always be reviewed.

Question 5

3-53   Petrus, a newsagent, is the registered owner of a modest property in Burleigh Heads. Petrus's chartered accountant, Royce, keeps custody of all of Petrus's important documents, including his business records and the certificate of title to his Burleigh Heads property.

In February 2011 Royce forges a transfer of Petrus's Burleigh Heads property to Quick Cash Pty Ltd. Quick Cash Pty Ltd, a company owned and controlled by Royce, becomes registered as owner of the Burleigh Heads property. After Quick Cash is registered, Royce approaches Mario about a loan of $500,000 based on inflated valuations showing the land was worth $600,000. The loan is secured by a registered mortgage over the Burleigh Heads property in late February 2011. Mario complies with the s 11A Land Title Act 1994 (Qld) provisions about the identity of Royce and Quick Cash Pty Ltd. The 'valuations' were in fact manufactured by Royce. Mario is mildly concerned by one of the 'valuations', but he continues with the loan nonetheless. The property's market value as at the date of the registration of the mortgage is in fact $200,000. Royce absconds to Brazil with the loan moneys.

In July 2011 Petrus discovers the actions of his accountant. Mario is preparing to exercise his power of sale. Due to buyer demand in the Burleigh Heads area, the property's market value has increased to $300,000. Petrus approaches you for advice:

(a)   Advise Petrus fully in regard to his ability to recover compensation.

(b)   Assume that in February 2011 Royce does not forge the transfer but instead obtains Petrus's signature on a blank transfer by telling Petrus that it is a tax minimisation strategy. Petrus has some concerns about this, but signs anyway. Royce then proceeds to enter his company's name onto the signed transfer and the facts proceed as stated above. Would this alter your answer to (a)?

Time allowed: 60 mins

Answer Plan

3-54 This question focuses on compensation for a holder of fee simple after partial deprivation of interest through fraud by a third party. It is a straightforward task of examining each of the different dates at which compensation can be calculated and determining which would be applicable here and how much the claimant is likely to be awarded.

Answer

3-55 At the end of the transfers Petrus has equitable and legal fee simple, indefeasible upon registration: s 37 Land Title Act 1994 (Qld) (LTA). He is bound by the registered mortgage: s 184(1) LTA.

(a) Petrus's compensation

This question deals with the issue of compensation. As Royce has been fraudulent in transferring the land to his company, clearly the interest of the company is defeasible: s 184 (3) LTA. As Royce has control of that company, his fraud would be imputed to the company.

Petrus would regain his land subject to Mario's mortgage, due to Royce's fraud. This mortgage would be indefeasible as there is no evidence Mario was involved in a fraud. Petrus has now suffered partial deprivation of his interest in the land which will entitle him to compensation: *Heron v Broadbent* (1919) 20 SR (NSW) 101; s 188 LTA. The mortgage is indefeasible as s 11A LTA is satisfied but s 189A LTA may arise as the power of sale had been exercised where the mortgagor was fraudulently registered. It should be noted that recovery of costs of sale may be restricted by the interest rate charged.

The problem in determining quantum is that the amount secured by the mortgage is $500,000 while the property was valued at $200,000 at the time of the loan, but a few months later is valued at $300,000.

Under *Spencer v Registrar of Titles* (1908) AC 235, the goal is to restore parties to their pre-deprivation position, and *Registrar of Titles v Crowle* (1947) CLR 191 suggests the appropriate date for assessment of compensation is the date of deprivation of interest. In this case that would be the creation of the indefeasible mortgage.

In *Registrar General v Behn* (1980) 1 NSWLR 589 the Court of Appeal distinguished those cases and said the relevant date was the date of the trial, though acknowledging each case had to be considered on its own facts. This approach appears to have been supported on appeal in the High Court in that judgment: *Registrar General v Behn* (1981) 148 CLR 562.

Gibbs J stated:

> Plainly the intention of the legislature is that a successful plaintiff can recover damages commensurate with the loss he [she] has sustained in consequence of the wrongful deprivation — damages that will put him

[her] in the same position, so far as money can do it, as if the deprivation had not occurred ...

This would suggest that the relevant date for calculation of the compensation could be the date of trial. There appears to be some uncertainty on this point though Whalan J appears to favour the date of deprivation as the relevant date, while proposing that there should be a statutory provision to confirm the relevant date.

If the relevant date is the date of deprivation the value of the land at that time was $200,000 while the amount lent was $500,000.

In *Registrar of Titles v Keddell* (1993) QCR 54-455 the Court of Appeal said that damages recoverable when land is fraudulently subjected to a mortgage is usually the lesser of the amount secured by the mortgage or the value of the land, unless payment at a higher figure was reasonable between the parties. There the fact that the persons deprived wanted to stay in the property did not justify granting more than the value of the land.

The Court of Appeal granted the registered owners market value and a bit more to cover costs, also allowing for a small amount above the market value so they could purchase at the auction when the mortgagee exercised power of sale.

It would appear that the compensation payable would be $300,000 (if the relevant date was the date of trial) plus a small amount to cover the costs of Petrus bidding at auction. Mario would need to recover the balance from Royce's company.

If the relevant date for assessment of compensation is the date of the trial, a payment of $300,000 would be the relevant value of the land and this would limit the compensation payable to approximately that figure.

(b) Signature on blank transfer

3-56 In this example there would be no difference in the result in relation to the registration of the mortgage. The difference may be in relation to the ability to recover compensation as a result of s 189(1)(b) LTA where Petrus was contributorily negligent in signing the blank transfer or where the loss was caused by the act of the agent.

Under *Registrar of Titles v Fairless* (1997) 1 VR 404, a primary or substantial cause of the claimant's loss must be the claimant's own negligence, but here the primary cause appears to be the agent's actions. The facts in *RT v Fairless* are similar to this situation, though the question does not state how old and experienced Petrus is. It is likely that, unless he was very old or inexperienced, he would be denied compensation on this basis.

If the state raised the fact that Royce was his agent, Petrus could argue that Royce acted outside his agency role when committing the fraudulent acts, in order to avoid loss of compensation on the basis of someone acting as his agent. This was accepted in *RT v Fairless*.

Examiner's Comments

3-57 The answer clearly progresses through all the compensation options available. The relevant cases are examined and appropriate quotes cited. This is a straightforward question, and the only criticism could be that parts of the answer focus on the cases without referring back to the facts and parties in the question. Otherwise this answer satisfactorily deals with the issues.

Keep in Mind

3-58 Students should keep in mind the following:

- The most common error in this type of question is incorrectly identifying the date of deprivation. Students must check when equitable title actually passes, rather than just legal title.
- A straightforward question such as this will only produce a good mark if the student addresses all the appropriate options in good detail, as this answer has done. Due to the lack of complexity in the question, skimming detail will result in lower marks.

Chapter 4

Priorities of Interests in Land

Key Issues

4-1 From early consciousness it soon becomes apparent to any individual that human conduct is flawed. Rules regarding priority of interests came about precisely because of flawed human conduct. It might be outrageous fraud, as when A, the owner in fee simple of 'Greenland', conveys 'Greenland' to B and then later conveys 'Greenland' to C. Or A, the owner in fee simple of 'Greenland', conveys the property to B without disclosing to B that the property is leased to D. Or A, in reality the trustee of 'Greenland' for beneficiary X, conveys 'Greenland' to Y in disregard of the interests of X and in breach of trust. In each of these situations, the person defrauded will have a conflicting interest with the person who took that interest. The status of the parties and their interests must be determined.

The rules of priority were devised to establish the ranking of conflicting interests. Those conflicting interests might be between competing legal interests, competing equitable interests or competing legal and equitable interests. When considering the priority of interests other matters were taken into account. Those matters related to issues of notice, acting in good faith or postponing conduct (eg failure to secure title deeds).

In order to assist persons being caught unawares in relation to the existence of competing interests, the legislature devised registration legislation. This legislation typically required persons to register their interests at the risk of losing priority. The registration of interests made it possible for parties to search (prior to acquiring an interest) and ascertain whether their potential title was affected by other claimants. In New South Wales, this legislation is seen in s 184G of the Conveyancing Act 1919.

4-2 Before attempting the questions in this chapter, students should be familiar with the following:

The priority rules:
✓ primary general rule — *first in time stronger in law*;
✓ secondary general rule — *where the equities are equal the law prevails*;

✓ the principle of the *bona fide purchaser for value without notice*;

postponing conduct:

✓ fraud;

✓ estoppel;

✓ negligence with deeds;

Notice:

✓ actual;

✓ imputed;

✓ constructive;

✓ s 164 Conveyancing Act 1919 (NSW);

✓ s 184 Land Title Act 1994 (Qld);

Registration legislation:

✓ s 184G Conveyancing Act 1919 (NSW)

✓ s 178 Land Title Act 1994 (Qld).

The questions in this chapter are generally set on the basis that students will study them in progression. Each question presumes the student will be familiar with the preceding question and answer. Accordingly, the answers become briefer regarding those aspects covered in the preceding material as the questions progress and some later answers will detail some area of legal principle that was covered briefly in a preceding answer.

 # Question 1

4-3 Section 184G of the Conveyancing Act 1919 (NSW) provides:

(1) All instruments (wills excepted) affecting, or intended to affect, any lands in New South Wales which are executed or made bona fide, and for valuable consideration, and are duly registered under the provisions of this Division, the Registration of Deeds Act 1897, or any Act repealed by the Registration of Deeds Act 1897, shall have and take priority not according to their respective dates but according to the priority of the registration thereof only.

> (2) No instrument registered under the provisions of this Division or the Registration of Deeds Act 1897 shall lose any priority to which it would be entitled by virtue of registration thereunder by reason only of bad faith in the conveying party, if the party beneficially taking under the instrument acted bona fide, and there was valuable consideration given therefor.
>
> What is the effect of the section in respect of the rules affecting the priority of competing interests in land?
>
> **Time allowed: 2 hours**

Answer Plan

4-4 The question is aimed at the student's understanding of the priority rules both before and after registration legislation as seen in s 184G. The answer requires an examination and explanation of the priority rules followed by an explanation of the section and its effect. An outline of the answer would be:

- primary general rule regarding both legal and equitable interests;
- secondary general rules regarding competing legal and equitable interests;
- principle of the bona fide purchaser for value;
- s 184G: effect of the section,

as well as interests generally, whether registered or unregistered.

Answer

4-5 Questions of priority of ranking of interests arise between persons claiming conflicting or inconsistent interests in land. Often they arise because those persons have been subject to trickery or some impropriety as a result of the actions of some third party. Various rules were devised to resolve the issues arising between these conflicting interests. Section 184G of the Conveyancing Act 1919 (NSW) (and its predecessors) were designed to simplify the resolution of conflicting interests and, although they largely succeeded, there are still situations where the priority rules still apply. It is proposed to deal with the question by discussing the effect of the rules prior to the introduction of the section (and its predecessors) and then to discuss the effect of the section upon the rules.

Primary general rule: 'first in time stronger in law'

Competing legal interests

4-6 The first rule, known as the 'primary general rule', provided that an interest that was first in time took precedence over an interest that was created after it. This meant that the holder of a prior legal interest took priority over a subsequent conflicting legal interest. So if A granted a legal mortgage of 'Greenland' to B, then later conveyed 'Greenland' to C, the interest of B prevailed over the interest of C, B being first in time.

However, it may well be that a subsequent legal interest might be found non-existent. For example, if A conveyed 'Greenland' to B by deed in fee simple and later purported to convey 'Greenland' by D to C in fee simple, the later conveyance by virtue of time would rank behind the earlier conveyance. But, on examination, the later conveyance would be seen to be a nullity because after A has conveyed the fee simple to B, there is no further fee simple to convey to C. The conveyance to A has exhausted the fee simple, hence the principle *nemo dat quod non habet*, literally no-one can give what they don't have.

Competing equitable interests

4-7 The primary general rule also meant that the holder of a prior equitable interest took priority over a subsequent conflicting equitable interest. So that if A agreed in writing to sell 'Greenland' to B and subsequently A also signed a contract to sell 'Greenland' to C, the equitable interest in 'Greenland' created by the contract between A and B would take priority over the equitable interest in 'Greenland' created by the contract between A and C.

The principle *nemo dat quod non habet* was less applicable (if applicable at all) to equitable interests, as equity took a more flexible approach to equitable interests. While, at common law, the granting of a legal mortgage would make a second legal mortgage of no effect (under the *nemo dat quod non habet* rule), in equity the second of two equitable mortgages would not be struck down but ranked second, taking up any equity not exhausted by the first interest. Equity, when ascertaining the ranking of interests, would look to all the circumstances of the creation of interests. So the equitable interest of a prior holder might be postponed to the interest of a later holder if the conduct of the prior holder brought about a belief in the later holder that no prior equitable interest existed. (An obvious example of this would be fraud or a representation or inducement by the prior holder to the later holder that no prior interest existed.)

Secondary general rule: 'Where the equities are equal the law prevails'

4-8 Where a legal and an equitable interest were in competition a further rule applied, namely, 'where the equities are equal the law prevails':

> Equality means the non-existence of any circumstances which affects the conduct of one of the rival claimants and makes it less meritorious of that of the other. (*Bailey v Barnes* [1894] 1 Ch 25 at 36)

Accordingly, where a legal and an equitable interest have competing equal claims to be recognised, the holder of the legal estate prevails, the equitable estate being postponed.

Prior legal interest subsequent equitable interest

4-9 The holder of the prior legal interest will lose priority to a subsequent equitable interest where the prior interest holder has committed fraud such as induced the holder of the subsequent equitable interest to take that estate:

> ... the general principle resulting from the leading cases on the subject is, that in order to postpone a prior mortgagee, it is necessary to prove against him fraud, or actual notice or negligence so gross as to amount to fraud. (*Peter v Russell* (1716) 1 Eq Cas Abr 321; 23 ER 1076)

The issue of 'negligence so gross' amounting to fraud troubled the court in *Northern Counties of England Fire Insurance Co v Whipp* (1884) 26 Ch 482, on the basis that negligence is carelessness and fraud requires intention or design. The court appeared to resolve the issue on the basis that the negligence required needed to be so gross as to indicate complicity in the fraud. Certainly any carelessness needed to be more than mere negligence in order to occasion postponement. In the *Northern Counties* case the fact that the mortgagor manager of the mortgagee company had access to the title deeds and used them to create an equitable mortgage was held not to be gross negligence on the mortgagee company's part. (Of course, between two equitable interests such conduct would have been postponing.)

A legal interest will be postponed to a subsequent equitable interest where the legal owner has given authority to a person to deal with a third party and that authority is exceeded:

> In my opinion any conduct on the part of the holder of the legal estate in relation to the deeds which would make it unequitable for him to rely on his legal estate against a prior equitable estate of which he had no notice, ought also to be sufficient to postpone him to a subsequent equitable estate the creation of which has only been rendered possible by the possession of deeds which but for such conduct would have passed into the possession of the owner of the legal estate. (*Walker v Linom* [1907] 2 Ch 104 at 114 per Parker J)

It follows that the legal owner will be postponed when that owner has been the creator of the instrument of creation of the subsequent equity.

Prior equitable subsequent legal

4-10 An equitable interest first in point of time will prevail over a subsequent legal interest unless the holder of the legal interest acquired it bona fide for valuable consideration without notice of the equitable interest.

The holder of the legal estate must be precisely that to benefit from the rule: the doctrine is not applicable to equitable interests. There must also be valuable consideration. It need not be adequate, but it must be more than nominal (nominal being consideration 'not necessarily paid': *Midland Bank Trust Co v Green* [1981] AC 513 at 532). The requirement of 'bona fide' is generally satisfied by lack of notice, however:

> ... it would be a mistake to suppose the requirement of good faith extended only to the matter of notice, or that when notice came to be regulated by statute, the requirement of good faith became obsolete. Equity still retained its interest in and power over the purchaser's conscience. (*Midland Bank Trust Co v Green*)

When it came to notice it might be actual knowledge of the facts which derived the purchaser of bona fide, or imputed notice (notice in the hands of one's agent which is then imputed to the principal–purchaser) or constructive notice (deemed notice to the purchaser). Constructive notice might result from not making the inquiries expected of a reasonable purchaser in a like situation — a pathway across the property a purchaser is buying, leading to the adjoining property, might be expected to raise an inquiry as to its purpose and whether it had status as an easement. The concept of constructive notice finds its statutory expression in s 164 of the Conveyancing Act 1919 (NSW). (Section 53(3) of the Conveyancing Act has the effect of limiting notice by its stipulating a good root of title need only be 30 years old.)

At what point in the transaction will notice affect the purchaser taking the interest? The authorities indicate that a purchaser will not be affected by notice received after valuable consideration has been furnished. If title is taken after the furnishing of consideration and notice is received after the furnishing of consideration, then the notice will not affect the title taken: *Pilcher v Rawlins* (1872) LR Ch App 259 at 267.

Registration: s 184G

4-11 The effect of the section is to rank interests in accordance with their date of registration of the instrument creating the interest. It makes no distinction between legal or equitable interests. It is not concerned with the date that instruments are made so far as their ranking is concerned. The instrument that is first registered (subject to the other requirements of the section), whether it be equitable or legal and irrespective of its date, will attain priority over later registered competing instruments (irrespective of their date of execution). Accordingly, the section is not concerned with the primary general rule and the secondary general rule. The section is its own source of priority ranking.

However, to attain priority on registration, the instrument creating the instrument must 'be executed or made bona fide, and for valuable consideration'. An instrument that is fraudulent will not be executed or made bona fide. However, the bona fides required are those of the person taking the interest under the instrument. The fact the conveyor lacks bona fide will not of itself deprive the instrument from priority upon registration: s 184(2). For the purposes of the section there will be no bona fides in respect of an instrument in relation to which notice of an outstanding interest has been received: *Marsden v Campbell* (1897) 18 LR (NSW) Eq 33. Notice received after title is taken, but before registration (and notice received after consideration has been furnished and before title is taken), will not preclude priority in registration. If:

> ... a person has become owner of property, bona fide and honestly, and hears that there is a prior deed in existence relating to the same property, it is a perfectly honest thing for him to promptly register his conveyance. That is what the law intends. The object of the law of registration is to keep people awake, and make them alive to their duties. It will not disentitle the registering vendee to the benefit of the Act. (*Burrow v Crimp* (1887) 8 LR (NSW) L 198 at 210)

Where the instrument creating the interest is voluntary then registration will not protect the interest from a competing instrument for value, prima facie. However, if the holder of the interest from the competing instrument for value has notice of the voluntary instrument, the holder might be hard pressed to argue the interest was taken bona fide. A person taking an interest in old system land is deemed to have notice of any registered interest affecting the land. Registration acts as notice of what interests are operative in relation to the title to land being taken. Registration does not give instruments any efficacy, nor remedy their defects; it merely decides their priority.

Where instruments are not registered their priority will be decided in accordance with the priority rules. Where they are registered they will rank according to date of registration (subject to them being executed or bona fide and made for value). A registered interest (executed or made bona fide for value) will have priority over an unregistered interest.

Where interests are not created by instrument (such as an interest created by part performance and not evidenced in writing, or an equitable mortgage by deposit of deed), they will not be affected by s 184G (the section referring only to *instruments*). Priority of these interests will rank according to the priority rules (*abstracting from registration*).

4-12 The position in respect of the priority rules may be summarised as follows:

- A legal interest that is acquired bona fide for value and registered takes priority over a competing unregistered interest or subsequently registered interest (whether it be legal or equitable) irrespective of the date the latter interest is created.
- An equitable interest that is acquired bona fide for value and registered takes priority over a competing unregistered interest or subsequently registered interest (whether it be legal or equitable) irrespective of the date the latter interest is created.

- An interest legal or equitable that is registered but not made bona fide or not made for valuable consideration has no more standing than an unregistered interest with this proviso: its registration serves as notice of its existence to any subsequent acquirer of the interest and places that person on subsequent acquisition as taking *mala fide*.
- An unregistered legal interest has priority over a later competing interest, legal or equitable (subject to any postponement arising out of fraud, estoppel and gross negligence with title documents).
- An unregistered equitable interest will take priority over a subsequent unregistered legal interest unless the latter has been acquired bona fide for value and without notice of the equitable interest (in which case the unregistered legal interest will take priority).
- An unregistered equitable interest takes priority over a later competing unregistered equitable interest (subject to postponement for fraud, estoppel or negligence with title documentation).

 ## Examiner's Comments

4-13 The answer basically follows the structure of the answer outline. It deals with the application of the primary general rule regarding legal interest (referring to the *nemo dat* principle) and equitable interests. It then takes up the secondary general rule dealing with competing legal and equitable interests. It alludes to the postponement of an interest arising out of conduct, highlighting the strict view taken of what is required to postpone a legal interest to a later equitable interest. In dealing with the postponement of an equitable interest to a later legal interest, it discusses the principle of the bona fide purchaser for value without notice. It distinguishes the concepts of 'bona fide' and 'notice' and discusses the various classifications of notice.

In discussing s 184G of the Conveyancing Act 1919 (NSW), the answer deals with the terms 'valuable consideration' and 'bona fide' and 'instrument' (interests must be created by instrument to come within the parameters of the section). Within the section 'bona fide' will be lacking where there is notice. The receipt of notice is delineated; voluntary instruments are discussed; priority of interests not created by instruments is dealt with.

Keep in Mind

4-14 Students should keep in mind the following:

- When explaining the terms of the section it is important to point out that valuable consideration does not apply to voluntary instruments. However, this does not mean voluntary instruments may be ignored. A registered voluntary instrument will place the person taking an interest on notice in relation to the voluntary interest. The question of notice will then make the voluntary instrument relevant under the issue of bona fide.

- Students sometimes fail to explain that the notice to be applicable under the section is notice received up to the time valuable consideration is paid by the conveyee. Notice after consideration will not affect the conveyee. It is also important to point out that bad faith in the conveyor will not affect the conveyee. It is bad faith in the conveyee that is crucial for the section.
- The fact the section applies only to instruments creating interests is often overlooked. Interests created outside instruments (eg by part performance) will not have their priority affected by s 184G, and their priority will be determined by the ordinary rules.

Question 2

> **4-15** Leo purchased the fee simple in Zak and Zelda's Brisbane land (Lot 1) and lodged the transfer document for registration on 20 March 2012.
>
> Gerald lodged a caveat over Lot 1 on 19 March 2012. Gerald is the registered owner of the adjoining Lot 2. Gerald claims that he is entitled, under an easement agreement, to use a six-metre-wide strip of land on Lot 1 as an alternative access to a nearby road. Gerald has a copy of his easement agreement with Zak and Zelda dated 1 May 2011. He is adamant that Zak and Zelda lodged the easement agreement for registration. Yet the Queensland Land Registry's current records do not show any registered easements on Lot 1.
>
> Leo wants to use the alleged easement area as an additional parking area for Lot 1. He is also negotiating with a bank to mortgage Lot 1 to secure a loan to fund his wedding and honeymoon. However, the bank will not lend Leo any money unless and until he becomes the registered owner of Lot 1.
>
> On 29 March 2012 a neighbour tells Leo that Gerald lodged the caveat over Lot 1 primarily because he wanted to buy Lot 1 and was furious that Zak and Zelda sold Lot 1 to Leo instead of to him. Advise Leo.
>
> **Time allowed: 45 mins**

 # Answer Plan

4-16 This question is testing Leo's status as holder of an equitable fee simple interest (equitable due to lack of registration), against the status of Gerald as an equitable easement holder (equitable due to lack of registration of the easement agreement), and as alleged holder of a caveatable interest. The principles of competing interests as discussed in Question 1 need to be applied by identifying the following:

- the equitable interests present and their comparable status;
- any postponing conduct by any of the parties and its effect;
- the effect of a caveat and how it may be removed and any associated consequences.

A logical outline for the answer to the question would be to consider:

- the status of the easement:
  - is it an omitted easement?
  - if it is, can it be registered and how, and if not, does Gerald have any interests to caveat?
- the status of the parties' interests after determining whether the easement is valid having regard to the caveat:
  - what is the effect of the caveat?
  - is there a caveatable interest?
  - is lodgment of the caveat valid?
  - how can the caveat be removed?
  - is any compensation payable?

 Answer

4-17 This answer will address the various equitable interests raised in this question by first addressing the status of Gerald's unregistered easement by determining whether it is an omitted easement and can thus be registered. After determining the status of the easement, this answer will address Gerald's caveat and determine: the consequences of his caveat; whether he has a caveatable interest; whether the caveat should stay or be removed; how it can be removed; and any compensation that arises from its removal.

Easement

4-18 Gerald's apparently unregistered easement is, prima facie, not binding on Leo if Leo becomes the registered owner (RO) of Lot 1 (s 184(1) Land Title Act 1994 (Qld) (LTA)), as Leo would not be bound by any unregistered interests once he became indefeasible through registration; s 37 LTA; *Breskvar v Wall* (1971) 126 CLR 376. The easement is not on the register and will not be binding unless it can be put on the register which will only occur if it is an omitted easement.

Gerald's easement would fall outside the s 185(1)(c) LTA omitted easement exception if it was never lodged for registration: *Stuy v BC Ronalds* Pty Ltd [1984] 2 Qd R 578. However, if Gerald's easement was indeed lodged for registration as he claims, but has never been registered because of the registrar's error, then it would be protected by the omitted easement exception to indefeasibility under s 185(3)(c) LTA and would become binding on Leo (s 185(4) LTA), preventing him from being able to use the area as a car park. The registrar would have the power to register Gerald's easement under s 15 LTA.

Not enough information is given to determine conclusively whether the document was lodged for registration or not, so before the registrar could determine whether the easement could be lodged, an enquiry may need to be held under s 19(a) and (b)(i) LTA. This would uncover whether it was lodged for registration and why it remains unregistered, allowing the registrar to reach a conclusion on whether the register is incorrect: s 15(2)(b) LTA.

If Gerald's easement falls within the omitted easement exception, then the registrar can register the easement notwithstanding any prejudice to Zak and Zelda who are the current ROs, and Leo the pending RO: s 15(3)(a) LTA and s 15(4) LTA.

4-19 Gerald's caveat prevents Leo from becoming the RO of Lot 1 under s 124(1) LTA. Gerald's right as holder of a valid easement would be considered an 'equitable interest' and more than a 'mere equity'. This is determined with reference to *Commissioner of Stamp Duties (Qld) v Livingston* (1960) 107 CLR 411, which led to the Livingston Indicia which defines an equitable interest as a beneficial interest *in* property which satisfies the four indicia being: recoverable, assignable, enforceable against third parties, and subject to competing interests. A 'mere equity' only has some of the indicia which could be binding against a third party with notice, while a personal equity satisfies none of the indicia and would have no enforceability. Thus if it is determined there is a valid easement then Gerald can caveat under s 122(1)(a) LTA as he has a caveatable and equitable interest in Lot 1 by virtue of his easement agreement with Zak and Zelda.

In the meantime, Leo clearly wants Gerald's caveat removed as it is preventing him from registering his fee simple and obtaining his mortgage. Leo could wait for the caveat to lapse, which it would after three months if Gerald did not act on it, but that is a long timeframe. (Note: if this had occurred in NSW there is no provision for lapsing without applying to the courts to lapse a caveat, otherwise they stand indefinitely.) If Gerald refuses to withdraw his caveat under s 125 LTA, then Leo may serve a notice on Gerald under s 126(2) LTA and thereby cause Gerald's caveat to lapse 14 days after the notice: s 126(4)(a)(i) LTA.

Alternatively, Leo may apply for the Supreme Court's removal under s 127 LTA. Gerald would then bear the onus of proving to the Court there is a serious issue to be tried, and justifying his caveat's retention on the balance of convenience: *Re Jorss' Caveat* [1982] Qd R 458; *Abraham v Abraham* [2012] NSWSC 254.

The serious issues arising from Gerald's unregistered easement include: (a) whether the easement falls within the s 185(1)(c) LTA omitted easement exception; and (b) if so, whether the registrar can register or restore the easement under s 15 LTA.

The Supreme Court may retain Gerald's caveat pending the registrar's inquiry and decision. On the other hand, the Supreme Court may remove Gerald's caveat to enable Leo's registration on the balance of convenience, given that Leo's unregistered fee simple is superior to Gerald's unregistered easement, and given that the omitted easement exception and the Registrar's powers already adequately protect Gerald's easement: *Bli Bli #1 Pty Ltd & Anor v Kimlin Investments Pty Ltd & Ors* [2008] QSC 289.

Leo may claim compensation from Gerald under s 130 LTA, if he can show that he has suffered any loss or damage as a result of Gerald's caveat, perhaps through his inability to obtain his mortgage and thus obtain the funds for his wedding and honeymoon.

Gerald appears able to prove that he had reasonable cause to lodge the caveat under s 130(3) LTA, as he had an honest and reasonable belief that he had an easement agreement representing a caveatable interest: *Bedford Properties P/L v Surgo Pty Ltd* [1981] 1 NSWLR 106.

However, it appears that Gerald's ulterior motive for wanting to buy Lot 1, assuming the neighbour's allegation is true, may represent a primary and improper purpose for lodging a caveat. Regardless of whether s 130 LTA requires reasonable cause (*Farvet Pty Ltd v Frost* [1997] 2 Qd R 39), Gerald's improper purpose may render his caveat without reasonable cause: *Hillpalm Pty Ltd v Heaven's Door Pty Ltd* (2004) 220 CLR 472.

Examiner's Comments

4-20 The answer identifies and examines the different equitable interests of each person. It explores the omitted easement exception, and how the registrar can affect registration upon determination thereof. The answer also examines the different kinds of interests and which ones are caveatable. This is then followed by an examination of how to get rid of a caveat having determined its validity, and how postponing conduct can result in compensation, even when a valid caveat has been lodged under an honest and reasonable belief.

The answer is succinct and addresses the necessary legislation and common law. More could have been provided concerning the consequences had Leo obtained registration, or had the easement proven to be invalid.

 # Keep in Mind

4-21 Students should keep in mind the following:

- When answering questions of this nature, it is important to identify the individual interests and their validity. Equality of interests is irrelevant if one is invalid or, if one interest is an interest in land and the other a personal right, then the superiority of the interest in land makes other issues moot.

- When addressing a caveat such as this, students should discuss the following, as leaving out parts of this discussion will result in incomplete analysis:
  - ◆ validity of the caveated interest;
  - ◆ effect of the caveat;
  - ◆ removal of the caveat;
  - ◆ retention of the caveat;
  - ◆ purpose of the caveat;
  - ◆ compensation.

Question 3

> **4-22**   Peter is seised of an estate in fee simple in 'Greenland', a property in New South Wales under old system title. Peter writes to his Uncle Arthur for a loan, which Arthur agrees to in a letter of response to Peter subject to receiving a mortgage over 'Greenland'. Peter writes back agreeing to the mortgage, saying he will have his solicitor draw up the necessary documents and send them to Arthur with the title deeds. Arthur forwards the loan moneys to Peter.
>
> Peter does not send the deeds to Arthur after receiving the loan moneys. Instead he hands them to Mick, his solicitor, as security for a further loan. Mick places the deeds in his safe.
>
> Robyn is Mick's secretary. She forges Peter's signature on a contract for sale and sells the property to Emma. Emma's solicitor searches the Registry of Deeds and finds the title in Peter's name. Robyn completes the sale to Emma and hands over, on settlement, the deeds she obtains from Mick's safe together with a conveyance to Emma upon which she has forged Peter's signature. She then catches a plane to Rio with her boyfriend.
>
> Arthur meanwhile has made numerous requests to Peter for the title deeds. He decides (after consulting his solicitor) that he must protect his interest as mortgagee. He registers his letters evidencing his agreement with Peter in the Registry of Deeds.
>
> The next day Emma's solicitor lodges the conveyance for registration.
>
> Discuss the competing interests.
>
> **Time allowed: 1 hour**

Answer Plan

4-23   The same approach to the answer outline is taken as that taken for the answer to Question 2. The answer again seeks to refine the student's understanding of the relevant principles. It is calling for identification of:

- legal and equitable interests;
- postponing conduct;
- the effect of a fraudulent and void transaction before and after registration;
- the effect of notice;
- the effect of registration particularly in respect of an unwritten equity.

The answer outline should be in the following form:

- the type of interest held by each party;
- the priority of that interest;
- postponing conduct affecting the party's interests;
- the effect of the fraudulent dealing.

These matters should be specifically addressed both before and after registration. In dealing with the 'after registration' situation, the effect of registration upon the unwritten equity should be discussed.

 # Answer

4-24 In answering this question the position of each of the parties will be dealt with before and after the fact of registration. Each party's interest will be determined and then examined as to its ranking.

Parties' interests prior to registration

Arthur

4-25 Arthur and Peter have an agreement in writing for a loan and mortgage. The agreement in writing will create an equitable interest in Greenland: s 23C(1)(a) Conveyancing Act 1919 (NSW). However, Arthur has made the loan advance without securing the title deeds, trusting on Peter's promise to send him the deeds (a trust that has proven misplaced). In not securing the deeds he has left Peter in a position to represent to another that the property is unencumbered:

> A common illustration of conduct on the part of the owner of an equity which postpones his interest is the arming of a third person with the indicia of title. (*Heid v Reliance Finance Corp Ltd (1983)* 154 CLR 326 at 339 per Mason and Deane JJ)

Equity will look to all the circumstances when considering conduct that might lead to postponement of an interest; however, Arthur's conduct would indicate postponement of his interest if Peter is able to represent the deeds are unencumbered (which in fact he does).

Mick

4-26 By making the loan and taking possession of the deeds, Mick has an equitable mortgage: *Bank of New South Wales v O'Connor* (1889) 14 AC 273 at 282. He secures the deed in his safe and certainly has not been negligent in his custody of them. It is only because of Arthur's omission in securing the deeds that Peter is able to secure the loan from Mick. It is not indicated in the question whether Mick searched the registry, but even if he did it would make no difference, as Arthur had not registered his agreement. Just as in *Abigail v Lapin* [1934] AC 492, failure to search the register on Abigail's part made no difference to the final outcome, in view of the fact no caveat had been lodged by Lapin in respect of their interest. Mick had no notice of Arthur's interest, constructive or otherwise. Arthur's conduct in not obtaining the deeds would be enough to see his interest postponed to Mick, even though prima facie it would have priority, being first in time: *Latec Investments Ltd v Hotel Terrigal Pty Ltd* (1965) 113 CLR 265.

Emma

4-27 Emma, prima facie, takes a legal interest in good faith for valuable consideration without notice. She is not a party to Robyn's fraudulent activities and she has no actual notice of the other interests. Her solicitor (as her agent) has searched the registry on her behalf without finding any outstanding interest. No constructive or imputed notice can be maintained against her. Prima facie she falls within the principle of the bona fide purchaser for value, who has taken the legal estate without notice of any prior equitable interest. However, the 'legal interest' she takes (and any 'equitable interest' on execution of the contract) is as a result of the fraudulent conduct of Robyn. As vendor and conveyor, Robyn has no interest to pass and no power to pass Peter's estate. Robyn falls into the *nemo dat* principle. The conveyance to Emma by Robyn (and the contract) is a nullity. Emma takes no interest and will have to look elsewhere for a remedy.

Accordingly, prior to any registration the priority of interests will be determined: Mick, Arthur, Peter (and Emma who in fact has no interest).

Parties' interests after registration

Arthur

4-28 Arthur is the first person to lodge the instrument evidencing his interest. Under the provisions of s 184G of the Conveyancing Act 1919 (NSW), his interest will take priority if his registration is bona fide for value and without notice. He seems to fulfil these requirements. He takes title for value and at that time does so in good faith and without notice of any outstanding interest. As the first instrument registered, Arthur will take priority.

Emma

4-29 Emma's instrument is registered after Arthur's. Accordingly, her interest will rank after Arthur's in accordance with s 184G. However, she takes her interest under a void instrument and her interest is a nullity in any case. Section 184G does not cure any defects in instruments upon registration. Her interests will be defeasible until deregistered.

Mick

4-30 Mick's interest is equitable, but not evidenced in writing. It is an interest that cannot be registered. Section 184G is applicable to interests created by instruments. An interest not created by an instrument is outside the scope of the section.

In *White v Neaylon* (1886) 11 App Cas 171, the respondent's brother had verbally agreed that the respondent should take title to some land (a crown lease) in settlement of their partnership dispute. However, the respondent's brother (in whose name title to the land stood), sold and transferred the property to the appellant. The appellant had notice of the respondent's claim prior to contract. The relevant South Australian Registration Act (5 Vict, No 8, 53) provided that all unregistered written agreements were void against a subsequent registered agreement, notwithstanding the purchaser had notice of the prior unregistered agreement at the time of conveyance.

On registration of the conveyance the appellant maintained that the registered interest, by virtue of the statute, gave him priority over the respondent's unwritten equity, notwithstanding his notice. The respondent maintained the statute referred to written agreements. It was silent about unwritten agreements and accordingly did not apply to his unwritten equity. The Privy Council held in favour of the respondent, on the basis the statute referred to written agreements and the respondent's equity was unwritten.

Mick's interest is not evidenced in writing; it is not created by instrument. Section 184G refers to instruments: 'All instruments (wills excepted)'. Therefore Mick's interest will not be affected by s 184G. His priority will be determined as if the section had not been enacted. In other words, the ranking of his interest will be subject to the priority rules unaffected by the provisions of s 184G. Arthur's registration will not affect the priority of Mick's interest. Arthur will be in the same situation regarding Mick's interest as Arthur was prior to registration. In other words, Arthur's interest, although first in time, will rank after Mick (because of his postponing conduct in not securing the deeds), notwithstanding Arthur's subsequent registration (and Mick's lack of registration).

One of the anomalies that was discussed in *White v Neaylon* was the priority that an unwritten equity might maintain over an interest, notwithstanding the latter's registration, when the same equity on reduction to writing would lose priority to the registered interest. The Privy Council indicated that it was for the legislature to correct the anomaly. The effect of the anomaly is that there may be situations where it is more advantageous to leave an unwritten equity in that state, rather than reduce it to writing.

Examiner's Comments

4-31 This question develops further the student's understanding of registration of instruments and identifying interests. The elements the answer addresses are the equitable interest created by the agreement, the equitable interest created by the deposit of deeds, and the fraudulent sale. These matters are identified and analysed in the answer. The further matters of postponing conduct and the unwritten equity are also analysed and discussed. It is important to discuss the position of the unwritten equity in relation to a competing registered interest. (This was an aspect of the law of priorities which was only briefly dealt with in the previous answer.)

Keep in Mind

4-32 Students should keep in mind the following:

- As in the previous answer, it is important to take each interest and analyse it, having regard to its position both before and after registration. In dealing with the registered conveyance, it is important to realise the instrument was void. Students sometimes confuse registration under s 184G of the Conveyancing Act 1919 (NSW) and registration under the Torrens system (particularly in the intense pressure of a written exam). Their confusion sees them making comments that registration will perfect the void instrument. It is essential to grasp that registration under s 184G does not add any perfection to an instrument. It does not correct any fault in an instrument. Registration merely gives priority over a subsequent instrument. The validity of an instrument will depend on the instrument, not on registration.

Question 4

4-33 Horatio and George were neighbours. George loved flying remote-controlled planes and in 1960, Horatio, who is the owner of deeds registration acreage land, agreed to allow George access over his land to provide a starting point for his remote controlled plane-flying competitions. Horatio and George signed an easement agreement confirming their arrangement and George paid Horatio $1,000. They agreed to register the easement and Horatio took it home to give to his solicitor when he next saw him.

Horatio's sister, Hermione, watched them sign the document and commented: 'I might buy this property from you one day, as long as those cute remote-controlled plane pilots keep coming round!

George never followed up with Horatio whether the agreement was registered on the deed but continued to use the easement area as agreed. In January 1977 Horatio applied to have the land registered pursuant to the Land Title Act 1994 (Qld). A certificate of title was issued in Horatio's name as registered owner of an estate in fee simple with no mention of the easement.

In 2010 Horatio decides to retire to the coast and sells the land to Hermione, his sister, under a written contract of sale for $100,000. There is no reference to the easement in the contract of sale. Hermione becomes the registered owner of the land in late March 2010. One week later she builds a large fence around the property and refuses George access to the property.

Hermione writes to George in April, 2010. 'I am the owner now and I need not acknowledge any of your rights under this fanciful easement document. No access to my property is allowed'.

Advise George if he can enforce the easement agreement against Hermione and advise whether the registrar is entitled to make this change to the register.

Time allowed: 45 mins

Answer Plan

4-34 This answer needs to address the changing status of rights, as the easement was originally granted by written agreement on old system land. However, when the land was registered under the Torrens system the easement was not carried over, resulting in potentially an equitable easement. The status of this must be contrasted with the rights of the registered fee simple owner of what is now Torrens land. The answer must examine:

- the original granting of the easement by written agreement;
- the status of the easement on old system land;
- the effect of the notice of Hermione as a witness to the agreement under the old system;
- the transfer of the land to Torrens without the easement and the effect of this on the status of the easement;
- Hermione's position as holder of registered fee simple title and the effect of that on the unregistered easement.

Answer

4-35 The easement document signed between Horatio and George is signed when the property is on old system land. Accordingly, it is an equitable easement and is never registered. Although the land is converted to Torrens land in 1977, the registration contains no reference to the equitable easement. Technically this has become an easement by prescription as it was never registered on the old deeds either.

In order to determine whether the easement can be transferred to the current title to the land, it must fall under one of the categories in ss 185

(1)(c) and 185(3)(a) Land Title Act 1994 (Qld) (LTA). This is an easement already undisputed and in existence when the land was brought under the provisions of the Torrens statute, though it is not reflected in the register.

4-36 Hermione's registered fee simple in Lot 3 is prima facie free from George's unregistered easement (s 184(1) LTA), unless George can raise the omitted easement exception of s 185(1)(c) LTA.

Does George's easement fall within the omitted easement exception?

There are various possibilities as to whether George's easement fits under s 185(3) LTA as an exception to indefeasibility due to the uncertainty of the facts given in the question:

- Under s 185(3)(a) LTA, if the easement was in existence when the lot burdened by it was first registered, but the easement particulars were never recorded in the freehold land register against the lot, then the easement will fall under the omitted easement exception and can be registered.
- If the easement instrument had been registered but was subsequently omitted from the register (ie the easement particulars in the register no longer include the easement particulars), then s 185(3)(b) LTA would apply and the easement would fall under the omitted easement exception. However, we are told the document was not registered so the easement would appear to fail this criterion.
- If the easement instrument was lodged for registration but was never registered because of a registrar's error, then s 185(3)(c) LTA would apply, but again, there does not seem to have been any attempt to register the document granting the easement.
- If the easement instrument was never lodged for registration, then it falls outside the omitted easement exception: *Stuy v BC Ronalds Pty Ltd* [1984] 2 Qd R 578. However, this applies to easements created after the land has been registered under Torrens.

If George's easement can fall within the omitted easement exception, as it seems likely to under s 185(3)(a) LTA, then Hermione would be bound by this easement: s 185(4) LTA.

There are a number of authorities that would indicate that this is an exception to indefeasibility as an omitted easement and the current registered proprietor would be subject to that easement document: *James v Stevenson* (1893) AC 162; *Beck v Aubach* (1986) 6 NSWLR454; and *Connellan Nominees Pty Ltd v Camerer* (1988) 2 Q R 248.

As an exception to indefeasibility the easement would be restored on the title. It is likely the registrar can make the amendment based on s 15(3) LTA as it was never registered. In any event, even without that provision it could be done on the basis of *James v Registrar General*, that it is an express exception to indefeasibility and in that sense there is no prejudice. The registrar could hold an inquiry under s 15(2) LTA to ascertain the facts and deal with the *Equitiloan* case which confirms the registrar may not make a correction that will prejudice a current interest holder, or await a Supreme Court order under s 15(3) LTA. Under s 189(1)(j) LTA there is no compensation for any change to the register.

The statement made by Hermione in 1960 may potentially raise an *in personam* action on the basis that she was bound by the statement which might be indicating she would continue to support the use of the land for remote plane flying as per *Bahr v Nicolay,* but perhaps the statement is a bit equivocal.

Examiner's Comments

4-37 This student has done a reasonable job of addressing the omitted easement issues. The answer has touched on the registrar's powers of correction in some detail as well, but there is a glaring omission in the failure to discuss Hermione's notice of the easement and agreement, due to her presence on the day. Had the easement failed to meet the criteria of an omitted easement, it could still have been added successfully to the title under s 15(8) LTA as there would be no prejudice to Hermione given her knowledge that the register was wrong, and how it was wrong. The rest of the answer is reasonably managed but more detailed arguments could have been presented.

Keep in Mind

4-38 Students should keep in mind the following:

- It is important that a student addresses each and every issue raised in a question. If information is given in the fact scenario, such as Hermione's presence at the signing of the agreement and her verbal comments, then this information should be addressed in the answer. Ignoring such a large piece of information in a question is bound to lead to a loss of marks.
- Students are often tempted to stop once they have found a legal solution to a client's problem, but they should always remember that often more than one solution is available, and all possible solutions should be addressed in an answer.

Chapter 5

Native Title

5-1 Native title represents recognition, under Australian law, of the indigenous system of law and ownership that pre-dates European colonisation. Native title was first recognised by the High Court of Australia in the decision of *Mabo v Queensland (No 2)* (1992) 175 CLR 1, and the Native Title Act 1993 (Cth) was the statutory embodiment of the principles espoused in that case.

The High Court declared the declaration of terra nullius by the initial settlers was incorrect, and confirmed that the indigenous inhabitants already had a system of cultural customs and rules in place when the settlers arrived. It was held that native title can be recognised where a traditional connection to land and waters has been maintained, and where intervening government acts have not extinguished those native title rights.

The native title rights of a particular group will depend on the traditional laws and customs of those people, and may include possession, occupation, use and enjoyment of the areas claimed. It may include a right of access to an area of land or water, or the right to participate in decisions concerning how the area is used by other people. Any native title rights and interests are subject to other existing rights (eg freehold or leases), and those other rights take precedence over native title rights. Thus native title rights, once established, are always defined by what other rights have been granted over the land since settlement.

Native title cannot be bought or sold. It can be transferred by traditional law or custom, or surrendered to government, which can then pay compensation to the native title holders in the same way as it does when acquiring rights to other property.

In answering native title problem questions, students should generally focus on assessing the potential for success of a claim, and then determine the impact of any government act over the same area on the indigenous rights claimed. It is important students fully understand the implications of the Racial Discrimination Act 1975 (Cth) and how it, in conjunction with the *Mabo* decision, led to the native title legislation.

5-2   Before attempting the questions in this chapter, students should be familiar with the following:

✓   Racial Discrimination Act 1975 (Cth);

✓   Native Title Act 1993 (Cth);

✓   Native Title Amendment Act 1998 (Cth);

✓   the concept of indigenous land use agreements;

✓   the National Native Title Tribunal, its role and functions;

✓   the definitions and application of past acts, intermediate acts and future acts;

✓   *Akiba on behalf of the Torres Strait Islanders of the Regional Seas Claim Group v State of Queensland (No 2)* [2010] FCA 643;

✓   *Bennell v State of Western Australia* [2006] FCA 1243;

✓   *Commonwealth of Australia v Yarmirr* (2001) 184 ALR 113;

✓   *De Rose v South Australia No 2* (2005) 145 FCR 290;

✓   *Fejo v NT* (1998) 195 CLR 96;

✓   *King v Northern Territory* (2007) FCA 994;

✓   *Mabo v State of Queensland* (1992) 175 CLR 1;

✓   *Members of the Yorta Yorta Aboriginal Community v Victoria* (2002) 214 CLR 422;

✓   *NT v Arnhem Land Aboriginal Land Trust* (2008) HCA;

✓   *Western Australia v Ward* (2002) 213 CLR 1;

✓   *Wik Peoples v Queensland* (1996) 187 CLR 1;

✓   *Wilson v Anderson* (2002) 213 CLR 401;

✓   *Yanner v Eaton* (1999) 201 CLR 351.

Question 1

5-3   Why was there a need for the Native Title Amendment Act 1998 (Cth) after the original Native Title Act?

Time allowed: 1 hour, 30 mins

Answer Plan

5-4 This question is concerned with why there was a need for further amendments to the original Native Title Act 1993 (Cth)(NTA). To answer this question, the student needs to look at how the original Native Title Act was created, including what native title is, and the circumstances surrounding the passing of the original Bill. Then the student needs to examine what happened after the first Act that prompted the need for an amending Act, how the amending Act came into being, and what key changes were made by the amending Act. The answer should look at the history behind native title, and also examine the social and political views at the time to put the legislation into context. This question asks the student to look at the social, political and historic events that prompted the legislative change.

A plan could be:

- What is native title?:
  - the history behind the concept of native title;
  - the difference between land rights and native title.
- How it came into being in Australia:
  - *Mabo v State of Queensland* (1992) 175 CLR 1;
  - the NTA.
- What was left out of the NTA?
- *Wik Peoples v Queensland* (1996) 187 CLR 1:
  - what was wrong with the Native Title Act?
  - the effect of *Wik*.
- The Native Title Amendment Bill:
  - the issues in the amendments;
  - the social and political circumstances.
- The Native Title Amendment Act.

Answer

5-5 In July 1998 the parliament passed the Native Title Amendment Act 1998 (Cth) after months of public debate about the issue of native title. Prior to 1998, most governments at state and federal level had passed some form of legislation recognising indigenous land rights. In June 1992, the High Court had handed down the *Mabo* judgment which had prompted the enactment of the NTA. Then in 1996 the High Court handed down another judgment (*Wik Peoples v Queensland* [1996] HCA 40), which reignited the debate over what many assumed had been resolved already under *Mabo* and the creation of the NTA, leading to the passing of the Native Title Amendment Act. In order to understand the need for an amendment Act, it is necessary to review the background, including what native title is, how *Mabo* came about, why the original Native Title Act was passed and why *Wik* caused such a furore.

5-6 Two key concepts underpin what native title is, and why it has become part of Australian law. One, native title did exist before *Mabo* and was not created by the High Court in that judgment, and two, *Mabo* did not grant new native title rights, it merely recognised them as rights which had been in existence for thousands of years. These two concepts identify the differences between land rights and native title rights. Land rights are created through the passing of legislation which grants rights to obtain land to indigenous Australians, in order to compensate them for land lost at colonisation. However, native title recognises rights that indigenous Australians have held since before colonisation, and which were not necessarily lost at the time of colonisation.

The recognition of native title has been part of English law for hundreds of years and is based on the principle that prior inhabitants of a territory had a right to retain their land against new arrivals, including English settlers. This did not occur in Australia because the initial British settlers did not recognise the indigenous laws and customs as comparable to their own system of property rights, and therefore felt no need to recognise them. At the time, Australia was declared terra nullius, which allowed the settlers to freely impose their own laws and customs in their entirety upon the land (sovereignty), as well as to take ownership of all the land, without any acknowledgement of any prior cultural system.

Despite becoming aware that terra nullius was not an appropriate designation, that approach was confirmed in 1889 by the Privy Council which held in *Cooper v Stuart* (1889) 14 App Cas 286 that in 1788 Australia was 'a tract of territory practically unoccupied without settled inhabitants', and this remained the legal position until *Mabo* in 1992. In *Mabo*, the judges held that it would be unjust for the common law of Australia to maintain the fiction that Australia was terra nullius in 1788. The High Court, in a majority judgment of six to one, stated a number of broad principles:

- Upon colonisation, the British Crown acquired sovereignty to take full or beneficial ownership over the land, but it was not automatically granted. If the Crown chose not to exercise its authority over an area by an act which unequivocally demonstrated the Crown's intention to claim full ownership of that land, for example by granting freehold rights, then that land continued to belong to the indigenous people in accordance with their laws and customs.
- Where native title continues to exist, the laws and customs of the indigenous people who have the connection with that land determine both the rights conferred under native title, and who may exercise those rights.
- If the indigenous population in an area loses its connection with the land, then those native title rights are extinguished.
- Native title rights may not be assigned or transferred other than by surrender to the Crown in exchange for a grant of freehold over that land, or monetary compensation.

Thus *Mabo* opened the way for Aboriginal peoples on the mainland to make claims in respect of their traditional land. However, for Aboriginal people to establish all the factors required to prove that their native title entitlement continues to exist to the current day, extensive research must be undertaken, covering such disciplines as history, anthropology, linguistics and genealogy; a chain of title must be established back to 1788 to see whether the Crown has undertaken any act demonstrating a clear and unequivocal intention to extinguish native title; and all of that evidence must be presented in court. This is a lengthy, time-consuming and expensive process. Moreover, because *Mabo* only offers broad principles for native title, many cases need to be referred to higher courts for determination of the individual variances of each set of circumstances.

Once native title rights were recognised, *Mabo* also implied that the Aborigines retaining those rights could veto any future dealings with that land which might extinguish or impair their native title. This meant that once an application for native title rights was made concerning a particular piece of land, any dealings on that land had to be put on hold pending the outcome of what was likely to be a protracted journey through the courts. If native title was eventually established, then the native title holders could presumably veto any development on their land at their discretion. Clearly it was in the interests of all concerned that a system be established to enable quick processing of claims at reasonable costs, preferably by conciliation and agreement rather than litigation. It was also in the interests of the wider community that procedures be put in place to enable land to be made available for future developments. The government responded to these issues by passing the Native Title Act in 1993 (NTA). Representatives of Aboriginal and non-Aboriginal interests spent months of consultation and negotiation working out a compromise and the result was the NTA.

The NTA has the following features:

- The NTA limits extinguishment of native title rights to those manners set out in the Act itself, that is specific procedures which governments must follow before native title may be extinguished or otherwise affected, as opposed to those methods identified in *Mabo*.
- The right of the Aborigines to veto future developments on their land was compromised in exchange for retaining rights to compensation and, in some instances such as mining, the right to negotiate compensation for the duration of the lease, and the later resumption of native title. The right to negotiate begins once a claim is submitted, not once it is accepted. This gives Aborigines the right to oppose, but not veto, certain future acts.
- The NTA formalises the means by which native title can be established, reducing costs and time, and enables assistance, via various bodies, to provide the funding and technical expertise necessary to prepare a native title claim to the Aboriginal communities.

- The NTA validates any past government acts which may be invalid because of the existence of native title. Under *Mabo*, the Racial Discrimination Act 1975 (Cth) (RDA) made it unlawful for governments to carry out any acts which extinguished native title (eg granting freehold title over land). The decision meant that for almost 20 years governments had been doing various acts in relation to land which, after *Mabo*, were considered unlawful and invalid. It was agreed that any such acts after the inception of the RDA and before the enactment of the NTA would be validated, and native title on that land extinguished and compensation deemed payable by the relevant government, for the value of any native title which was extinguished as a result.
- Establishment of an indigenous land fund for those indigenous people who would not benefit from native title because of prior extinguishment.

One question not addressed by *Mabo* was whether, at common law, the grant of a lease extinguished native title. General consensus was that granting of freehold would extinguish native title but the judges did not agree whether leases would act the same way. Three of the six majority judges held that the grant of a lease would extinguish native title, but the other three raised doubts as to whether that would always apply.

Most of Australia's land title is not freehold but is one or another form of Crown lease. Generally it is thought that certain types of Crown leases, such as the residential and business leases in the Australian Capital Territory, extinguished native title. The issue in debate was pastoral leases, a unique form of lease created in Australia to give the leaseholder the right to graze cattle or sheep. Pastoral leases usually cover large areas of land in fairly arid parts of Australia and are designed to minimise the land impact of livestock. Many felt that these activities were unlikely to interfere with Aboriginal use of the land under native title, so it was unlikely that the grant of such leases would be inconsistent with the continued existence of native title. However, others disagreed, arguing that at common law a lease generally confers exclusive possession on the tenant, and the tenant's right to exclusive possession is therefore necessarily inconsistent with the Aborigines' native title right to possession of the same land. They suggested that since the Crown's sovereignty could extinguish native title by granting inconsistent rights, the grant of a lease extinguished native title. The matter was not settled under the NTA as the parties involved could not agree, and they left it to the High Court to determine a case already before it, the *Wik* case.

In *Wik*, the Wik and Thayorre peoples of northern Queensland had claimed native title over lands which, in the past, had been the subject of pastoral leases. It was argued by those opposed to the claims that the granting of the pastoral leases had extinguished native title. The High

Court was asked to decide a number of questions that had been referred to it by the judge who was hearing the native title claim. The High Court has been criticised for answering precisely those questions, and not addressing wider issues. The principle question which was answered was, in effect, 'Did the granting of the pastoral leases under consideration in that case (*Wik*) necessarily extinguish all native title rights and interests that might otherwise exist?' The High Court, by a majority of four to three, answered in the negative, and held that:

- The pastoral leases under consideration in the case did not confer exclusive possession on the pastoralist.
- The leases therefore did not necessarily extinguish all native title rights and interests.
- Determination of whether there was any extinguishment or impairment of native title can only be determined by considering the nature of the native title rights and interests which the Aborigines can establish in relation to the land.
- Where native title rights and interests can co-exist with the statutory rights of the pastoralist then they survive, but, to the extent of any inconsistency, the rights of the pastoralist prevail.

In reaching their decision, the High Court examined the legislation under which the leases were granted, and declared neither the legislation nor the leases granted demonstrated a clear and unequivocal intention by the Crown to extinguish native title. The court reviewed the history of pastoral leases and found that the legislation granting pastoral leases was not intended to deprive Aborigines of their land, but was designed to provide a means by which the rapid expansion of the pastoral industry could be regulated and controlled, while providing some degree of security from claim jumping, as was common at the time of their inception.

There was already pressure on the government to amend the NTA. Practice of the Act had brought to light deficiencies in its operation and administration. The recent case of *Brandy v The Human Rights and Equal Opportunity Commission* (*Brandy*) (1995) 183 CLR 245 had cast doubt on the ability of the National Native Title Tribunal (NNTT) to make determinations of native title and compensation, and the decision of the High Court in *North Ganalanja Aboriginal Corporation v Queensland* (*Waanyi*) (1996) 185 CLR 595 had shown that native title claimants could get the benefit of statutory rights, such as the right to negotiate, without having to demonstrate that they were likely to succeed in their native title claim. The right to negotiate was triggered by the making of a native title application, so with no effective filter, claimants with no likelihood of success still obtained the benefit of the right to negotiate. Now, after *Wik*, the rights of third parties also had to be taken into account. If native title was confined to vacant Crown land, then generally the only interests to be considered were those of the native title holders and the Crown, and, where Crown land was to be the subject of mining, mining companies. While *Wik* held that the rights of pastoralists prevailed over the rights of native title holders where they conflicted, applying that principle practically could be an expensive, time-consuming business. For example, under most state legislation, pastoralists could apply to the relevant state authority for permission to diversify their activities. After *Wik*, some state governments decided that until a native title claim had been finalised, no such applications could be granted.

The government had assumed that granting a pastoral lease extinguished native title and, under this misapprehension, believed approximately 36% of Australia was potentially available for native title claims. However, if native title could be claimed where pastoral leases had been granted, that percentage increased to 78%. This also meant a correspondingly large increase in the NNTT's workload, particularly in terms of mining leases and the right to negotiate, which meant providing more resources which would cost more money.

Due to the intense public debate generated by *Wik,* many Australians, especially farmers, mistakenly believed that the *Wik* decision meant that Australians would lose farms, and even suburban land in cities. The government was put under pressure to pass legislation to extinguish native title on pastoral leases, which they resisted because of the compensation that would engender. Instead, the government announced the 'Ten Point Plan' in May 1997, which did include a number of provisions to either extinguish native title in particular circumstances, or to cut back significantly statutory rights which native title holders had obtained as part of the NTA compromise in 1993. This was met with outrage by the indigenous people and their supporters.

The Native Title Amendment Bill 1997 (NTAB) was introduced into the House of Representatives in September 1997 and passed through the lower house. At the time the government held minority numbers in the Senate. When it reached the Senate, members called for major amendments to some of the core elements, and the Bill was defeated.

There were four big issues on which the Senate and government disagreed. The government wanted a sunset clause to limit all claims for determination of native title under the NTA to be made within six years, which was rejected as unreasonable by the Senate. A threshold test was suggested by the NTAB to allow claims likely to succeed to be registered. The Senate approved the idea but felt the government's test was too restrictive. The Senate wanted an amendment that the NTA be read and construed in accordance with the RDA, which the government felt would create uncertainty. The biggest issue between the government and the Senate was the right to negotiate (RTN) on pastoral leases. The government proposed allowing abolition of RTN on pastoral leases by state governments. The mining industry and pastoralists supported the plan.

Ultimately, the Senate rejected the Bill three times, and a double dissolution followed by an election appeared to be the only way to break the impasse. In June 1998, the One Nation party secured 23% of the vote in Queensland and the Coalition realised they might lose government in an election. It became apparent a compromise with the Senate was a better alternative than a race-based election, and negotiations began between the government and the Senate in earnest. On 1 July 1998 the details of the compromise were finalised and announced, and the following week the NTAB passed through the parliament.

Ultimately, there was no sunset clause. The government's threshold test was relaxed to make allowance for the registration of claims by the children of the 'stolen generation' and victims of 'locked gates' practices to have their native title claims registered. The Senate's amendment requiring the NTAA be read and construed subject to the RDA was retained, and the right to negotiate on pastoral leases was retained. The states could, however, introduce their own procedures to manage mining, and some compulsory acquisitions on pastoral lease lands on which native title existed, as long as those procedures met the strict federal criteria, giving native title holders and claimants substantive rights of negotiation.

A multitude of other changes were implemented in the NTAA, but none that caused the debate and argument engendered by the ones discussed here. The *Wik* judgment brought to a head the various problems with the original Act, but also exposed the conflicts that exist in Australia between respect for the indigenous heritage and the commercial interests that support much of the economy. Ultimately, it was fear of losing power completely that persuaded the government to capitulate and negotiate. The next questions, of course, are what other unresolved issues remain to be exposed in native title, and will any of them have the same impact on the legal landscape, or is the current legislation sufficient to manage the process moving forward.

Examiner's Comments

5-7 The answer follows the outlined plan in structure. It is a good examination of the history and events surrounding native title, its creation, and the later public arguments that created the Native Title Amendment Act. The structure would have benefitted from headings, an introduction outlining where the paper intended to go, and a thesis covering the general proposed topic. These all would have assisted the reader in navigating what is ultimately a fairly long discourse. The paper would also have benefitted from some references to the actual judgments in questions, with some quotes from the relevant judges who made some notable and apt quotes on the issues mentioned. The points that caused the tension in parliament are the focus of the essay, but there were many other important changes in the amendment Act that would have been worth mentioning. Perhaps the student could have spent slightly less time on the history and a little more on the amendment Act itself. However, ultimately the student addressed the topic and gave a thorough accounting of the events that led to the changes: a good effort.

Keep in Mind

5-8   Students should keep in mind the following:

- In an answer this long, it is a good idea to have an introduction that provides a clear thesis statement of what the essay will discuss, the material to be covered, and the order of the discussion, to give the reader a map to such a broad topic.
- Answers of this type benefit from headings and the student should always try and break the subject matter into subject-based chunks, clearly marked with relevant headings.
- Although this topic covers a lot of non-legal information, the student should remember that ultimately this is a law essay, and should always come back to the effect of the law on the situation, or vice versa.

Question 2

5-9   Samuel is part of the Jagadju people who made a native title claim over an area in Queensland in 1996.

The claim covers the following:

- freehold interest over a farm and acreage, held by the Baxter family;
- Ninety-nine-year crown pastoral lease granted to the Baxter family. The conditions of the lease include non-intensive sheep grazing, the right to build on the leasehold area, and the right to exclude unauthorised persons, only after permission to do so is granted by the Crown;
- The township of Succotash comprising:
  - ♦ wetlands and a park;
  - ♦ police station built in 1958;
  - ♦ school built in 1976;
  - ♦ a total of 162 assorted houses, all on freehold blocks, including Candice and Jimmy Baxter's house in town.

The Jagadju people are spread out throughout Succotash and the surrounding areas, although some have moved and work and live in Metro City, about 180 kilometres south of Bunda Mountain. The clan meets twice a year to celebrate family, culture and hunt kangaroos. However, the local elders are upset that some of the younger generation living in Metro City are disinterested in their Aboriginal heritage and fail to attend the clan gatherings.

Advise the Jagadju people whether their native title claim over the township of Bunda Mountain is likely to succeed.

(Note: For the purpose of the question, assume that all grants were made between 1980 and 1992.)

Time allowed: 1 hour

Answer Plan

5-10 This an introductory question, focusing on the concepts of native title, and how to manage multiple varieties of interests in respect to land in one question. The answer should address:

- proving the existence of native title:
- any potential extinguishment of each of the individual grants; each grant should be assessed separately:
  - ♦ freehold interest;
  - ♦ pastoral lease;
  - ♦ properties in the town.

Answer

Establishing native title

5-11 In order to prove their right to native title, the Jagadju have to satisfy the criteria laid down in *Mabo* and legislated in s 223 of the Native Title Act 1993 (Cth) (NTA). The legislation specifies that they will only succeed if their rights and interests are possessed under traditional laws acknowledged, and the traditional customs observed, by their clan; laws or customs must have a connection with the land or waters; and those rights and interests must be recognised by the common law of Australia. The Jagadju seem to have maintained fairly strong physical ties with the area, in that the majority of the clan still live locally, and still practise their traditional customs in the area twice a year. Although the youth involvement seems to be decreasing, at this stage there does not appear to be any difficulty in them establishing their continued presence and links with the land, or their ongoing practice of traditional customs. A number of federal agencies are available to assist them in establishing proof, using archaeological, historical and anthropological evidence. Their claim can then be determined either by a trial, litigated determination or a negotiated settlement of claim, that is by consent.

Extinguishment of native title

5-12 The next hurdle for the Jagadju to overcome is whether any of the Crown grants have extinguished the native title rights.

The NTA provides for validation of past acts by the Crown, that would have been invalid due to the existence of native title. The Commonwealth can only validate past Commonwealth actions, each state has been authorised to pass its own legislation, on identical terms, to validate past state actions:

- **Freehold interest over farm and acreage held by the Baxter family:** Under NTA and under *Mabo*, native title cannot co-exist where a freehold or fee simple interest has been granted, and the native title rights are thus extinguished. Native title cannot be revived after it has been extinguished: *Fejo and Mills v Northern Territory and Oilnet (NT) Pty Ltd* [1998] HCA 58. Therefore native title cannot exist over the Baxter farm, nor can it be revived in the future, and the Jagadju cannot make a successful claim over this land. Since the freehold interest was granted after 1975, this will be a Category A past act under s 229 NTA, and the Jagadju will be entitled to compensation under s 17(1) NTA.
- **Ninety-nine year Crown pastoral lease held by the Baxter family:** This lease was granted between 1980 and 1992, so it was before the *Mabo* decision. However, if any or all of the native title rights in the area under the lease have been extinguished by the granting of the lease, the Jagadju might be entitled to compensation as this would be a Category A past act if the lease was granted between 1975 and 31 December 1993. The definition of a 'past act' is in s 228 NTA. If the dealing took place between 1 November 1975 (Racial Discrimination Act 1975 (Cth) (RDA)) and 31 December 1993, as here, then the dealing would have been invalid, because it purported to extinguish native title in a manner inconsistent with the provisions of the RDA. As a result it is a past act which is retrospectively validated by force of the native title legislation. The validating provision in Queensland is s 8 NTA (Qld). In *Western Australia v Ward* (2002) 213 CLR it was held that, if the Crown granted a leasehold estate over previously unallocated land to a third party, and native title rights and interests existed at the time of the grant but were not given a right to compensation in respect of their extinguishment at the time, then a right of compensation is extended to the native title holders. There is no right of compensation if the lease was granted before 1975, as there is no entitlement to compensation for rights granted prior to the enactment of the RDA. It is not clear from the facts when the lease was granted, so the Jagadju would have to rely on assistance from government agencies to determine when the Crown first allocated rights and interests in the land under a lease; though given it was 1980 they can be sure they fall under the Category A past acts in s 299 NTA.
- **Properties in the Town of Succotash:** The question states that all Crown grants were between 1980 and 1992, so only past acts (grants between 1975 and 1992) need to be considered.
  - ◆ **Wetlands and park:**
    Reserves and national parks do not automatically extinguish native title. There is still room for debate on whether native title

can be claimed over public land in an urban area. In *Bennell v State of Western Australia* (2006) 230 ALR 603 rights over an urban foreshore were recognised, subject to normal principles of extinguishment. However, this case was overruled on appeal, and the Full Court declined to reach a final determination on whether native title existed in the area. It is unlikely the court will find the Jagadju people have a right to the use and enjoyment of the lands outside of the rights enjoyed by the general population.

♦ **Police station built in 1958:**
The police station was built prior to the implementation of the RDA, so no compensation is due as any government act, whether partially or fully extinguishing native title, is not recognised as a breach of the RDA pre-1975.

♦ **School built in 1976:**
This is classified as a Category A past act under s 229 of the NTA as it is defined as construction of a public works under s 299(4) NTA. Therefore native title will be extinguished, but the Jagadju can claim compensation under s 17(1) NTA.

♦ **Assorted houses:**
All of the houses are under freehold grants which extinguish native title under s 229 NTA. Once native title is extinguished it cannot be revived; s 237 NTA; *Fejo and Mills v Northern Territory and Oilnet (NT) Pty Ltd* [1998] HCA 58.

Examiner's Comments

5-13 The answer generally followed the answer plan. This is a straightforward question which requires addressing each of the granted interests and determining their effect on the Jagadju native title claim. The student has addressed each in turn, which is the simplest and clearest way to answer the question. The grants have been clearly identified under their categories and the correct statutory and case law applied. The answer would have benefited from a conclusion, summarising the Jagadju's ultimate position with respect to their claim and any relevant remedies. More mention could have been made of the process required to make a claim, and the associated organisations and bodies. More attention could have been paid to compensation and the application of the different categories of act. Ultimately it was a straightforward question and the student has managed the answer clearly and concisely in the topics addressed, but the answers should go further.

Keep in Mind

5-14 Students should keep in mind the following:

• A native title question generally requires confirming that the claimants have the right to native title, so students should make sure they address the establishment of native title under s 223 NTA, rather than make assumptions.

- It is common to answer a native title question that deals with multiple different Crown grants by lumping together the various interests and trying to assess them all together under one native title claim. Not only does separation of the interests make the answer cleaner and easier to read in terms of structure, it also allows for recognition of the individual way the law deals with different categories of interests, and makes it less likely students will make errors.
- Never assume a straightforward question is easier. It should still have a plan, an introduction, a middle body of reasoning and a conclusion. It should be answered thoroughly with reference to statute and case law. Straightforward questions leave less margin for error and should not be handled carelessly because they seem simpler.

 # Question 3

5-15 The Kanjimup people approach you and state they intend to lodge a claim with the National Native Title Tribunal (NNTT) in relation to a parcel of land in North Queensland.

The Kanjimup elders seek native title recognition over an area covered by two adjoining pastoral leases, known as Downdale farm and Little Down Dale, 'the claim land'. Most of the clan live in nearby towns, and have not moved from the area. None of the land has been claimed by the Crown, other than by the two grants, described below.

Jason Jallup, the current tenant of both pastoral leases, has made clear his opposition to the native title claim. The Downdale farm lease covers 25 hectares, and was granted for use as a 'cattle feed lot' in 1974, under the Land Act 1962. A 'cattle feed lot' is a change of land use from agricultural activities to intensive animal keeping. Since the granting of the lease, the land has been used for intensive grazing for an average of 3,500 cattle at a time. In 1989 Jallup was granted a lease for Little Down Dale under a farm rationalisation program, introduced under the Land Act 1962. These leases were granted to allow smaller producers to increase the size of their properties by giving them access to land for non-intensive grazing purposes only, to make their businesses more viable. Therefore the purpose of the lease over Little Down Dale was non-intensive cattle grazing over an area of 30 hectares.

The Kanjimup people have been present in the area since before colonisation, and claim they have traditionally hunted kangaroos and emus on the lands covered by the granted leases. Every five years the Kanjimup people make a pilgrimage to the centre of Little Down Dale to view the constellations on the summer equinox from the valley, when the moon and stars light a particular path across the outback, which is followed by all young male tribe members between 15 and 18 to mark the start of their spiritual journey to becoming a man. The rocks alongside this path are marked with Aboriginal rock art.

Local historical archives record a fierce battle between the Kanjimup and government troops in 1818 on Little Down Dale. The battle was over access to water, that is Lake Yulli, a lake in the centre of Little Down Dale. Clan members who had suffered a setback or difficulties, or had committed a wrong, would swim through the lake as a symbol of their rebirth and a fresh start — a break from the past. In the last few years drought has dried up Lake Yulli, and an alternative ceremony was held in the centre of the dry pan with basins of water. However, recent rains have filled the lake again, and the Kanjimup are planning a return to the traditional ceremony.

Jallup claims that he has been on the leased land since 1980, and in that time he has not had any knowledge of a relationship between the Kanjimup people and the land. He says there has been little tribal presence in the area at all, since he introduced his cattle. He acknowledges that in 1980 he gave permission to some elders of the tribe to hunt on his land, but outside of that occasion, he states that he has no knowledge of any connection between the Kanjimup people and the land, and has only seen them when he has visited the local townships. Jallup has also pointed out that under the terms of the leases, he has been obliged to put up fencing, which would have prevented access to some parts of the pastoral leases.

Advise the Kanjimup elders on any matters you consider relevant, based on these facts.

Time allowed: 1 hour

Answer Plan

5-16 This question raises issues relevant to the extinguishment of native title and the nature of native title. Some time should be spent discussing native title generally: the content of native title is based on the laws and customs of indigenous peoples. Entitlement to native title rights must be established using the criteria of s 223 of the Native Title Act 1993 (Cth) (NTA).

After establishing an entitlement to native title, the Crown grants need to be addressed to determine their effects on the native title rights claimed and, if they extinguish native title, whether there is any opportunity for compensation.

This question involves two areas that were unclaimed Crown land until the following grants:

- a pastoral lease (Downdale farm) for 25 hectares granted in 1974 for a cattle feedlot; and
- a pastoral lease (Little Down Dale) for 300 hectares granted in 1989 for non-intensive cattle grazing.

The categories for these acts and their effect on native title rights can be found in the NTA. The conclusion should summarise the position of the Kanjimup people.

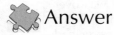 Answer

Is native title in existence?

5-17 Under the NTA, claims for recognition of native title rights should be assessed under s 223 NTA, rather than the definition in *Mabo and Others v Queensland (No 2)* (1992) 175 CLR 1. This view was supported in *Western Australia v Ward* (*Ward*), and *Members of the Yorta Yorta Aboriginal Community v Victoria* (2002) 214 CLR 422 (*Yorta Yorta*). Under s 223 NTA, 'native title ' means the communal, group or individual rights and interests of Aboriginal peoples or Torres Strait Islanders in relation to land or waters, where:

- the rights and interests are possessed under the traditional laws acknowledged, and the traditional customs observed, by the Aboriginal peoples or Torres Strait Islanders;
- the Aboriginal peoples or Torres Strait Islanders, by those laws and customs, have a connection with the land or waters; and
- the rights and interests are recognised by the common law of Australia.

In *Yorta Yorta* the court confirmed that if the laws and customs practised by a society at the time of sovereignty ceased to exist, then the rights and interests in land which would be occasioned by those practices, would also cease to exist. Even if a later society adopted those same laws and customs, it would not be a continuation of the first society, but rather laws and customs rooted in the new later society, and not in pre-sovereignty traditions and customs. Bearing in mind the s 223 NTA criteria, and the effects of the *Yorta Yorta* ruling, it is necessary to turn to the facts and examine the history of the Kanjimup people to see how well they meet the criteria, and if there has been a break in customs which would end their claim entitlement.

Here the Kanjimup people can show evidence of a spiritual connection to the claim area, and evidence of regular visits until they were forced to change their practice fairly recently, due to drought, which is similar to *De Rose* where a temporary break forced by natural changes was not deemed to extinguish a connection. The Kanjimup people have also claimed they follow traditional practices by hunting kangaroo and emu. The issue is whether this is enough to comply with the NTA requirements. It is likely to satisfy the criteria given there is both a physical and spiritual connection with the land, and both have run consistently on the land with only a very recent hiatus in practice. Unlike *Yorta Yorta*, this is not an instance where the connection was lost generations ago.

If the Kanjimup people meet the criteria, then they can make an application under s 61 NTA, which requires the relevant evidence to be provided to the National Native Title Tribunal (NNTT). It is possible a connection to the land and the possibility of a spiritual connection would be sufficient by itself. Although a spiritual connection was not sufficient in *Yorta Yorta,* it may not be authority to suggest it is never sufficient to base a native title claim. Under s 190A NTA, the registrar must accept the claim if it meets the criteria for the merits of the claim under s 190B NTA, and complies with the procedural requirements under s 190C NTA. The merits of the claim under s 190B NTA can be assessed with regard to historical, anthropological and archaeological evidence, and probably evidence from an elder and any other respected sources of local history.

The registrar must be satisfied that:
- there is a factual basis to support the claim;
- a prima facie case has been established;
- the claim includes a member with a current physical connection to the land, or one who would have such a connection but for exclusion (usually due to being part of the stolen generation or being 'locked out' of the land);
- there is compliance with formalities;
- native title has not been extinguished.

The evidence from Jallup, that he has not seen the claimants on his land for many years, could cast doubt on some of the claims. However, this would be contrasted with whether the evidence of a physical and spiritual connection with the land can be established. The fact the Kanjimup people have requested permission from Jallup to hunt on the land before, gives credibility to their claims. The rock art alongside the path walked by the young men to start their spiritual journey is evidence of both their physical presence on the land and their connection to that particular area, and the spiritual custom and its practice, which work in the claimants' favour. The historical records of Little Down Dale, evidence of the clan's long historical association with the area and the fact there was a battle, support the strength of their connection to the land.

That they have been forced to adapt their practices due to the drought could indicate an abandonment which would be an issue. However, under *De Rose v South Australia No 2* (2005) 145 FCR 290, a temporary break in the physical connection with the land is not necessarily fatal to a claim. If the claimants have been unable to access parts of the property because of fencing over an extended period, that could represent partial extinguishment of the native title rights, bearing in mind *Wik People v State of Queensland* [2000] FCA 1443 (*Wik*), which suggests that native title must give way to the lease provisions where there is inconsistency. However, under the Native Title Amendment Act 1998 (Cth) (NTAA), if the claimants or their parents were locked out from the land due to government policy, the claimants can ask the Federal Court to endorse their application. Given Jallup has claimed he was obliged to put up fencing under the terms of the leases, further examination is required to determine if the resultant locking out of the Kanjimup people from particular areas was as a result of government policy enforced through the leases, or if the fencing was required under some other rationale.

It seems that overall it is likely the Kanjimup would be able to successfully claim native title rights over the areas covered by the two leases.

Have the leases extinguished the native title entitlements?

5-18 In *Wik* it was held that native title was not necessarily extinguished by a pastoral lease. The High Court majority placed Crown leases into a separate category of leases, as a creature of statute, and said whether a lease did extinguish native title was subject to a number of considerations:

- the language of statute under which the lease was granted;
- the terms of the lease;
- the activities of the tenant — it should be noted that since *Ward* the more popular view is that the determinant factor is consideration should be given to the substantive rights granted by the lease, and not the rights as utilised and enforced by the tenant;
- the nature of the native title claimed.

If there is inconsistency between the native title rights claimed and the substantive rights granted by the leases, then native title must yield to the rights granted under the pastoral lease, but only to the extent of any inconsistencies. In *Wilson v Anderson* (2002) 76 ALJR 1098 it was established based on the facts, including the history and intention of the legislation, that the perpetual lease granted was deemed to extinguish native title, as it was seen as comparable to a grant of determinable fee simple.

Downdale farm

5-19 Applying the rules and legal reasoning outlined above to this scenario, the Downdale farm lease was granted under the Land Act. As this lease was granted in 1974 it was prior to the Racial Discrimination Act 1975 (RDA), and the concepts in *Wik* can apply with full effect, as it does not fall within the category of a past act under the NTA. If the lease has had no impact on the native title that existed at the time of granting, then the native title will continue uninterrupted. *Wik* recommends assessing certain criteria to determine whether there is extinguishment.

Beginning with the statute, the Land Act does not provide much guidance. However, the nature of the substantive rights granted under the lease for a cattle feedlot, which involves intensive feeding of cattle in a small area, would strongly suggest complete extinguishment. It is unlikely any kind of native title entitlement could be practised in the same space as the high intensity activity of a cattle feedlot. If the conclusion is that the native title is extinguished due to the extent of the inconsistency between the lease and the native title, then there can be no compensation for the Kanjimup people as the lease was granted prior to the RDA: *Mabo*.

Little Down Dale farm

5-20 Continuing with the same reasoning and applying it to the land under the granted lease, it is clear this lease is potentially caught by the RDA and may be a past act as it was granted in 1989. This lease was granted under the authority of the Land Act 1962 for the promotion of non-intensive grazing. The proposed use of the land could suggest a statutory intention not to extinguish, as it is a use with minimal impact upon the land. If the lease has no impact on the native title that existed at the time of the grant, then the native title will continue uninterrupted. Under such circumstances the lease would not be a past act as it would not be an act made invalid by the existence of native title; therefore, it would not need to be retrospectively validated by the legislation. However, this is unlikely, and again one must turn to the *Wik* criteria to determine whether there is extinguishment.

Here the nature of the native title rights claimed might suggest there has been complete extinguishment, but given the apparent occasional use of the land by the Kanjimup people for their spiritual ceremonies, there is unlikely to be any impact on those practices. The use of the land for ceremonies, hunting and general visits could suggest some inconsistency between the two leases, but this needs to be examined on a practical basis by determining the impact of the hunting and general visits on the non-intensive grazing cattle.

If native title has been extinguished, even only partially, then this pastoral lease is defined as a Category A past act, under s 228 and s 229 of the NTA. This is because the act, that is the granting of the lease, occurred after 1975 and before the enactment of the NTA in 1994. A past act would be invalid as it would breach the RDA, but is now validated by s 14 NTA (Cth) or s 8 NTA (Qld). A pastoral lease past act, that is one that at least extinguishes native title even a little, has the effect under statute of extinguishing native title entirely under s 15 NTA, and the extinguishment will raise a compensation claim under s 17(1) NTA. For grants of pastoral leases after 1975 that are past acts, any extinguishment will result in full extinguishment based on the provisions of the NTA, and will entitle the claimants to compensation.

The result here is extinguishment in both areas but there is only potential for compensation for the native title rights affected by the lease granted over Little Down Dale farm. Of course, if Jallup was prepared to negotiate an indigenous land use agreement (ILUA), and reach agreement on both parties exercising their rights over the land without a finding as to native title being extinguished, then an ILUA might be entered into to confirm continuing native title access.

Examiner's Comments

5-21 The answer covers all the material raised in the answer outline. It treats in some detail the elements required to determine native title, with reference to both the relevant statue and case law, and applies them to the facts. The issue of extinguishment of the different leases is dealt with, and a reasonable discussion given of the different views and how each lease results in a different conclusion. There is probably more detail than could be managed under exam conditions, but it is a thorough treatment of the issues involved. The structure could be better and as an essay answer, the tone needs work, but in terms of content it is a reasonable effort.

Keep in Mind

5-22 Students should keep in mind the following:

- Students must be careful of the dates involved in classifying Acts under the Native Title Act, and the effects of that categorisation upon native title entitlements — getting the categorisation wrong would completely change the status of the final determination.
- It is important to discuss all the possible evidence for establishing native title, both for and against, and assessing it against the relevant case law, as there is no single overarching consideration but rather it tends to weight of evidence.

Chapter 6

Co-Tenancies

Key Issues

6-1 Co-tenancy, also known as 'co-ownership', is the ownership of a property by more than one tenant. In encompasses both joint tenancy and tenancy in common. In order to attempt these questions, students need to be familiar with both forms of co-tenancy. The common denominator for both forms of co-tenancy is the unity of possession. Under Australian law, co-tenancies can exist under common law, statute or in equity.

It is important for students to note that the law relating to co-ownership focuses on defining the property rights of the parties, and the legal consequences of those rights, rather than regulating the interaction between the co-tenants. An excellent discussion of the rules relating to the rights of co-tenants (including contributions for maintenance and capital, rights of occupation and rights where one co-owner excludes another co-owner from possession) during the existence of the co-tenancy is enunciated by Meagher JA in *Forgeard v Shanahan* (1994) 35 NSWLR 206.

When creating a joint tenancy, there is a presumption at law in favour of a joint tenancy. Conversely, equity favours the creation of a tenancy in common because of the operation of the survivorship rule. In some jurisdictions, it is important to note that there is the statutory presumption of the creation of a tenancy in common when a co-tenancy is established (such as in Queensland).

Joint tenancy

6-2 Under joint tenancy, the tenant owns the whole estate, and is entitled to the use, possession and enjoyment of the whole of the land, and is subject only to the rights and interest of the other tenants. Joint tenancy is premised on two important concepts. The first is the four unities: unity of time, unity of interest, unity of title and unity of possession. Students must comprehend the effect of the four unities — when one of these unities has been broken, the joint tenancy will be broken, although it may still survive for the other joint tenants. The second is the right of survivorship (*jus accresendi*). Several jurisdictions have established a presumption of seniority to establish order of death and therefore the survivor when uncertainty exists regarding the survivor (such as when all joint tenants die in a car crash). It is essential that students understand the nature of *jus accresendi* as the hallmark of a joint tenancy.

An important consideration for any student that is studying co-tenancies is how severance of a joint tenancy occurs. Severance can occur either at law (such as in mutual agreement between joint tenants or in the course of dealings between joint tenants), or in equity (such as unilateral severance). Students must note that the transfer of the interest of joint tenant to another person will destroy the unity of title between that joint tenant and the remaining joint tenants, although the joint tenancy between the remaining joint tenants (where there are two or more) will still remain.

Tenancy in common

6-3   Under tenancy in common, a tenant is deemed to own a distinct yet undivided share in the land. This means that although the tenants hold distinct interests, the land itself is physically indivisible, with no tenant able to claim physical possession of a portion of land over another tenant. Unlike joint tenants, tenants in common are able to hold uneven interests (or shares) in the land. There is no right of survivorship between tenants in common. Instead, each tenant's share is fixed, and upon the death of a tenant in common his or her interest is granted to the beneficiary under a will, or if no will exists, according to the rules of intestacy.

6-4   Before attempting the questions in this chapter, students need to familiarise themselves with the following concepts:

✓	the nature of a joint tenancy;
✓	the four unities required in a joint tenancy;
✓	the right of survivorship (*jus accresendi*);
✓	section 35 of the Conveyancing Act 1919 (NSW) and s 65 of the Succession Act 1981 (Qld); and
✓	severance of a joint tenancy.

 # Question 1

6-5   Fred and Molly have been living together in blissful harmony since 2005 as registered joint tenants of a property in Surfers Paradise in Queensland. Lately they have been arguing a lot, and Fred decides that he wants to leave Molly since they have been arguing about many things for the past few months.

Fred decides to give his share of the tenancy to his sister Sally. He gives Sally an instrument of transfer, asking her to organise the transfer since he is very busy. The relationship between Fred and Molly comes to a head one stormy night, and they are heard arguing by the neighbours. The argument reaches a crescendo when Molly screams out:

> ... I wish you would drop dead Fred!

After the argument, Fred immediately leaves the house. The next afternoon the neighbours, concerned that Fred has not been seen, report Fred's disappearance to the police. His body is eventually found in a ditch on the side of the road, with severe bruising and abrasions. The coroner's report on the cause of death is inconclusive. Sally contacts police, claiming Molly murdered Fred. Sally also makes claim for Fred's half of the house as he had transferred it to her, and in any case, she is the sole beneficiary under Fred's will. Molly argues that house is now hers.

Who owns the property, and why?

Time allowed: 1 hour

Answer Plan

6-6   This question seeks to test a student's understanding of severance of a joint tenancy and the issue of survivorship between two tenants. Since the property is located in Queensland, the Property Law Act 1974 (Qld) (PLA), the Land Title Act 1994 (Qld) (LTA) and the Succession Act 1981 (Qld) should be applied.

The answer should deal with the following:

- the nature and constitution of a joint tenancy under the four unities of possession, interest, time and title;
- the characteristics of joint tenancy flowing from the unities (the right of survivorship);
- the unilateral severance of a joint tenancy in equity;
- the unilateral severance of a joint tenancy in Queensland under the PLA and the LTA; and
- the determination of joint tenancy under survivorship.

Answer

Nature of a joint tenancy

6-7   The nature of a joint tenancy is that it is characterised by the four unities: unity of time, unity of title, unity of possession and unity of interest, as well as the right of survivorship.

In *Peldan v Anderson* (2006) 226 CLR 471, the High Court described the nature of a joint tenancy:

> Joint tenants were generally regarded as together composing one single owner, each seised *per my er per tout* and consequently having nothing to convey to the other. However, in *Wright v Gibbons*, Dixon J doubted that this proposition could be regarded as an unqualified truth because "the

aliquot share of each [joint tenant] existed in contemplation of law as a distinct and ascertained proprietary interest" for the purposes of alienation, including alienation to a co-owner.

Upon Fred's death, two primary questions are raised. First, has the joint tenancy been severed by Fred? This gives rise to the second question of whether the right of survivorship still exists, and has Fred's interest in the property passed to Molly, the surviving joint tenant?

The four unities

6-8 In order for the joint tenancy to be created there must be the presence of the four unities. If one is absent, then a joint tenancy will not exist; instead a tenancy in common will be created, although it must be remembered that just because the four unities exist, it does not mean that a joint tenancy has been created. Other factors may indicate a tenancy in common has been created.

Unity of time means that the co-tenants must take their interest simultaneously and from the same source. This is distinguished from unity of title, which requires that the co-ownership interests be created by a single instrument. Unity of possession means that each joint tenant is equally entitled with the other co-tenants to possession of the whole of the land. The unity of possession is common to both joint tenancy and tenancy in common. In both forms of co-tenancy, if the unity of possession is absent, there is no co-tenancy. The unity of interest requires that the co-tenants must have the same kind of interest (estate) as the others. This means that one tenant can't hold a fee simple interest, while another holds a leasehold interest. For unity of interest to exist there must be identity in the nature, extent and duration of the interest held by the joint tenants. Therefore, it follows that the co-owners cannot be joint tenants if they hold unequal shares in the joint tenancy. Fred and Molly each have a half-share interest, and their interests are held as joint tenants.

Severance of the joint tenancy

6-9 A joint tenancy may generally be severed in three ways: by agreement, by the conduct of the joint tenants or by death of a joint tenant (severance of that tenant's interest): see *Williams v Hensman* (1861) 1 J & H 546.

Severance by agreement

6-10 Where joint tenants enter into a valid agreement to hold as tenants in common, there will be a severance in equity, with the legal estate being held in joint tenancy. Upon registration, a legal tenancy in common is created. Once a joint tenancy is severed by agreement it cannot be revived if that agreement is rescinded or terminated. It is important to note that the agreement does not need to be specifically enforceable or binding as a contract in law, as noted in *Abela v Public Trustee* [1983] I NSWLR 308.

The filing of an application under s 79 of the Family Law Act 1975 (Cth) will not operate as an agreement to sever, since the filing of the application is not irrevocable as at any time prior to hearing the parties may withdraw the application. If Fred and Molly had made an agreement to sever by filing an application under s 79 of the Family Law Act 1975 (Cth), and their application is one for approval of that agreement (an application under s 87), then severance has occurred because of their agreement, as noted in *Pertsoulis v Pertsoulis* (1980) FLC 175-265. In the facts of this question there is no issue of agreement between the parties severing the joint tenancy.

Severance by conduct

6-11   Severance by the conduct of Fred is an issue to be considered in this question. Fred seeks to transfer his interest to Sally, and gives her an instrument of transfer, asking her to organise the transfer since he was busy. This raises the question that, in giving Sally the instrument of transfer, has Fred effectively alienated his interest thereby severing the joint tenancy? Under the authority of *Milroy v Lord* (1862) 4 De GF & J 264; 45 ER 1185 at 1189, the voluntary alienation of an interest in a joint tenancy requires the donor:

> ... to have done everything which, according to the nature of the property required in the settlement was necessary to be done in order to transfer the property and render the settlement binding upon him.

This view held in *Milroy v Lord* was considered in *Corin v Patton* (1988) 13 NSWLR 15 (Ct App); (1990) 64 ALJR 256 (HCA), in respect of land under the Real Property Act 1900 (NSW). The NSW Court of Appeal addressed the principle enunciated in *Milroy v Lord*. It concluded the issue was not whether the donor had divested him or herself of the interest, or done all that was within power to be divested of the interest, but whether the donor had so placed the donee that the latter had the right to register a transfer, a right which the donor could not impair. In contrast, the High Court took the view (in *Corin v Patton* (1990) 92 ALR 1) that if the donor had done all that was necessary to affect a gift of a transfer of legal title (which included registration), then equity would recognise the gift. In dissent, Mason CJ and McHugh J took the view that if the donor had done all that was necessary to effect a gift of a transfer then equity would recognise the gift. In *Corin v Patton*, the certificate of title had not been handed to the donee when the gift of the instrument of transfer was made, nor had its production to the benefit of the donee been authorised by the donor. For different reasons, both the New South Wales Court of Appeal and the High Court held that the gift had not been completed and the joint tenancy still existed.

Considering the reasoning of the High Court in *Corin v Patton*, Fred as donor needs to do all that is necessary in order to effect a gift of legal title. This requires the delivery of a signed instrument of transfer, a certificate of title and registration. On the facts, Fred delivered an instrument of transfer to Sally, although it is not known whether the instrument was signed. He did not deliver a certificate of title. Furthermore, registration has not taken place. Therefore, according to the reasoning in *Corin v Patton*, the transfer of the interest from Fred to Sally will fail and the joint tenancy will not be severed.

A number of statutory amendments in the Queensland jurisdiction breathes some life into the possible transfer of Fred's interest to Sally, and therefore the severance of the joint tenancy. The minority view of Mason CJ and McHugh J in *Corin v Patton* has been imbued in statute in Queensland. Section 200 of the PLA deems a voluntary assignment of property to be effective in equity and complete when the assignor has done everything that is necessary on order to transfer the property to the assignee, even if the assignee still needs to re-register the transfer in order to complete the transfer. Furthermore, when an interest in land is registered in Queensland under the LTA, the certificate of title in paper form is no longer automatically created and issued by the registrar. Rather, when the existing certificate of transfer is lodged with a dealing, it is cancelled, unless the registrar directs otherwise: s 45 LTA. Since the registration of the property to Fred and Molly occurred in 2005, it is likely that the certificate of title has been recorded on the register and the paper certificate cancelled. As such, if Fred signed the instrument of transfer, and the certificate of title is lodged at the register, then Fred as donor has done everything necessary in order to effect the transfer, and the transfer will be deemed complete in equity under s 200 PLA.

Should Fred have not signed the instrument of transfer, and therefore the transfer has not been complete in equity, it is possible that the conduct of Fred may indicate severance. According to *Williams v Hensman* (1861) 1 J & H 546 at 557–8, in order for conduct to indicate severance there must be a:

> ... course of dealing sufficient to intimate that the interests of all were mutually treated as constituting a tenancy in common. When the severance depends on an inference of this kind without any express act of severance, it will not suffice to rely on an intention with respect to the particular share declared only behind the backs of the other persons interested.

According to *Williams v Hensman*, the unilateral declaration by Fred to gift his share to Sally, thereby demonstrating an intention to sever the joint tenancy was not sufficient to determine the joint tenancy.

This was re-affirmed by the High Court in *Corin v Patton* (contrary to the views expressed by the members of the Court of Appeal in *Burgess v Rawnsley* [1975] Ch 429), which noted that a course of conduct must be mutual in order to sever the joint tenancy. Accordingly, Fred's unilateral conduct in handing the instrument of transfer to Sally and asking her orally to organise the instrument of transfer in order to complete the gift will not suffice. Molly's declaration that she wished for Fred to drop dead, and the constant fighting serves as evidence of mutual disharmony, but in themselves they do not necessarily indicate a mutual desire to regard the joint tenancy as severed. Furthermore, the making of wills does not sever the joint tenancy unless it is part of an agreement to so sever: see *Re Wilford's Estate* (1879) 11 Ch D 267, where the agreement was the severing action.

If the conduct of Fred is sufficient to sever the joint tenancy then his interest in unit will pass in accordance with the terms of his will. However, it is likely that under s 200 of the PLA the gift has not been complete, and therefore severance has not occurred.

Survivorship

6-12 Flowing from the four unities, the unique characteristic of joint tenancy is the right of survivorship (*jus accresendi*). Each joint tenant has a right of survivorship, which operates against the other joint tenants as a matter of law. When a joint tenant dies, his or her interest in the property is extinguished and the surviving joint tenants' share is enlarged equally. This rule operates automatically upon the death of a joint tenant and cannot be overridden by will or by the laws of intestacy. As noted by Latham CJ in *Wright v Gibbons* (1949) 78 CLR 313 at 323:

> If one joint tenant dies, his interest is extinguished, He falls out, and the interest of the surviving joint tenant is correspondingly enlarged.

The right of survivorship existing in the surviving joint tenant will be maintained, despite any stipulation in the deceased tenant's will to the contrary. Only an effective severance by agreement or by conduct during the life of the joint tenant can the rule of survivorship be circumvented.

Determination of Fred's interest in the joint tenancy

6-13 Fred attempted to sever the joint tenancy by gifting his half of the property to Sally. However, if he did not sign the instrument of transfer and the gift was not effective, then Fred's attempt to circumvent the right of survivorship has failed. Consequently, Molly's interest in the property will be enlarged, in this instance by Fred's entire share since there are no other joint tenants. In addition, since Molly is the only surviving joint tenant the joint tenancy will be terminated. Molly will own both her half of the unit she held as a joint tenant with Fred as well as Fred's half interest in the joint tenancy. Effectively, Molly will be the sole owner of the property.

Where a joint tenant murders another joint tenant, the murder does not prevent the operation of the survivorship principle. According to the facts, Molly and Fred had a fight, with Molly wishing Fred was dead. Less than 24 hours later, Fred is found dead in suspicious circumstances. Sally indicates that she thinks that Molly murdered Fred, although the coroner's report is inconclusive. If Molly was found guilty of the homicide of Fred, his interest would still be transferred to Molly (as per *Re Stone* (1989) 1 Qd R 351) even though she is a murderer. However, as a matter of public policy, a person is not entitled to benefit from their crime (see *Cleaver v Mutual Reserve Fund Life Association* (1892) 1 QB 147). As such, Molly would not receive the benefit of murdering Fred. Rather, equity would impose a constructive trust to the extent that Fred's share of the joint tenancy would be held by Molly for the beneficiary of the constructive trust. As Sally is the beneficiary of Fred's will, it is likely that Fred's interest would be held in constructive trust for her.

If the killing of Fred by Molly was unlawful, but did not constitute murder, there is a question whether public policy considerations would similarly preclude Molly from benefiting from her crime. In *Re Barrowcliff* (1927) SASR 147, the court held that the right of survivorship does not arise where a joint tenant has unlawfully killed another joint tenant. Similarly, in *Troja v Troja* (1994) 33 NSWLR 269 the New South Wales Court of Appeal held that there should be no personal gain by one person from the killing of another. This decision has been somewhat overruled by the Forfeiture Act 1995 (NSW), which provides that except in the case of murder, the forfeiture rule may be modified by the presiding justice if the situation requires it to be modified.

Conclusion

6-14   Since the joint tenancy was unlikely to be unilaterally severed by Fred's incomplete gift to Sally, it is likely that the death of Fred enlarged Molly's share of the joint tenancy. Molly would now hold both her's and Fred's share of the joint tenancy. The only exception to this would be if Molly was found guilty of Fred's murder. In such an instance, Fred's interest would still be transferred to Molly; however, public policy considerations would compel the court to establish a constructive trust for Fred's interest for his beneficiaries.

If the gift had been completed in equity prior to Fred's death, Sally and Molly would hold their interests in the property as tenants in common, since the unities have been severed.

Examiner's Comments

6-15   The answer in this question focused upon the two major issues related to joint tenancy — the unities and the right of survivorship. It provided a detailed consideration of the severance of a joint tenancy, including the possible severance by homicide as a result of Molly's actions. It did not consider the severance of the tenancy by court order under the Family Law Act 1975 (Cth).

It focused on severance by agreement and severance by conduct of the parties. In particular, it provided a detailed consideration of the law in relation to unilateral severance in equity arising from the conduct of the joint tenants. Necessarily, the answer considered the principles regarding a transfer by way of gift of an interest of land, as set forth in *Corin v Patton*, considering number of judicial views on the matter. It also considered the statutory position of unilateral severance in Queensland, where a gift is considered effective under s 200 of the PLA once the donor has done all things necessary to complete the gift. This represents the Mason CJ and McHugh J view in *Corin v Patton*.

Keep in Mind

6-16   Students should keep in mind the following:

- Often in this type of question many students fail to adequately consider severance by conduct, and that the content does not satisfy the requirement for determination in joint tenancy.
- Students often fail to recognise that in Queensland the certificate of title is often on the register. As such the donor is only required to sign and deliver an instrument of transfer. In addition, many students fail to recognise the importance of s 200 of the PLA, which will recognise a transfer in equity.
- Many students confuse the right of survivorship, and presume that a testamentary disposition will override the right of survivorship. Students need to be aware that the right of survivorship will be maintained despite any testamentary disposition, unless the joint tenancy was severed during the life of the joint tenant.
- Students will often fail to provide an adequate discussion of unilateral severance in equity as considered in *Corin v Patton*.

Question 2

6-17   Karri, Samantha, Miranda and Charlotte have been friends since grade one. After completing university the girls decide to purchase a unit together as joint tenants at Varsity Reserve on the Gold Coast. The purchase price was $750,000.

Things go well for the girls, until Samantha becomes deeply involved with Adrian, a handsome sports coach with killer arms and a smile to match. After several months, Samantha and Adrian become engaged, with Samantha declaring:

> I love him so much he is perfect ... we do everything together and he has encouraged me to train for marathons.

Miranda is devastated, as she has secretly had a crush on Adrian since he was her soccer coach in grade 12. Unable to cope with seeing Samantha and Adrian together, Miranda decides to leave the household. She discusses it with the other girls, who all agree that it is the best thing to do. Miranda signs an agreement with Karri that states:

> I shall give Karri my interest in the unit, and in return Karri shall give me $200,000.

After Karri gave the money to Miranda, and signed the instrument of transfer, Miranda leaves the household. Karri duly registers the transfer.

Glad that Miranda has left, Adrian marries Samantha. He then purchases Miranda's share of the property from Karri and commences living with the girls. Adrian's happiness is short-lived; Samantha dies from cardiomyopathy after a particularly intense fitness session with Adrian.

As Samantha's surviving spouse, Adrian claims Samantha's share of the house. Karri and Charlotte contest his claim.

Advise Adrian.

Time allowed: 45 minutes

Answer Plan

6-18 This question seeks to test a student's understanding of severance and survival of a joint tenancy where there are multiple co-tenants (in this instance four), and the issue of survivorship between the remaining tenants. Since the property is located in Queensland, the Property Law Act 1974 (Qld) (PLA), the Land Title Act 1994 (Qld) (LTA), and the Succession Act 1981 (Qld) should be applied.

Since the nature and constitution of a joint tenancy under the four unities were considered in Question 1 above, it is necessary to only provide a cursory consideration of:

- the characteristics of joint tenancy when one of the tenants severs his or her interest within the joint tenancy (by a consideration of the law in *Wright v Gibbons*);
- the severance of a joint tenancy by agreement;
- the unilateral severance of a joint tenancy in Queensland under the PLA and the LTA; and
- the determination of joint tenancy under the rules of survivorship.

Answer

Nature of the joint tenancy

6-19 The joint tenancy in this question is characterised by the four unities of possession, interest, title and time. To establish a joint tenancy it is necessary to demonstrate that the four unities are present. In this question the friends bought the property at Varsity Reserve on a single deed at the same time, and all have equal interests. The facts state that the friends purchased as joint tenants. Therefore the four unities are present. In addition, since a joint tenancy exists, the right of survivorship is present.

In Queensland there is a statutory presumption that upon registration the co-tenants own their interest as tenancy in common: s 56(1) LTA. As the friends have created a joint tenancy, they would have to expressly request the establishment of a joint tenancy. Each of the friends hold a one-quarter interest in the joint tenancy.

Alienation of Miranda's interest to Karri

6-20 Whilst a joint tenancy cannot be disposed of in a will, it may be severed by the joint tenant and therefore converted to a tenancy in common during the co-tenants' lifetime. Where a joint tenant enters into a valid agreement to sever their interest as a joint tenancy (severance by alienation) there will be a severance in equity, with the legal estate being held in joint tenancy. Upon registration, a legal tenancy in common is created. Once the joint tenancy of a party is severed by agreement it cannot be revived, even if that agreement is rescinded or terminated. It is important to note that the agreement does not need to be specifically enforceable or binding as a contract in law, as noted in *Abela v Public Trustee* [1983] 1 NSWLR 308.

A legal interest in land may be disposed of at law by a binding contract for value entered into by a joint tenant and a third party, which would sever the joint tenancy for that co-tenant: *Public Trustee v Pfeiffle* [1991] 1 VR 19. Where there are multiple joint tenants in a joint tenancy, and one joint tenant alienates their interest to another party, the party receiving the interest will hold the interest as a tenancy in common with the remaining joint tenants, since there is no longer any unity of title. In order for the joint tenancy to be severed at law, the transfer of legal title must be registered: *Wright v Gibbons* (1949) 78 CLR 313.

In this question, Miranda alienated her interest to Karri. Upon the alienation of Miranda's share to Karri, the joint tenancy between Samantha, Karri and Charlotte will continue to exist, since their individual relationship has not been severed, and the four unities have been preserved. Each of the three friends will continue to hold a one-quarter share of the property, each as joint tenants. The remaining one-quarter interest in the property that Karri purchased from Miranda will be held by Karri as a tenant in common with the joint tenancy that exists between Charlotte, Samantha and Karri. In order for the severance of Miranda's share of the joint tenancy to be severed at law, the transfer of the interest from Miranda to Karri needs to be registered.

The question of the survival of a joint tenancy after severance by alienation was considered by the High Court in *Wright v Gibbons* (1949) 78 CLR 313. In this case, a document purporting to re-transfer and re-register the interest of two joint tenants to each other (cross-transfer) was designed to create a new joint tenancy between the two parties, and effectively severing the joint tenancy between the two joint tenants and the third joint tenancy. However, the court held that although the transfer and registration resulted in each joint tenant acquiring a unity of interest, they received the interest pursuant to different title documents, since each transfer was registered sequentially rather than simultaneously. As such the joint tenancy was severed, and the parties held their interests as tenancy in common. In this instance, there is no cross-transfer, and

Karri's interest in the joint tenancy is preserved. She merely acquires an extra interest that, because of a lack of unities, the additional interest is held as a tenancy in common with the joint tenancy.

Purchase of a portion of the property by Adrian

6-21 Karri's share of the co-tenancy that she purchased from Miranda is held as a tenancy in common. A tenancy in common holds an undivided share in property that is distinct, although the tenancy may be held in unequal shares with the other tenants: *Nullagine Investments Pty Ltd v Western Australian Club Inc* (1993) 177 CLR 635.

The tenant in common is entitled to the use and enjoyment of the land, but is also entitled to dispose of their interest: as such, Karri has the right as a tenant in common to dispose of her interest to Adrian if she so wishes. As such, Adrian's purchase of Miranda's original share of the property from Karri will create a tenancy in common between Adrian and the joint tenancy held by Karri, Charlotte and Samantha in equal shares. At this point the joint tenancy will continue to survive, as the four unities between the three girls will continue.

Samantha's death and the right of survivorship

6-22 Under the law relating to joint tenancy, each joint tenant has a right of survivorship that operates as a matter of law against each other. When a joint tenant dies, his or her interest is extinguished and the surviving joint tenants hold the property (see **6–12** above).

Since the joint tenancy survives the severance of Karri's interest. The right of survivorship exists. Upon Samantha's death, her one-quarter interest in the joint tenancy will be extinguished. This one-quarter interest will be equally divided between the two remaining joint tenants, Karri and Charlotte, who will each receive a one-eighth share, enlarging their share in the joint tenancy to three-eighths each. The remaining joint tenancy will hold the interest with Adrian's one-quarter as a tenancy in common.

It is possible that the death of Samantha could be seen as suspicious, since Adrian is a sports coach, and therefore he should be aware of heart conditions of those he trains. However, on the facts there is no indication that Adrian is responsible for the unlawful death or murder of Samantha. Even if Adrian is responsible for Samantha's death, since he is not a joint tenant, and does not benefit by Samantha's death, his actions will have no bearing on the joint tenancy.

Conclusion

6-23 Adrian's claim to Samantha's share of the unit will not succeed. Instead, Samantha's share of the joint tenancy will be subject to the law of survivorship. Under the law of survivorship, Samantha's interest cannot be disposed of by will since the right of survivorship takes precedence over any disposition made by will, and any provision regarding disposition by will is ineffective: *Carr-Glynn v Frearsons* [1999] Ch 326. Rather, her interest will be divided equally between Karri and Charlotte, whose joint tenancy interest will be enlarged, and each will hold a three-eighths share in the property. Adrian will continue to retain his one-quarter share he purchased from Karri (and who purchased the share from Miranda), which was held as a tenancy in common with the joint tenancy of Charlotte and Karri.

 ## Examiner's Comments

6-24 Although there are similar elements to those arising in **Question 1**, this question focuses on the capacity of a joint tenancy to continue to exist when one of the parties in the joint tenancy severs his or her interest. It also focuses on a detailed consideration of the concept of a member of the joint tenancy able to hold an additional interest as a tenancy in common with the remaining joint tenants.

Most students get extremely confused about the concept of a co-tenant being able to continue to hold an interest as a joint tenant as well as one as a tenancy in common. It is vital that students understand this concept.

This question did not consider the issue of mortgages in a joint tenancy. Students may examine the law relating to mortgages in a joint tenancy.

 ## Keep in Mind

6-25 Students should keep in mind the following:

- A very common error in this question is that many students presume that the severance of Miranda's share to Karri will sever the joint tenancy for all of the parties. At this point the student presumes that Samantha holds her interest as a tenancy in common, and is no longer subject to the right of survivorship.
- In making the assumption that the joint tenancy does not survive, students incorrectly conclude that Adrian will receive Samantha's share.

 ## Question 3

6-26 Mike and Kate are naval officers. They are also the registered owners of an estate in fee simple pursuant to the Real Property Act 1900 (NSW). They contributed equal amounts of money to the purchase of the property, which was purchased without the need for a mortgage. The property is a run-down three-bedroom house. However, Kate is transferred to Cairns naval base. Mike remains in the property in Sydney, and rents out the remaining two rooms to fellow sailors from the local naval base,

HMAS Hawkesbury. He receives the rents from the two rooms and carries out renovations to the house. Following several complaints from tenants he has replaced the hot water system in the house. However, tragedy strikes; Mike dies in a workplace explosion.

Mike's daughter Jenny from a previous relationship is the sole beneficiary of Mike's estate. She claims that she is entitled to reimbursement for the money spent on renovations and the replacement of the hot water system. In addition, she wishes to claim in respect of the income from the two tenants in the house. Kate decides to sell the house, since she has been transferred to HMAS Kanimbla in Cairns.

Kate seeks your advice. Advise Kate whether Jenny has a claim for the moneys.

Time allowed: 1 hour

 ## Answer Plan

6-27 The question considers the rights between parties in a tenancy in common. These rights that the parties enjoy exist in both equity and common law and both will be considered.

In order to address the rights of Kate and Jenny, it is essential to consider the rights of the co-tenants for the duration of the tenancy in common, including their:

- rights to occupation;
- rights regarding the distribution of income;
- rights regarding costs and expenditure, including improvements; and
- rights in relation to the sale of the house.

In answering this question, the principles of co-tenancy at common law that existed during the co-tenancy should be outlined and analysed based on the facts in this question. This should be followed by an outline and analysis of how the principles equity imposed on partition apply to the facts of the question.

 ## Answer

Nature of tenancy in common

6-28 In a tenancy in common, each co-tenant has a distinct interest in the property, similar to a joint tenancy. However, this interest is not an entitlement to a separate physical possession of the property. Rather, it operates similar to a joint tenancy, where each tenant in common is entitled to possess all the property, but no entitlement to any distinct part of the property. This entitlement was considered in *Nullagine Investments Pty Ltd v Western Australia Clubs Inc* (1992) 177 CLR 635 at 656, noting that:

... the distinct "interest or share" of one of two or more tenants in common of a freehold estate cannot, on any approach, be equated with the land itself. Indeed an essential feature of the "interest or share" of a tenant in common, and a condition precedent of its existence or survival, is that the tenant in common does not own the freehold estate and is unable alone to deal with "the land".

Mike and Kate, as co-tenants in common enjoy unity of possession, but unlike joint tenants, lack unity of time, title and interest. Therefore, there is no right of survivorship. Rather, Mike is free to dispose of his interest in the land. In this question, under a testamentary disposition, Mike has disposed of his entire estate to his daughter Jenny.

Mike and Kate are able to exercise their rights as co-tenants between and against each other. Importantly, Mike is entitled to dispose of his interest whether by sale, gift or otherwise, without reference to Kate: *Pralle v Sharka* (1978) 2 NSWLR 450. Generally co-tenants, whether they are tenants in common or joint tenants, have four rights against each other, as outlined in *Forgeard v Shanahan* (1994) 335 NSWLR 206 at 222 onwards:

- right of occupation;
- right to share rent and profit;
- right to compensation for improvements; and
- right to be jointly liable for the debts jointly incurred.

Occupation and occupation fee

6-29 Since each co-owner has an undivided share in the land, each co-owner and his or her invitees have a right to use and occupy the whole land: *Thrift v Thrift* (1975) 10 ALR 332 at 338–9. However, if one co-owner chooses not to be in occupation, and the other co-tenant is in occupation, the occupier is not required to pay rent to the non-occupier: *Luke v Luke* 1936 26 SR (NSW) 310. This means that a non-occupying co-tenant could only claim rent from an occupying co-tenant if there had been ouster or exclusion or if the occupier was claiming an amount for improvements on partition (or like proceedings). Other than that, no occupation fee was payable: *McMahon v Burchell* (1846) 2 Ph 127; 41 ER 889 at 892 per Lord Cotlenham LC. In *Luke v Luke* (1936) 36 SR (NSW) 310 at 315, Long Innes CJ reasoning was that:

> ... the effect would be, that one tenant in common, by keeping out of the actual occupation of the premises, might convert the other into his bailiff; in other words prevent the other from occupying them, except upon the terms of paying him rent.

The rationale of an occupation fee being payable by the occupying co-tenant when exclusion or ouster had occurred in respect of other co-tenants was an example of equity following the law. The occupying co-tenant had committed a legal wrong to the co-owners and on any partition suit (or like proceedings) equity would see that the wrong was righted.

Equity requires an occupation fee to be paid by the occupier if the occupying co-tenant seeks an amount for partition, as enunciated by North J in *Re Jones; Farrington v Forrester* [1893] 2 Ch 461 at 478:

> ... he was not to be allowed to have the equitable assistance of the court to get any part of his expenditure repaid, unless he was willing to be charged with what he could not by the rules of law, as distinguished from equity, be made liable for. It was merely a case of imposing terms: a man who comes into equity must do equity.

Therefore, although no occupation fee can be extracted at common law from the occupying co-tenant, on partition (or like proceedings) equity would seek payment of an occupation fee if there was a claim for improvements or repairs by the co-owner in occupation. That claim, however, has to relate to lasting improvements (or substantial repairs):

> I think that those accounts must be reciprocal, and unless the defendant is charged with an occupation rent, he is not entitled to any account of substantial repairs and lasting improvements on any part of the property. (*Teasdale v Sanderson* (1864) 33 Beav 534; 55 ER 476 per Romilly MR)

Right to compensation for improvement

6-30 At law there is no requirement that co-owners who benefit from the repairs and improvements made to the property by another co-owner should make a contribution to the expense in the absence of an agreement to that effect: *Leigh v Leigh* (1884) 15 QBD 60. However, in equity an allowance is made for a co-owner who has paid for such improvements when there is a claim for moneys. The rationale for this, as outlined in *Brickwood v Young* (1905) 2 CLR 387 at 394–5 is:

> No remedy exists for the money expended in repairs by one tenancy in common, so long as the property is enjoyed in common; but in a suit of partition it is usual to have an inquiry as to those expenses of which nothing can be recovered so long as the parties enjoyed their property in common; when it is desired to put an end to that state of things, it is then necessary to consider what has been expended in improvements and repairs; the property held in common has been increased in value by the improvements and repairs; and whether the property is divided or sold by the decree of the court, one party cannot take the increase in value, without making an allowance for what has been expended in order to obtain the increased value ... There is, therefore, a mode by which money expended by one tenancy in common for repairs can be recovered, but the procedure is confined to suits of partition (and sale).

In order for recovery to occur, improvements and repairs must be lasting. Mere repairs and maintenance will not be allowed. What will constitute mere repairs or maintenance will depend on circumstances, but in *Forgeard v Shanahan,* insurance premiums and pest control costs were held as not claimable as recoverable improvements, although they may be recoverable under other proceedings or remedies, but not as part of proceedings to which partition rules apply. The effect of the sale would act in the same manner as a partition.

In considering Jenny's claim (as Mike's beneficiary) for the improvements (renovations) and repairs that Mike made to the property when he was alive, it is necessary to consider who paid for the improvements.

As demonstrated above, there is an entitlement to reimbursement for lasting improvements and repairs. The house is lasting, therefore the claim for improvement by Jenny is legitimate. Replacement of the hot water system could also come under the heading of 'lasting'. As a result, Jenny is able to claim moneys from Kate for the renovation on the house. She may be able to claim for replacement of the hot water system, if it is not categorised as maintenance or improvements. Any other maintenance that Jenny claims would have to be assessed to determine whether it was 'lasting' or not.

It is important to consider whether the improvements were financed by Mike only, or by moneys jointly provided by Mike and Kate. On the facts, there is no clear indication where the moneys for the renovations arose.

If Mike financed the improvements himself, the contribution payable by Kate to Jenny would be half the lesser of the amount expended by Mike, and the amount by which the improvements enhanced the value of the property. If the improvements were financed by Mike and Kate, then Kate would not be liable to pay Jenny any amount of moneys. However, if the property was sold, Kate would only realise half of the amount of the property, with the other half realised by Jenny as beneficiary of Mike's estate.

Right to rent and profits

6-31 In *Squire v Rogers* (1979) 27 ALR 330, the court held that where the cost of improvements has been financed by rents and profits received by the co-tenant in occupation, the tenant not in occupation seeking an account for the rents and profits must allow the occupying co-owner an amount in respect of all moneys spent (and not just for the value by which the property is enhanced). The amount that is allowed to the tenant who has effected repairs or improvements is the lesser of the value of the enhancement of the property, and the cost of effecting the repairs (*Forgeard v Shanahan* (1994) 35 NSWLR 206 at 223), against which amount will be set off any occupation fee, not to exceed the value or cost of the improvements (as the case may be): *Brickwood v Young* (1905) 2 CLR 387.

If the rents and profits Mike collected from the renters funded the improvements, Jenny is entitled to apply the rents and profits to the total amount expended on improvements. Any residue remaining would be accountable to Kate, who may have a claim in respect of income and will succeed to that extent.

As Jenny is making a claim for improvements, Kate is entitled to make a claim for an occupation fee (the two claims are reciprocal — 'no rent if no improvements': *Forgeard v Shanahan,* at 225). The occupation fee, however, will be payable to the extent that it does not exceed the value of the improvements. The amount of occupation fee to be adjusted would be one-half of the market rent value of the unit occupied by Mike. It is likely that the courts could consider it equitable to deduct an amount representing Mike's labour costs for work carried out by him during his occupancy.

Conclusion

6-32 Generally, each co-tenant has an individual share in the property which is not physically divisible. Therefore when one tenant is not in occupation, the occupier is not required to pay rent to the non-occupier. As such Jenny is not required to pay rent to Kate. Since the improvements Mike made to the property are 'lasting', it is possible for Jenny to recover moneys. If Mike solely paid for all of the renovations, Kate would be liable to Jenny for half the lesser of the amount of the money expended by Mike, the amount the improvements have increased the value of the property. If the improvements were paid for by rents and profits received by Mike, Jenny is entitled to apply the rent and profits to the amount expended. Since Jenny is making a claim for improvements, Kate is entitled to make a claim for an occupation fee, since the two claims are reciprocal.

 ## Examiner's Comments

6-33 This question seeks to test the students' level of understanding of relevant principles relating to the rights of co-owners against each other. It especially seeks to test whether the students have a firm understanding of the principles at common law and in equity.

It is important to note that these principles are applicable regardless of whether it is a tenancy in common or a joint tenancy.

A deeper consideration of the question might be to analyse whether any particular item or activity undertaken as part of the renovation (the term 'renovation' in the question is very vague) might or might not be an improvement.

The answer did consider the applicability of the rules of partition. These rules were criticised by Kirby P in *Forgeard v Shanahan* as being out of touch and reflecting 'utterly different social conditions': at 211. However, an answer of this nature does not allow scope for such a jurisprudential issue, and in any case, the facts as presented probably would not call for any rules other than those applied.

Keep in Mind

6-34 Students should keep in mind the following:

- Many students will fail to provide an adequate conclusion. The question asks the students to advise Kate. In an exam, if the 'client' is not advised, then the question has not really been answered. Therefore, a conclusion that answers the question is vital.

- When discussing the claim for improvements, it is important to note that they must be 'lasting' improvements. In addition, a claim for improvements may be made whether or not a claim for an occupation fee is made, although a claim for an occupation fee may only be made if there is a claim for improvements.

- This is a question upon which students need to reflect carefully in order to cover the ground. It requires a detailed knowledge of the rights of tenants against each other. These rights are outlined in detail in *Forgeard v Shanahan* (see Meagher JA's judgment).

Question 4

6-35 Bec and Mim are two sisters who own the property Sago Plains, as joint tenants with their stepmother Tanya. Bec is 26 years old, and recently widowed. She has triplets Isabella-Joyce, Joshua and Carson. They are the only beneficiaries of her estate, and will take the whole of Bec's estate in equal shares. Mim is 24 years old and is engaged to a fellow dentist. Tanya is also a widow, although she met a delightful geologist on a recent trip to central Queensland to investigate the last remains of the Muttaburra dinosaur.

Tanya's romance progresses well and she decides to marry Steve, the delightful geologist, and move to Perth. Before leaving for Perth, Tanya decides to transfer her interest in equal portions to Bec and Mim.

Upon completion and registration of the transfer, Bec and Mim place the certificate of title in a safety deposit box in a Sydney bank. The bank requires the signature of both Bec and Mim to open the safety deposit box.

Mim decides that she wants to leave the property and live in the city, as her and her fiancé want to open a dental practice. She decides to sell her share of the property to Bec. Mim duly signs the instrument of transfer. However, she finds out that her fiancé is having an affair with the dental nurse they had employed for the new dental practice.

The two sisters drive to Sydney to collect the certificate of title, as Mim decided not to sign the form for opening the safety deposit box until they arrived at the bank.

Unfortunately, Bec and Mim were involved in a major car accident on the M2 motorway and were killed instantly.

Who owns Sago Plains, and in what shares?

Time allowed: 45 mins

Answer Plan

6-36 This question raises a number of issues, with the question directed towards the following issues:

- legal severance of an interest in a joint tenancy;
- severance of an interest in equity;
- simultaneous death of the joint tenants, and the determination of the survivor for disposition of the interest in the property.

Necessarily, this will require a consideration of s 35 of the Conveyancing Act 1919 (NSW), since the sisters died simultaneously.

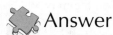

Answer

Nature of the co-tenancy

6-37 A joint tenancy in this question is characterised by the four unities of possession, interest, title and time. To establish a joint tenancy it is necessary to demonstrate that the four unities are present. In this question the joint tenants bought Sago Plains on a single deed at the same time, and all have equal interests (one-third share each). On the facts, the sisters and their stepmother purchased as joint tenants. Therefore a joint tenancy exists.

Severance of the joint tenancy

6-38 An existing joint tenancy may be severed in three ways: by agreement, by the conduct of the joint tenants, or by death of one or more joint tenants: see *Williams v Hensman* (1861) 1 J & H 546. In this question, each of these forms of severance will be considered.

Severance by agreement

6-39 A joint tenant's interest may be severed in equity by agreement between the co-tenants. This is a common method of severance. In severance by agreement, one joint tenant will alienate their interest to another party. Where a joint tenant enters into a valid agreement to sever their interest as a joint tenant (severance by alienation) there will be a severance in equity, with the legal estate being held in joint tenancy. Upon registration, a legal tenancy in common is created between the tenants in common and the other parties, regardless of whether the other parties hold their interest as joint tenants or tenants in common. Once the joint tenancy of a party is severed by agreement it cannot be revived, even if that agreement is rescinded or terminated. It is important to note that the agreement does not need to be specifically enforceable or binding as a contract in law, as noted in *Abela v Public Trustee* [1983] I NSWLR 308.

A legal interest in land may be disposed of at law by a binding contract for value entered into by a joint tenant and a third party, which would sever the joint tenancy for that co-tenant: *Public Trustee v Pfeiffle* [1991] 1 VR 19.

In this instance, Tanya has chosen to alienate her interest by agreement between her two stepdaughters. Since there are multiple joint tenants in the joint tenancy, Tanya's action of alienating her interest to Bec and Mim will mean that Bec and Mim hold the interest they received from Tanya as tenants in common. In this question, Tanya alienated her interest equally to Bec and Mim, granting each sister a one-sixth share in the land, in addition to the one-third share they each hold as joint tenants. Upon the alienation of Tanya's share to Bec and Mim, the joint tenancy between Bec and Mim will continue to exist, since their individual joint tenancy relationship has not been severed, and the four unities have been preserved. The sisters will continue to hold a one-third share of the property each as joint tenants. The remaining one-third interest that Tanya divided equally between the two sisters will be held by Bec and Mim as tenants in common with Bec and Mim's joint tenancy.

In order for Tanya's joint tenancy to be severed at law, the transfer of legal title to Bec and Mim must be registered: *Wright v Gibbons* (1949) 78 CLR 313. According to the facts, registration has occurred. Therefore the severance is effective at law.

Severance by conduct

6-40 Mim seeks to transfer her interest in Sago Plains to Bec. In order to transfer her interest, Mim signs an instrument of transfer, and presumably gives the signed instrument to Bec. This raises the question that by giving Bec a signed instrument of transfer, has Mim effectively alienated her one-third interest in the joint tenancy, thereby severing the joint tenancy? Under the authority of *Milroy v Lord* (1862) 4 De GF & J 264; 45 ER 1185 at 1189, a voluntary alienation of an interest in a joint tenancy requires the donor:

> ... to have done everything which, according to the nature of the property required in the settlement was necessary to be done in order to transfer the property and render the settlement binding upon him.

The case of *Corin v Patton* (1990) 92 ALR 1 also considered the issue of severance by conduct. The court held that if the donor had done all that was necessary to effect a gift of a transfer of legal title (which included registration), then equity would recognise the gift. In dissent, Mason CJ and McHugh J took the view that if the donor had done all that was necessary to effect a gift of a transfer, the court would recognise the gift. In *Corin v Patton*, the certificate of title had not been handed to the donee when the gift of the instrument of transfer was made, nor had it been produced for the benefit of the donee. Both the New South Wales Court of Appeal and the High Court (for different reasons) held that the gift had not been completed, and therefore the joint tenancy still existed.

Considering the High Court's reasoning in *Corin v Patton*, Mim as the donor needs to do all that is necessary in order to effect a gift of legal title. This requires her to deliver the signed instrument of transfer to Bec, as well as the delivery of the certificate of title, and registration of the transfer.

On the facts, Mim delivered a signed instrument of transfer to Bec. However, Mim decides not to sign the document to enable the safety deposit box holding the certificate of title to be opened. Instead, she wishes to drive to the box herself. As such, she has not yet delivered the certificate of title to Bec.

However, it is possible to determine Mim's intentions to sever the joint tenancy on the basis of her conduct. According to *Williams v Hensman* (1861) 1 J & H 546 at 557–8, in order for conduct to indicate severance there must be a:

> ... course of dealing sufficient to intimate that the interests of all were mutually treated as constituting a tenancy in common. When the severance depends on an inference of this kind without any express act of severance, it will not suffice to rely on an intention with respect to the particular share declared only behind the backs of the other persons interested.

Applying *Williams v Hensman*, Mim's reticence to sign the document that will open the safety deposit box, combined with her distress at finding out her fiancé is having an affair with the dental nurse, indicate that Mim may not wish to complete the transfer of the property to Bec, either at law or in equity.

The position in *Williams v Hensman* was re-affirmed by the High Court in *Corin v Patton* which noted that a course of conduct must be mutual in order to sever the joint tenancy. As such, Mim's reticence to sign the document does not demonstrate mutual conduct to transfer her joint tenancy interest to Bec. Mim's failure to deliver the certificate of transfer to Bec in order to complete the severance of her interest in the joint tenancy means that the severance will fail. Not only does it fail to meet the requirements for severance that was articulated by the majority in *Corin v Patton*, it also fails to meet the lesser standard for severance (no requirement for registration) as laid out by the majority. Furthermore, the severance of the one-third share that Mim holds as a tenancy in common with Bec will also fail. Hence, Mim and Bec remain joint tenants, each holding a one-third interest. In addition, each holds the one-sixth interest they received from Tanya as tenants in common.

Severance by death

6-41 The simultaneous death of joint tenants can pose difficulties for the disposition of the property. At common law, there was no presumption as to who survived whom. However, many jurisdictions, including New South Wales, have introduced legislation that provides for the order of death. Under s 35 of the Conveyancing Act 1919 (NSW), where two or more persons have died simultaneously and there is uncertainty as to who died first, the deaths are presumed to have occurred in order of seniority, with the younger person surviving the older.

According to the facts, both of the sisters were killed in a motor accident on the M2 motorway and killed instantly. Therefore, it is impossible to determine whether Mim or Bec died last, and therefore receive the other sibling's share of the property. In such instances, s 35 of the Conveyancing Act will intervene, since the property is located in New South Wales.

At the time of the siblings' deaths, each held a one-third share in joint tenancy, since the severance of Mim's share of the property to Bec was incomplete. Furthermore, the severance of Mim's one-sixth share as a tenancy in common is also incomplete.

Applying s 35 of the Conveyancing Act, the younger party is presumed to have died last. Since Mim is the youngest sibling, the law would presume that she had died last. As Bec's death precedes Mim's, upon Bec's death her one-third interest in the property as a joint tenant will go to Mim under the law of survivorship. This will enlarge Mim's share of the property to five-sixths: her one-third portion of the joint tenancy, Bec's one-third of the joint tenancy that Mim received upon Bec's death, and her one-sixth share Mim received upon Tanya's severance by agreement. Bec's share of the property will comprise the one-sixth share she received upon Tanya's alienation of her interest in the land. This one-sixth share can be disposed to the beneficiaries of Bec's estate.

Conclusion

6-42 The alienation of Tanya's interest in the joint tenancy was effective at law, and granted Bec and Mim each a one-sixth interest in Sago Plains. The joint tenancy that had initially been established between Bec and Mim still remained, with each sibling holding another one-sixth as tenancy in common. Mim's attempt to sever the joint tenancy in equity failed for lack of completion, in a similar manner to the failed transfer in *Corin v Patton*. Furthermore, there is a lack of evidence to indicate that the severance was mutual. Consequently, Mim's interest in the land was not transferred to Bec. As a result of this failure to transfer Mim's interest to Bec, Mim is deemed to be the last to die under s 35 of the Conveyancing Act. Mim's joint tenancy interest is enlarged by Bec's interest. Combined with Mim's one-sixth interest she holds as tenancy in common, Mim's estate holds a five-sixth interest in the land. Bec's estate holds a one-sixth interest.

Examiner's Comments

6-43 This question seeks to test the students' level of understanding of the application of the principles of joint tenants and tenants in common. It is important that students realize that both tenancy in common and joint tenancy can co-exist.

A deeper consideration of the question might be to analyse whether the use of an electronic register (such as the land title system in Queensland) will have any effect on the perfecting of a gift in equity.

The answer considers the application of *Corrin v Patton*. Students need to be aware of the application of such principles in their jurisdiction of study, and the use of statute to clarify the common law position.

Keep in Mind

6-44 Students should keep in mind the following:

- Many students will fail to provide an adequate conclusion. The question asks the students to determine who owns Sago Plains. Students should be sure to provide the portions of ownership and the parties. In an exam, if the portions of ownership are not provided, then the question has not really been answered. Therefore, the conclusion should answer the legal question posed.

- When discussing whether the joint tenancy exists, it is important to note that some jurisdictions have a presumption of joint tenancy, whilst others tenants in common. Students should be aware of the presumption in the jurisdiction of study.

- This is a question upon which students need to reflect carefully on the principles enunciated in the case law, especially *Corrin v Patton*, and the application of the case law to individual circumstances. It is only through an understanding of the principles of the case law that students will be able to effectively answer the question.

Chapter 7

Mortgages

Key Issues

7-1 A mortgage is a legal document under which the borrower (mortgagor) transfers an interest in real property to the lender (mortgagee) as security for a debt. Under old system land the borrower gave title of the land to the lender, in the form of a deed, upon execution of the mortgage. This meant the mortgagor had no legal title but instead retained an equitable interest: the equity of redemption, which entitled the borrower to the return of title once the debt was paid.

The mortgage transaction was one that lent itself to abuse. Mortgagees attempted to avoid the reconveyance by enforcing the common law acceptance of time being 'of the essence'. Sometimes mortgagees disregarded mortgagor's rights when exercising power of sale, or punished defaulting borrowers with penalty interest rates. Much of this behaviour was regarded as inequitable and many equitable principles have now been incorporated into and enhanced by statute.

Under the Torrens system, the lender holds an interest in the land but no longer the title. The mortgagee's interest is known as a 'security' or 'charge over the land', and can and should be registered to protect the lender's interest in the land and to make their rights legally enforceable. An unregistered mortgage will not be invalid but will only be enforceable in equity *J & H Just (Holdings) Pty Ltd v Bank of NSW* (1971) 125 CLR 546. The mortgagor may transfer ownership of the property, but the mortgage must be discharged before the land can be registered under the new purchaser's name. If it not discharged, the new owner can be bound by the registered mortgage. The borrower's rights include: the equitable right to recover full right to the property, that is remove the mortgagee's interest under the equity of redemption upon repayment of the debt; the right to possession; the right to receive rents and profits if in possession; and the right to lease (often subject to the mortgagee's consent). The mortgagee's rights include: the right to sue on personal covenants; appoint a receiver; and take possession of, and exercise the power of sale over the property if the mortgagor defaults on repayments. Exercising of these rights is predominantly covered by statute, which also contains hefty penalties for mortgagees who disrespect or disregard borrowers' rights.

7-2 Before attempting the questions in this chapter, students should be familiar with the following:

✓ nature of a mortgage and its effect under old system title and Torrens title;

✓ the concept of the equity of redemption and the equitable right to redeem;

✓ the principles relating to clogs on the equity of redemption;

✓ duties of the mortgagee on exercising the power of sale;

✓ equitable principles regarding interest in mortgages;

✓ section 93 of the Conveyancing Act 1919 (NSW);

✓ the Property Law Act 1974 (Qld);

✓ Schedule 1 The National Consumer Credit Code of the National Consumer Credit Protection Act 2009 (Cth);

✓ the following cases:

- *Australian & New Zealand Banking Group Ltd v Bangadilly Pastoral Co Pty Ltd* (1977) 139 CLR 195;

- *Biggs v Hoddinott* [1898] 2 Ch 307;

- *CAGA v Nixon* (1981) 152 CLR 491;

- *Cholmondeley v Clinton* (1820) 37 ER 527;

- *Cuckmere Brick Co Ltd v Mutual Finance Co Ltd* [1971] Ch 949;

- *Fairclough v Swan Brewery* [1912] AC 565;

- *Farrar v Farrars Ltd* (1888) 40 Ch D 395;

- *Forsyth v Blundell* (1973) 129 CLR 477;

- *G & C Kreglinger v New Patagonia Meat & Cold Storage Co Ltd* [1914] AC 25;

- *Kennedy v De Trafford* [1897] AC 180;

- *Knightsbridge Estates Trust Ltd v Byrne* [1939] Ch 441;

- *Latec Investments v Hotel Terrigal Pty Ltd* (1965) 113 CLR 265;

- *McKean v Maloney* [1988] 1 Qld R 628;

- *Noakes v Rice* [1902] AC 24;

- *Pendlebury v Colonial Mutual Life Assurance Society Ltd* (1912) 13 CLR 575;

- *Samuel v Jarrah Timber & Wood Pacing Corp Ltd* [1904] AC 323;

- *Steindlberger v Mistroni* (1992) 29 NSWLR 351;

- *Stocks and Enterprises Pty Ltd v McBurney* (1977) 1 BPR 9521;
- *Wanner v Caruana* [1974] 2 NSWLR 201;
- *Warner v Jacob* (1882) 20 Ch D 220;
- *Westfield Holding Ltd v A C Television Pty Ltd* (1992) 32 NSWLR 194;
- *Wily v Endeavour Health Care Services Pty Ltd* [2003] NSWCA 312.

 # Question 1

7-3 (a)   On 27 January 1998, Paul borrows $100,000 (the principal sum) for 10 years from Archie, secured on Paul's property Mummulgum (being land under the Real Property Act 1900 (NSW)). Interest is calculated at the rate of $10 per centum per annum (reduced to $8 per centum per annum, if paid within seven days of the due date for payment) and payable quarterly.

The principal sum is due and payable on 16 January 2008. No provision is made in the mortgage for early repayment of the principal sum. On 27 January 1999, Paul wins the Boystown Art Union Award. He wishes to pay the secured debt to Archie with the proceeds of his winnings. Archie requires payment of interest calculated to 26 January 2008.

Advise Paul.

(b)   Now alter the facts so that instead of paying the debt to Archie, the following occur:

- On 26 January 1999, Paul defaults on a quarterly interest payment due on that date and fails to make payment thereafter.

- There is a clause in the mortgage that 'on default in payment of principal and interest, the principal sum hereby secured shall immediately become due and payable and it shall be lawful for the mortgagee to sue for recovery of the principal sum and interest although the time for payment shall not have arrived'.

- Archie gives a notice to Paul (in view of the default), requiring payment of principal in the sum of $100,000 plus interest calculated to 26 January 2008, referring to s 93 of the Conveyancing Act 1919 (NSW).

- Paul has entered into a contract of sale to sell the property and seeks advice on his liability to Archie.

Advise Paul.

Time allowed: 60 mins

Answer Plan

7-4 This question involves an understanding of the contractual nature of a mortgage, particularly in regard to the payment of interest. Accordingly, the answer should first deal with an explanation of the mortgage contract and the implications of the contractual date for redemption.

The question of interest payments arising out of the contract should then be discussed. In New South Wales, s 93 of the Conveyancing Act 1919 significantly alters the contractual effect of a mortgage. This section should be discussed in terms of early redemption and its significance for payment of principal and interest. Any relevant case law should be referred to. The issue of penalties in a mortgage should also be clarified in view of the provision allowing reduction in interest rate for prompt payment.

In the second part, the answer should discuss the liability for interest on default. Equitable principles affect this liability and need discussion. Section 93 of the Conveyancing Act 1919 (NSW) will need discussing in terms of the section's applicability to a mortgagor's request for early repayment. The section is not available for the use of mortgagees against defaulting mortgagors and the answer should explain this aspect.

Answer

7-5 A mortgage is an agreement for loan for some specified period secured on an interest in property, real or personal. It is secured at law by a conveyance of the legal estate in the property by the owner (mortgagor) to the lender (mortgagee), with the proviso that on the contractual date for repayment of the loan (and only on that date), the mortgagee is to reconvey the interest secured to the mortgagor. Equity gave the mortgagor the right to redeem the mortgage after the contractual date for repayment had expired. Equity's purpose was to alleviate the harsh effect of the common law requiring redemption on the contractual date. However, there was no right to demand redemption prior to the contractual date for repayment as:

> ... it might be attended with extreme inconvenience to mortgagees, who generally advance their money as an investment. (*Brown v Cole* (1845) 14 LJ Ch 167 at 169)

As explained by the court in *O'Reilly v Heydon* (1893) 10 WN (NSW) 39 at 40:

> ... the court regards the transaction as an investment by the mortgagee which ought not to be disturbed before the date on which the parties have agreed that the investment is to be at an end.

In respect of the date for the investment being at an end, Lord Parker in *Kreglinger (G & C) v New Patagonia Meat & Cold Storage Co Ltd* [1914] AC 25 at 47-8 said: 'Till this date had passed there was no equity to redeem'.

In *O'Reilly v Heydon,* the court distinguished ordinary mortgages where the principal was not due until the contractual date for redemption and instalment mortgages (in that case a building society mortgage), where the principal was reduced by regular payments (in that case, monthly instalments). The court said that in the latter case it would 'be in a sense absurd' to argue that redemption could not take place until the end of the mortgage. The terms of redemption in this latter situation would be obtained by examining the contract between the parties (in *O'Reilly v Heydon,* the contract was affected by the rules of the building society).

In New South Wales the legislature has given mortgagors the right of early redemption by enacting s 93 of the Conveyancing Act 1919. This section provides that a mortgagor has an entitlement to early redemption, but must pay all moneys due under the mortgage together with interest for 'the unexpired portion of the terms of the mortgage'. The proviso is without prejudice to any collateral right of the mortgagee if the mortgage had run its full term. The provision applies notwithstanding any condition in the mortgage documentation to the contrary.

It has been held (*Steindlberger v Mistroni* (1992) 29 NSWLR 351) that the application of the provision 'notwithstanding any stipulation to the contrary' only applies to early redemption and not to the obligation to pay interest for the unexpired portion of the term (this case also made it clear the section was enacted for the interests of mortgagors). Accordingly, mortgagors and mortgagees can agree that on early redemption, interest for the unexpired portion of the term may not be payable in full (or at all), but they cannot stipulate that there will be no right to early redemption.

Equity will not allow a stipulation in a mortgage that is a penalty. A stipulation imposed for a purpose to enforce payment, rather than to estimate damages, flowing from a breach of a condition, is regarded as a penalty. So equity generally regarded a further sum being paid on default of payment (in addition to the agreed amount) as a penalty. A provision increasing the interest rate on default (or if the payment of interest was not made punctually) was regarded as a penalty. However, equity tolerated a provision that rewarded a mortgagor who paid punctually with a lesser rate of interest than the stipulated higher rate.

With reference to the facts in the question, the provision for interest reducible to 8% for punctual payment is accordingly valid. There is no provision for early redemption in the mortgage; however, Paul can take advantage of the provisions of s 93 of the Conveyancing Act 1919 (NSW) (which has no counterpart in the other Australian jurisdictions) and redeem the mortgage before the due date. However, the section, while allowing for early redemption, insists that interest for the unexpired portion of the term must be paid. In the absence of any agreement to the contrary, Paul must pay the interest calculated to 26 January 2008.

Under the altered facts

7-6 The mortgage terms are unclear as to the position in relation to payment of interest where the mortgagor is in default. The clause provides for recovery of principal and interest on default 'although time for payment shall not have arrived', but it is silent on whether a liability for interest is calculated for the unexpired portion of the term. It has been held that where default has arisen, the mortgage must disclose a 'contractual obligation on the mortgagor to pay interest at a point of time after the principal sum has been received in full by the mortgagees': *Stocks and Enterprises Pty Ltd v McBurney* (1977) 1 BPR 9521 at 9524.

Accordingly, where the conditions of the mortgage do not clearly stipulate the obligation to pay interest for a period after the date of receipt of the principal sum, then there will be no liability to pay (where there is an issue of default). In *Van Kempen v Finance & Investments Pty Ltd* [1984] 6 NSWLR 293 at 301 Holland J stated in respect of a similar situation, where the mortgage incorporated a schedule of repayments and on the mortgagor's default the mortgagee took action and sought to recover interest for the full term of the mortgage:

> ... there is, in my opinion, an equitable basis in a case like the present for denying the mortgagee future interest. Whatever the position where the mortgagee after default has made a mere demand, here the mortgagee has made the choice of not leaving the balance of the principal out at interest on the security of the mortgaged property but getting it in by realising the security. The mortgagee's action, justified though it was, has accelerated recovery by the mortgagee of the principal. Instead of remaining available to the use of the mortgagor to the end of the four years as contemplated by the mortgage, the money is already back with the mortgagee and available for his own use and, as a consequence, the operation of the repayment schedule has ceased to be applicable. As the mortgage can no longer continue as intended by its terms but does not define the rights of the parties in relation to its present discharge, the situation would seem to me to entitle either party to seek from the court an accounting on equitable principles to enable the mortgage to be discharged.

In this question, the mortgagee, Archie, has sought to justify the payment of interest for the unexpired period of the term on the basis of s 93 of the Conveyancing Act 1919 (NSW). However, the section applies to situations where the mortgagor wishes to redeem prior to the contractual date for redemption. In the question before us, the mortgagor has made no request for redemption. The mortgagor is on the contrary satisfying the demand of the mortgagee, 'and that situation is not the one to which s 93(1) is directed': Samuels JA in *Stocks & Enterprises Pty Ltd v McBurney*.

Paul has no liability to pay Archie interest, as demanded, in the absence of a contractual obligation in the mortgage conditions. Paul has no obligation to Archie under s 93.

Examiner's Comments

7-7 The answer to this question discusses the implication of the mortgage contract. It highlights that while equity would allow redemption after the contractual date, it was just as firm in not allowing redemption before the contractual date. The answer explains the rationale of a mortgage being viewed as an investment, and the very different situation that might arise in an instalment mortgage.

Equity expected mortgages to run their term. Section 93 of the Conveyancing Act 1919 (NSW) altered this position. The section is discussed in its three aspects of payment of interest, early redemption and its application in the face of any attempt to contract out of it. The answer further discusses the issue of mortgage penalties in view of the clause allowing an interest rate deduction.

Having outlined the principles applicable, the answer then applies them to the factual situation to answer the direct issues of the question.

The second part of the answer deals with liability to pay interest on default. It explains that a contractual obligation must be shown to exist. The citation from the judgment of Holland J explains the equitable principles behind the obligation to pay interest. The mortgagee has the investment back and is free to re-invest.

The answer discusses the purpose of s 93 and the fact that it is for the purpose of the mortgagor requesting an early discharge.

The answer was open to address the apparent conflict raised in the citation from Holland J. Equity regarded the mortgage as an investment, and for that reason there was no right to redeem until the contractual date. The citation rationalises the non-liability for interest (in the absence of a clear contractual obligation) on the part of the defaulting mortgagor, on the basis that the mortgagee has the investment back before the contractual date.

Keep in Mind

7-8 Students should keep in mind the following:

- In answering this question, it is not uncommon for students to neglect to deal with the interest rate deduction for early repayment and to discuss the principle that equity will regard a higher interest rate imposed for late payment as a penalty.
- It is important to explain why repayment prior to the contract date for repayment was not allowed.
- In dealing with s 93 of the Conveyancing Act 1919 (NSW), students tend to focus on the fact that the section requires payment of interest for the contractual term on early repayment. They neglect to explain the section has altered the law regarding repayment prior to the contractual date for repayment.

- The fact that the courts have held the proviso 'notwithstanding any provision to the contrary' is not applicable to interest should be explained.
- Section 93 of the Conveyancing Act 1919 and the cases that have dealt with the section indicate that it is for the benefit of mortgagors requesting early repayment. It is not for the use of mortgagees against defaulting mortgagors. However, it is easy to overlook the necessity to discuss the liability for interest on default. That liability requires the existence of a clear stipulation in the mortgage conditions, if after payment of the principal sum by the defaulting mortgagor, interest is to be payable for a period after that payment.

Question 2

> **7-9** Refer to Question 1. The facts are again altered so that now:
>
> - Archie and Paul are neighbours. Archie wishes to retire and sell his farm to Paul, but Paul does not have sufficient funds to pay the full purchase price of $500,000. In view of his poor health and his anxiety to sell, Archie reluctantly agrees to vendor finance in the sum of $100,000 secured by mortgage to ensure there is a sale to Paul. Archie would much prefer to receive the full purchase price of $500,000.
> - The default clause in the mortgage states that in the event of default 'the whole of the principal sum together with interest at the rate of $10 per centum per annum for the balance of the term up to and including 26 January 2008 shall immediately become due and payable, and it will be lawful for the mortgagee to sue and recover same'.
> - On 26 January 1999, Paul defaults on a quarterly interest payment due on that date and fails to make payments thereafter.
> - Paul enters into a contract to sell the property.
> - Archie requires payment of principal and interest calculated to 26 January 2008.
>
> Advise Paul.
>
> **Time allowed: 15 mins**

Answer Plan

7-10 This question follows on from Question 1 above. It examines the issue of interest and penalties in a mortgage. Contrasting the facts in the question with those in *Wanner v Caruana* [1974] 2 NSWLR 201 and considering the principles enunciated in that case provide a reasonable approach.

Answer

7-11   In *Wanner v Caruana* [1974] 2 NSWLR 301, a similar clause (in a similar factual scenario) was held by Street CJ to be a 'stipulation in terrorem'. There was no commercial advantage for the mortgagee in the mortgage running its full term. It was simply a case of a mortgage to secure the balance of purchase funds as part of negotiations to secure a sale of the property. It was not a case of an investment by the mortgagee. In fact, the reality was that rather than have an 'investment', the mortgagee would much prefer to have the funds in possession. In view of the original interest, the stipulation in the mortgage for interest in the situation of default arising did not reflect the structure of the parties' transaction. The clause (in *Wanner v Caruana*) did not reflect any of the justifiable principles relating to accelerated payment of interest as damages, because it did not indicate a genuine estimation of damages.

In *Wanner v Caruana*, Street CJ further pointed out that the mortgage did not attempt to aggregate interest as a lump sum to be paid by instalments. If that had been the case, it might have been viewed as 'an agreed present debt' being reduced by instalments, thus decreasing the likelihood of its challenge as a penalty. In the facts of the present question, the interest has not been aggregated and accordingly is challengeable as a penalty.

Equity always looked to intention. Equity will not allow a stipulation that is a penalty — a stipulation aimed at punishment rather than damages. Accordingly, even where there is an aggregation of interest in the mortgage payable by instalments, whether the balance of those interest instalments will be due on default will depend on the substance of the mortgage agreement viewed in totality.

Examiner's Comments

7-12   The question was seeking to bring to mind that equity will look at each situation. Here, there was no commercial reality in the mortgage other than as a security. It was never meant to be an investment, and to attempt to require interest on default was outside the mortgage purpose, apart from falling into the realm of penalty. The answer deals with these issues. Perhaps some further direct discussion on penalties and damages might have been included. The difficulty of aggregating interest and its effect on default is dealt with. The question was attempting to highlight the flexibility of equitable principles when it comes to the mortgage contract.

Keep in Mind

7-13   Students should keep in mind the following:

- The main issue regarding the lack of commercial intention in the transaction is fairly obvious. It is important to remember that some discussion is required of the issue of aggregation of interest in view of the comments of Street CJ in relation to this in *Wanner v Caruana*.

Question 3

7-14 In January, Susan and Jack Battle bought a two-storey beachfront property in Noosa. They have registered their title as joint tenants. They run their craft shop in the downstairs area, where they sell Susan's quilts and tables and chairs made by Jack, and use the upstairs level as their private residence. When they bought the property, they borrowed $250,000 from Jack's uncle, Lester Cubb, which is secured by a registered mortgage over the property. The mortgage document contains the following clauses:

Clause 2: The term of this mortgage is eight years.

Clause 3: Susan and Jack Battle, the mortgagors, grant to Lester Cubb, the mortgagee, an option to purchase the property. This option may not be exercised until six months before redemption of the mortgage, subject to Clause 7.

Clause 4: The interest rate is 7% per annum. A lower rate of 5% will apply if the mortgagors pay promptly three consecutive monthly instalments. In the event that the mortgagors default then the higher rate of 8% applies in respect of the amount in default.

Clause 5: The mortgagors shall not sell, assign or lease the property without the mortgagee's prior written consent.

Clause 6: In the event the mortgagors default in payment of principal and interest, the principal sum secured shall immediately become payable upon the mortgagee providing 30 days written notice, even though the time for payment shall not have arrived.

Clause 7: If the default continues after the 30 days notice period pursuant to Clause 6, the mortgagee shall be entitled to exercise the option to purchase the property.

Lester is also a carpenter, and he has a separate contract with Jack and Susan to sell his custom-made rocking chairs in the craft shop. Lester believes the shop has a great future as the area is becoming widely known for its crafts and organic produce, and he is keen to take over the property and expand.

Jack and Susan have been unable to make any mortgage payments since 1 May: Jack was diagnosed with chronic arthritis and had to stop work, and Susan has been unable to maintain her quilting as she has been caring for Jack. Susan and Jack have also been unable to comply with their agreement to sell Lester's rocking chairs as they have been forced to close the store because they cannot do the work to create new stock.

On 1 August Jack and Susan receive written notice from Lester, pursuant to Clause 6 of their mortgage agreement.

Lester wants to exercise his option to purchase under Clause 7. Jack and Susan want to keep the property.

Advise Jack and Susan. Would you change any of your advice if the National Credit Code applies to the mortgage agreement?

Time allowed: 1 hour, 15 mins

 Answer Plan

7-15
- Identify if this is a registered legal mortgage or an equitable mortgage. It appears that this is a registered mortgage and is therefore a legal mortgage.
- Look at each clause to determine validity and enforceability:
  - accelerated payments;
  - clogs on redemption.
- Does the National Credit Code (NCC) apply?
  - look at definition in s 5 NCC.
- Are there additional requirements if the NCC does apply?
  - consider obligations under NCC;
  - consider any restrictions concerning paying out the loan;
  - consider variations of interest rates;
  - consider restrictions on dealing with the property;
  - consider acceleration of the mortgage.
- Remedies available;
  - where NCC does not apply;
  - additional remedies if NCC does apply.

 Answer

7-16   In order to determine whether Lester can exercise any option, the status of the mortgage needs to be determined, assuming initially that the NCC does not apply as no dates are given.

The mortgage appears to be registered, therefore it is a legal mortgage. However, the fact that it is registered does not mean that all the clauses in the mortgage are valid or enforceable, as the mortgage does not have to be checked in order to be registered. Each clause in the mortgage must be assessed to determine validity and enforceability:

- **Clauses 3 and 7:** These clauses need to be assessed to determine if they are clogs on redemption. In *Wily v Endeavour Health Care Services Pty Ltd* [2003] NSWCA 312 it was held that an option to buy was not a clog on redemption nor unconscionable as it was an option agreement and did not offend the rule that a mortgagee

— 145 —

cannot take an option to purchase a property. Jack and Susan are likely to argue here that by subjecting Clause 3 to Clause 7, Lester can exercise such right relatively quickly and easily by accelerating their payment, and that as such it is related to and directly affected by the mortgage. If these clauses in operation together are viewed as an example of clauses conferring upon the mortgagee, on the mortgagor's default, a right to take over the mortgaged property in satisfaction of the debt then it would be unconscionable, a penalty and a clog on redemption: *Kreglinger v New Patagonia Meat and Cold Storage Co Ltd* [1913] UKHL 1. The other issue with Clause 7 is that if Lester exercises the option, Jack and Susan would be unable to exercise either their contractual or equitable right to redeem the property. This would be inconsistent with or repugnant to the equitable right to redeem: *Samuel v Jarrah Timber and Wood Paving Corporation Ltd* [1904] AC 323.

- **Clause 4:** This clause provides for variations of interest rates. An initial rate is set for the mortgage, a lower rate is allowed if the mortgagor pays promptly and a higher rate is applied to any amounts in default. The lower rate in the event of prompt payments has not been considered a penalty (*Strode v Parker* (1694) 32 ER 804) and is likely to be enforceable as analogous to the discount interest rate: *Wanner v Caruana* [1974] 2 NSWLR 301. The higher rate is also unlikely to be regarded as a penalty due to its apparently prospective, rather than retrospective, nature.

- **Clause 5:** Such restrictions on dealings with the mortgaged property are usually acceptable. Even s 66 of the Land Title Act 1994 (Qld) requires the mortgagee's prior consent to assignment and lease of the mortgaged property.

- **Clause 6:** This seems to be an accelerated payment. In *Wanner v Caruana* [1974] 2 NSWLR 301 a clause providing for payment of the outstanding principal, together with interest for the full period of the loan upon the mortgagor's default, was regarded as void as a penalty. In *Cityland and Property (Holdings) Ltd v Dabrah* [1968] 1 Ch 166 the court found that requiring the borrower to pay the full amount owed under the loan — in that case held to be a premium as the total amount was specified and not provided as an interest rate — was held to be such a collateral advantage that it was unconscionable. Here Lester is only seeking the remainder of the principal so there is no attempt to limit the borrower's equity in the security: *Kreglinger v New Patagonia Meat and Cold Storage Co Ltd*. However, this clause should be further considered under s 95 of the Property Law Act 1974 (Qld) (PLA).

Lester seems entitled to accelerate Jack and Susan's payment under s 95(1) PLA. However, depending on how the interest will be calculated, the accelerated amount may be unenforceable as a penalty. For example, a higher interest rate for the outstanding amount would not be a genuine pre-estimate of Lester's loss as required under *Wanner v Caruana*.

Depending on their financial position, Jack and Susan may tender payment of the outstanding amount (presumably the missed three months instalments plus interest) to Lester. If Lester accepts such payment, then they would be relieved from any accelerated payment under s 95(2) PLA. However, if Lester refuses to accept payment (which is likely because he is keen to exercise either the option to purchase or the right of foreclosure), then Jack and Susan could tender the payment to the court and obtain relief under s 95(3) PLA.

Separate contract to sell Lester's chairs

7-17 While this is a collateral advantage, it does not necessarily clog Jack and Susan's right of redemption (*Kreglinger* case). The agreement appears to be a separate contract but may be treated as part of the mortgage agreement if it is not genuinely independent or separate, akin to *Toohey v Gunther* [1928] HCA 19 where they held the collateral covenant had to be part of the mortgage transaction generally and not limited to the terms of the mortgage instrument.

The duration of the selling agreement is uncertain. It is more likely to be enforceable if it ceases before or upon Jack and Susan's redemption of their mortgage: *Biggs v Hoddinott* [1898] 2 Ch 307. If it continues after redemption, then it may still be enforceable, provided that it is a separate and independent agreement which is neither oppressive, unfair nor unconscionable (*Kreglinger* case).

Would it make any difference if the NCC (Sch 1 to the National Consumer Credit Protection Act 2009 (Cth)) applied?

7-18 The applicability of the NCC is uncertain due to the limited facts provided. Section 5 NCC provides the relevant definitions and application criteria. The NCC only applies to transactions from 1 July 2010. If this transaction occurred after that date, then the following must be considered.

The definition of 'credit purpose' in s 5 NCC

7-19 This definition requires the borrower be a natural person or corporation and that the credit is provided wholly or predominantly for personal, domestic or household purposes. The act allows for a charge to be made for providing the credit, but it requires the credit provider to provide the credit in the course of a business of providing credit or as part of the business of the credit provider.

One issue that might arise here is the purpose of the credit amount provided. The NCC definition may not be satisfied and the NCC may not apply if:

- The credit of $250,000 was not provided predominantly for Jack and Susan's personal, domestic or household purposes: s 5(1)(b). Here half of the property is used for the shop, while s 5(4) defines 'predominant purpose' as 'the purpose for which more than half of the credit is intended to be used'. There is no information provided about how Jack and Susan are using the $250,000.

- There is also the problem that Lester did not 'provide the credit in the course of a business of providing credit': s 5(1)(d). No information is given about the nature of Lester's business or even if he has any outside of making rocking chairs for sale.

However, if the NCC did apply, then the following additional matters would need to be considered:

- **Clause 4 variations of interest rate:** The position here would be the same as the common law position outlined above, but it is further supported by s 30(2) NCC. The lower rate is likely to be enforceable by analogy with a discount interest rate: *Wanner v Caruana*.

The higher rate is still unlikely to be regarded as a penalty due to its apparently prospective rather than retrospective nature. It also seems consistent, or at least analogous, with s 30(2) NCC which requires that 'the higher rate is imposed only in the event of default in payment, in respect of the amount in default, and while the default continues'.

- **Clause 5: Restriction on dealings with the mortgaged property.** Again, the same comments apply as set out above, as s 51(1) NCC also requires the mortgagee's prior consent to assignment and lease of mortgaged property.

Additionally, the NCC requires the mortgagee, as the credit provider, to do the following:

- Make pre-contractual disclosure under s 16 NCC by giving a pre-contractual statement containing those matters specified in s 16(3) and (4) NCC. This must be given to the mortgagor before the contract is entered into: s 16 (2) NCC;
- Ensure that the credit contract contains all matters referred to in s 17 NCC;
- Provide a copy of the credit contract to the mortgagor within 14 days under s 20 NCC;
- Ensure the mortgagor has the right to pay out the loan at any time under s 82 NCC;
- Ensure that no acceleration clause within the mortgage is actioned until the proper procedures have been followed and the notices given as specified under ss 92–94 NCC.

While it is clear the correct notices have not been given for Lester to successfully activate the acceleration clauses, it is not known on the facts provided whether the pre- and post-contractual requirements were complied with, or whether the contract does contain all the necessary information.

Examiner's Comments

7-20 The answer covers all the matters raised in the answer plan. The scope of this question is wide. Not all of the information required to reach a conclusion on certain issues is provided in the question, but the student has done the right thing by identifying the legislation or common law that would apply while acknowledging the gaps in the material. Most of the issues are straightforward and the authorities are clear and relevant. The issue of foreclosure, while an option for Lester, is not directly addressed by this question and is best left to the later version of the question provided below, given the scope of the question already.

Keep in Mind

7-21 Students should keep in mind the following:

- It is a good idea to break the question down and deal with each clause individually, and to deal with pre- and post-NCC separately, as this student has done. Trying to put them all together often leads to details being missed.
- Students sometimes forget the common law references and focus instead on just statute references. It is important to remember common law often clarifies and specifically defines how the statute will be applied, and should always be reviewed alongside the statute.
- Students must be careful not to put forward just one party's perspective, but remember that if the other party could have a counter-argument, it should be presented as well.

Question 4

7-22 Refer to the facts in **Question 3** above. Alter the facts so that instead of accelerating payment by Susan and Jack and exercising his right to purchase their Noosa property, Lester intends to either foreclose their right of redemption or sell the Noosa property. Assume the National Credit Code applies to the relevant mortgage. Advise Susan and Jack of their legal options in the following two separate and independent scenarios.

Scenario 1

Lester notifies Susan and Jack of his planned foreclosure. The current market value of the Noosa property is $500,000 while the loan amount is $250,000.

Scenario 2

Lester duly notifies Jack and Susan of his intention to sell the Noosa property if the couple fails to pay their outstanding instalments. The default continues after the expiry of the notice period. Lester then appoints Brisbane Realty to handle the sale of the Noosa property by public auction. The manager of this Brisbane-based firm is a good friend of Lester's.

After setting the reserve price at $500,000 (which is also the current market value), Brisbane Realty advertises the Noosa property twice in the Brisbane Courier Mail a week before the auction. The auction is held at 4 pm on the Brisbane Show Day (which is also a Friday). Lester's friends bid up to $500,000 at the auction. Brisbane Realty then let Buy Les (a company partly owned by Lester) put in the winning bid at $510,000.

Buy Les has signed the contract to purchase the Noosa property and will settle within a month.

Time allowed: 1 hour, 15 mins

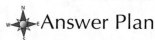# Answer Plan

7-23 *Foreclosure*

- Does the mortgagee have the power to foreclose?
- What are the writing requirements for the mortgagee to foreclose?
- What actions can the mortgagor take to defer or prevent foreclosure?

7-24 *Power of sale*

- Does the mortgagee have the power to exercise the power of sale?
- What are the writing requirements for the mortgagee to exercise their power of sale?
- How can the mortgagor prevent the registration of the sale of the property?
- How can the mortgagee have the sale set aside?
    - ♦ Assess the actions of the mortgagee:
        - good faith at common law;
        - reasonable care — statutory requirements;
        - can notice be imputed into the sale (express or implied)?
    - ♦ Assess mortgagee behaviour and notice by examining:
        - appointment of agent, advertising of auction, timing and location of sale, sale itself (bidding), valuation, sale price and sale to purchaser.
- Remedies.

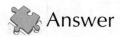# Answer

Scenario 1: Foreclosure

7-25 Foreclosure is a right that can be exercised by a mortgagee and is implied under statute: s 78(1)(c)(ii) Land Title Act 1994 (Qld) (LTA). The mortgage agreement between Lester and Jack and Susan does not exclude this right, in fact it specifically entitles Lester to purchase the Noosa property under certain prescribed circumstances. However, Lester must comply with s 88(2) of the National Credit Code (NCC) before this right can be exercised. This entails serving Jack and Susan with a compliant default notice which allows them at least 30 days to remedy their default.

Several options are then available depending on Jack and Susan's financial position. They could:

- pay the outstanding mortgage instalments within the notice period and thus prevent Lester from proceeding with foreclosure;
- negotiate with Lester to postpone the foreclosure by obtaining his agreement to extend the due date for their payment under s 94 NCC, or by applying to the court for postponement under s 96 NCC, although Lester would still have the option of applying for a variation of the postponement order under s 97 NCC;
- apply for judicial sale of their Noosa property under s 99(1) Property Law Act 1974 (Qld) (PLA) if they were unable to repay the amount in arrears. The court might consider their application in this scenario, as the value of the Noosa property ($500,000) is substantially more than the loan amount ($250,000) and it could be considered inequitable for the foreclosure to proceed.

In order to exercise his power of foreclosure Lester must apply to the Supreme Court for an order nisi, under which the mortgagee seeks an account of the money owed. The order either directs the mortgagor to pay the debt within a specified time, or demands the land be transferred to the mortgagee. It should be noted the courts will not allow foreclosure if the mortgage is worth less than the land as is the case here, as this would represent a windfall for the mortgagee. If the mortgagor was ordered to pay the arrears and failed to do so, the mortgagee should then return to court to seek an order absolute, which vesting order would require the mortgagor to hand up possession. This is an expensive process as it necessitates going to court twice, and is also slow, so it would not be in Lester's interests to pursue this course of action.

Scenario 2: Mortgagee's power of sale

Section 83(1)(a) PLA implies the power of sale in favour of Lester. The facts suggest that Lester has notified Jack and Susan in accordance with the legislation under s 84 PLA and s 88 NCC. Both require Lester to give Jack and Susan at least 30 days to remedy their default. Lester can satisfy both sets of requirements under one notice: ss 88(6) and 183(2) NCC.

Jack and Susan want to prevent the completion of the sale to Buy Les, and if possible to set it aside. The best way for them to make sure the sale does not go through to registration until the relevant issues are resolved is to caveat under s 122(1)(c) LTA as the current registered owners of the Noosa property. Then they should begin court proceedings to restrain or set aside the sale to prevent the expiry or removal of their caveat. However, in order for them to support their right to caveat, they would need to demonstrate fraud on the part of the mortgagee. This would be difficult on the facts, but they might be able to make a case for Lester acting in bad faith as per *McKean v Maloney* [1988] 1 Qld R 628.

Under *Forsyth v Blundell* (1973) 129 CLR 477 Jack and Susan need to establish the following:

- Lester's improper exercise of his power of sale, preferably by proving a breach of his common law duty to act in good faith rather than a mere breach of his statutory duty to take reasonable care under s 85(1) PLA; and
- Buy Les's knowledge or notice of Lester's impropriety.

Lester's actions can be assessed to determine whether his behaviour is sufficient to establish these requirements.

- Appointment of Brisbane Realty: Lester has chosen an estate agent who is not local to the property. This leaves him potentially liable for breaching s 85(1) PLA despite such appointment. The duty to act in good faith requires the mortgagee to 'act without fraud and without wilfully or recklessly sacrificing the interests of the mortgagor but stopping short of exposing the mortgagee to liability for mere negligence or carelessness': Brennan CJ in *CAGA v Nixon* (1981) 152 CLR 491 at 522. Mere failure to appoint a local agent may not constitute a breach, provided that the agent is reputable and competent. However, this may be one of the reasons for finding the mortgagee has committed a breach of their statutory duty, as in *McKean v Maloney* [1988] 1 Qd R 628.
- Advertising: It is likely the advertising here will be found insufficient both in frequency and duration: *McKean v Maloney*. The mortgagee has a duty to allow sufficient time for advertising, generally four weeks, and with a reasonable number of occurrences.
- Timing of the auction: Friday would not generally be considered a good day for an auction (*Latec Investments v Hotel Terrigal Pty Ltd* (1965) 113 CLR 265) and holding it on the Brisbane Show day, when it conflicts with a public holiday and family events, almost guarantees there will be minimal attendance.
- Sale price: Although this slightly exceeds the market value, it does not reflect an independent or genuine sale, nor is it designed to test the market: *Latec v Hotel Terrigal*; *Forsyth v Blundell* (1973) 129 CLR 477. Given there were minimal independent attendees at the auction due to the lack of advertising, the inappropriateness of placement of advertising, and the bad choice of timing, the majority of attendees were known to the mortgagee. This means that regardless of the price achieved, this cannot be viewed as an independent sale. Lester asked his friends to increase the price by bidding at the auction, and then ensured the winning bid went to Buy Les at slightly above market value. This behaviour combined with the absence of independent attendees is strongly indicative of fraud or collusion between mortgagee and purchaser.

- The sale to Buy Les: given that this is a third party and not the mortgagee itself, but nonetheless a third party related or with transaction is not automatically invalid (*Farrar v Farrars Ltd* (1888) 40 Ch D 395), but the association places a heavy burden on Lester to prove the propriety and reasonableness of the sale as he partly owns Buy Les: *ANZ Banking Group v Bangadilly Pastoral Co Pty Limited* [1978] 139 CLR 195. The closer the parties' relationship, that is the relationship between mortgagee and the third party, the higher the burden to prove propriety on the part of the mortgagee.

Lester's conduct and knowledge are imputable to Buy Les, although further information about the extent of Lester's ownership of, and control over, Buy Les is needed before a final determination can be made.

Can Jack and Susan claim damages against Lester?

7-26   Since the sale price slightly exceeds the market value, Lester has arguably complied with s 85(1) PLA by taking 'reasonable care to ensure that the property is sold at the market value'. Damages are usually awarded under s 85(3) PLA to compensate for the difference between a higher market value and a lower sale price, unless exemplary damages are awarded against Lester's impropriety. Here it would be hard to claim damages, despite the issues with Lester's behaviour, as it would seem the sellers still realised a reasonable return on their property. Even if the sale does seem slightly rigged, it does not appear to have disadvantaged them and without a provable loss they would struggle to set aside the sale or lay claim to damages from Lester.

Can they restrain or set aside the sale to Buy Les?

7-27   The availability of this remedy is contentious under a breach of the duty in s 85(1) PLA. If Jack and Susan had suffered a measurable loss they would have a remedy in damages against Lester exercising his power of sale but it would not necessarily help them against Buy Les's title, as the title of the purchaser from the mortgagee is not impeachable solely on the grounds of a breach of this section (s 85(3) PLA), or on the ground of Lester's improper or irregular exercise of his power of sale: s 87(1)(d) PLA.

On the one hand, the literal interpretation of ss 85(3) and 87(1) PLA together with the judicial approach in *Cameron v Brisbane Fleet* Sales *Pty Ltd* [2002] 1 Qd R 463 at 470, which says the statutory duty of reasonable care subsumes the common law duty of good faith, may limit Jack and Susan's remedy to damages against Lester. On the other hand, the actual statutory provisions are silent on the common law duty of good faith. A purposive interpretation of these provisions should prevent Buy Les from unduly or unfairly benefiting from these provisions. The High Court has interpreted provisions comparable to s 87 PLA and yet has still set aside or restrained the relevant sale: for example *Latec v Hotel Terrigal* and *Forsyth v Blundell*.

Thus Jack and Susan may be entitled to this remedy if the sale to Buy Les can be proven to be fraudulent or in bad faith, and if Buy Les can be shown to have had notice of such fraud or impropriety. Jack and Susan could even get around proving Buy Les notice if the court favoured *Forsyth v Blundell*, where the High Court still restrained the mortgagee from completing the sale despite the purchaser's unawareness of the mortgagee's bad faith.

 ## Examiner's Comments

7-28 The answer needed to cover a number of very grey areas in the law. Many of the tests of the mortgagee's behaviour come down to what is reasonable and that can be affected by multiple external factors. A reasonable timeframe for advertising could vary depending on the current economy, how quickly sales are moving, the price and marketability of the house and so on. The important issue is for the student to recognise the different factors that can come into play rather than assume there is a strict rule for how each will be applied. A good answer will pay attention to the specificity of the property in question: location, marketability, economic climate and so on. This student has identified the key issues that must be assessed to determine the mortgagee's behaviour and validity of the final transaction. Further mention could have been made of determining market value and cases such as *Sablebrook Pty Ltd v Credit Union Australia Ltd* [2008] QSC 242.

 ## Keep in Mind

7-29 Students should keep in mind the following:

- Two matters are often overlooked in this type of question:
  - a brief introductory discussion of the source of the power of sale and how equity regulates it;
  - the statutory protection that is extended to purchasers from mortgagees.
- A further point to keep in mind is that any delay of sale by the mortgagee will ultimately be dictated by commercial realities having regard to both tests.

Question 5

7-30 Ryan Rearden is a financial broker with many successful self-employed clients for whom he finds it difficult to arrange finance from the traditional financial institutions. So much so that Ryan has started a side business lending these clients his own money, usually at an interest rate of around 4% above the market rate.

On 1 July 2011, Ryan lent $500,000 to Sam Swift to assist Sam complete the purchase of a $1 million luxury penthouse on Magnetic Island, as a holiday property for himself and his parents. Sam is a retired professional athlete and much of his income comes from public appearances and show performances for his sponsors. Ryan took a registered first mortgage over the property as security, under the Land Title Act (Qld) 1994.

The mortgage contained, inter alia, the following covenants:

- term — five (5) years;
- interest rate — 10.5%, payable monthly in arrears (but if the mortgagor is in default, interest will be payable at the higher rate of 14.5%);
- in the event of default, the principal and interest become immediately payable upon the mortgagee giving fourteen (14) days notice in writing to the mortgagor.

In September 2011, Sam broke his leg in a skiing incident in Switzerland. Sam quickly found himself in financial difficulty as he was unable to perform his contractual obligations and lost his sponsors and thus his income. Sam could not make the December interest instalment payment, and is now finding it difficult to maintain his other financial commitments.

On 1 January 2012, Ryan served notice on Sam that unless he remedies the default within fourteen (14) days, the entire principal will become due and owing. On 18 January 2012, Ryan served Sam with a notice of his intention to exercise his power of sale under s 84 of the Property Law Act (Qld) 1974.

The prices of real estate in the Magnetic Island area have been soaring and Ryan is now keen to purchase the property for himself at the best price he can, as he can see this will become an excellent long-term investment. Ryan plans to hire an old friend of his from university, Trevor, who now works as a real estate agent, to handle the sale for him and market the property. The real estate firm is a national franchise, and Trevor works out of the Cairns office.

Trevor puts together the following marketing plan:

- An advertisement will be placed in the property lift-out section of the *Townsville Bulletin* each Saturday for a period of four weeks.
- The property will be auctioned on the first day of the Sealink Magnetic Island Race Week. Ryan is pretty confident that most people will be busy competing or spectating and the island will be full of visiting tourists as it is a peak week for rentals.

> - The commission is set in accordance with the Real Estate Institute of Queensland scale, with an additional 1% of the purchase price, as an incentive.
> - A reserve of $100,000 above the market value has been set to enable Ryan to negotiate the purchase after the auction.
>
> The auction date is coming up and Ryan seeks legal advice regarding the outstanding loan and the arrangements he has put in place to buy the property at the best possible price.
>
> Advise Ryan.
>
> **Time allowed: 1 hour, 30 mins**

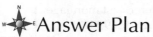 Answer Plan

7-31 An answer to this type of question should focus on the remedies available to the mortgagor, and requires advising the mortgagee of the consequences he will face if he continues with his planned actions. The mortgagee's actions and plans should be discussed from this perspective.

Applicability of the National Credit Code (NCC) must be determined, and statutory obligations discussed. Alternative actions that could be taken by Sam should also be reviewed. The answer must incorporate a review of the contractual terms as well as examine the application of the power of sale.

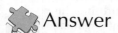 Answer

Does the National Credit Code apply?

7-32 The mortgage is registered so there is no doubt it is enforceable at law and is not an equitable mortgage.

The NCC is applicable as the loan was entered into after 1 July 2010. The definition of the 'credit purpose' in s 5 NCC requires the borrower be a natural person or corporation, and that the credit is provided wholly or predominantly for personal, domestic or household purposes: s 5(1)(b) NCC. Sam's purchase meets all the criteria and the loan has been granted as a mortgage which secures obligations under a contract: s 7(1)(a) NCC. There is also no doubt Ryan provided the loan in the course of business associated with his primary business as a financial broker.

Sam would have rights under ss 95(2) and (3) of the Property Law Act 1974 (Qld) (PLA) enabling him to tender the outstanding instalments to remedy the default, or seek an order of relief from acceleration from the court. Sam could have tried negotiating with Ryan under ss 94–97 NCC, or even applied to the court for postponement, an option available for loans up to $500,000. However, on the facts provided it does not seem Sam has taken up any of these options.

Sam is clearly in default and Ryan has accordingly exercised his right to demand accelerated payment under the mortgage. However, pursuant to s 93(1) NCC, Ryan is obliged to provide Sam with a default notice in the required format and the default must continue for a further 30 days. Ryan has only given 14 days notice and failure to provide adequate or correct notice is likely to deem the subsequent acts invalid.

Ryan then sought to increase the rate of interest from 10.5% to 14.5%. It is unclear from the contract wording whether he intends the higher rate to apply to all future payments, or just the amount in default. This may breach s 30 NCC unless it complies with s 30(2) NCC which allows acceleration in the event of default in payment, but only in respect of the amount in default and while the default continues. This clause is likely to be in breach of the legislation as it reads as if applying the penalty interest rate on the full amount of the loan and not just the amount in default. Regardless, the acceleration has not been done correctly as Ryan failed to follow the statutory notice requirements and thus any acceleration will be ineffective anyway.

Ryan has given Sam a s 84 NCC notice, but although this allows 30 days, on the facts given it is unclear whether the notice advises Sam of the details of the default and what actions he must take to get out of default. Further, Sam should have been provided with a default notice under s 88 NCC (which could have been included in the s 84 NCC notice) but this does not seem to have been issued.

It is likely, in light of the above, that Ryan has not successfully established his right to exercise power of sale and the sale will be invalid.

This sale is caught by s 85(1A) PLA as it seems to be a residence under reg 4 of Property Law Regulation 2003. The mortgagee has an obligation to satisfy s 85(1) PLA which says:

> (1) It is the duty of a mortgagee, including as attorney for the mortgagor, or a receiver acting under a power delegated to the receiver by a mortgagee, in the exercise of a power of sale conferred by the instrument of mortgage or by this or any other Act, to take reasonable care to ensure that the property is sold at the market value.

Satisfying the mortgagee's duty of care involves ensuring that the property is sold with proper advertising (*McKean v Maloney* 1988 1 Qd R 628) and also outlines all the various actions a mortgagee must undertake in order to fulfill their duty of care, including the obligation to advertise properly and obtain proper market value.

It is important for the mortgagee to realise that merely appointing a competent agent will not satisfy their duty under this section: *CAGA v Nixon* (1981) 152 CLR 491.

Here Ryan's buddy Trevor has been appointed as the agent. He is a real estate agent in a major national real estate agency in Cairns. *McKean v Maloney* suggests that a local agent should be appointed. In that instance an agent from Mackay had been appointed to accomplish a sale in Proserpine and this was found to be a factor in the finding that the mortgagee's duty had not be satisfied. This must create some concerns about the likelihood of market value being obtained.

An important issue in satisfying the mortgagee's duty is the question of whether advertising is sufficiently broad and well timed. Here Ryan and Trevor have booked four occasions for advertising for the local Townsville newspaper only, and have arranged to hold the auction on a day when other local events mean few people are likely to be available to attend the auction.

These facts are strongly indicative of a breach of the mortgagee's duty, and imply Trevor and Ryan are attempting to avoid their obligations. A property of this type, worth around $ 1 million, could easily justify state-wide or at least regional advertising, and would definitely require more than the advertisements contemplated. The advertising should be wider and over a much longer period. If it can be shown that the market value is not obtained at the sale — which would depend on valuation evidence — then the difference between the market value and the sale price would prima facie be the quantum of the damages recoverable by Sam under s 85(3) PLA. No information is given about how Ryan obtained the market value but the reserve price is overly inflated anyway, and seems set to doom the auction to failure: *Latec Investments Ltd v Hotel Terrigal Pty Ltd* (1965) 113 CLR 265.

A mortgagee cannot purchase land it is selling as a mortgagee exercising power of sale. Therefore Ryan will have to avoid purchasing the property himself. As North J held at 860 in *Martinson v Clowes* (1885) 52 LT 706:

> It is quite clear that a mortgagee exercising his power of sale cannot purchase the property on his own account, and I think it clear also that the solicitor or agent of such mortgagee acting for him in the matter of the sale cannot do so either … There must be a declaration that the sale and conveyance … are void.

However, a sale can possibly occur to a company owned by the mortgagee without being inherently invalid: *Farrar v Farrars* (1808) 40 Ch D 395. However, this increases the burden of proof placed on the mortgagee to show that nothing untoward has happened in the process of the sale: *ANZ Banking Group v Bangadilly Pastoral Company Pty Limited* [1978] 139 CLR. Here there would have to be very clear evidence that all the correct procedures were followed ensuring that proper market value was obtained and it is unlikely Ryan could meet that burden of proof under the current circumstances.

Note that just because the market value is obtained does not necessarily mean there can be no claim by the mortgagor to set aside the sale if Torrens title fraud has arisen, where the purchaser was aware of this fraud. The knowledge would likely be imputed to the purchaser if the company was controlled by the mortgagee.

The high reserve could suggest that there is no real intention to obtain a buyer at the auction. The difficulty Ryan faces would be in justifying a sale at below that reserve price after the auction. There should probably be two independent valuations to establish a valid reserve price but here it does seem to have been set in order to prevent a sale by placing the reserve well beyond the actual market value.

Giving Trevor the higher rate of commission would likely be a breach of s 6 of the Property Agents and Motor Dealers Regulation 2001. The maximum commissions chargeable under the Regulation are stated in Sch 1A. The standard commission would be the limit of the sum that could be deducted from sale proceeds before the balance is returned to the mortgagor under s 88 PLA.

Overall it is clear that Ryan's plans breach most, if not all, of his statutory duties and obligations and any purchase he made after the auction would be extremely unlikely to stand in these circumstances.

Therefore the question really requires an outline of the remedies available to Sam, so that the mortgagee can be given realistic advice concerning the consequences of his actions.

The obvious first issue is whether Sam could seek an order to set aside the sale. There is a general rule that an injunction restraining a sale by the mortgagee or setting aside a sale will not be granted unless the mortgagor pays an amount owing into court, confirmed by Walsh J in *Inglis v Commonwealth Trading Bank of Australia* (1972) 126 CLR 161 at 164. There are different rules however where:

- the mortgagor admits that the power of sale is exercisable; and
- the situation where the matter in dispute is whether the power is exercisable at all.

If the mortgagor admits the power of sale is exercisable (not the position here), the general rule requires payment into court of all principal and interest outstanding, and the mortgagee's costs, before an injunction restraining the sale can be granted. This applies because the mortgagee is apparently entitled to sell and the mortgagor can only be granted relief when:

- the mortgagor demonstrates its ability to pay the mortgagee's claim; and
- when the court considers it is fair and just.

Where the mortgagor disputes the power of sale is exercisable at all, for example where there is no default or s 84 NCC has not been satisfied — as probably applies here — the court will not require all principal interest and costs to be paid, but some payment will be required before a mortgagor can obtain an interlocutory injunction to restrain the sale (*Harvey v McWatters* (1948) 49 SR (NSW) 173), because the ordinary undertaking as for damages may be inadequate in a case involving mortgagor and mortgagee. Therefore, Sam will need to come up with some money to cover this requirement.

In terms of another remedy besides damages being available to Sam, he could consider a caveat to hold the status quo. In Queensland under s 121(1)(c) Land Title Act 1994 (Qld), a caveat could be lodged by Sam as the current registered owner.

If Sam sought an injunction after a contract had been signed by Ryan under his power of sale — as he could ultimately do here — Ryan could be met with the requirement that a court will not interfere in a sale after a contract is made by the mortgagee unless the mortgagee has exercised its power of sale in bad faith or demonstrated a reckless disregard for the mortgagor's interest: Walsh J in *Forsyth v Blundell* 1973 129 CLR 477 at 499–500.

This applies even if a breach of statutory duty is shown, that it is sold without reasonable care under the statutory test. There is some controversy on this point and some are of the view that an injunction will lie even when there is no lack of bona fides by a purchaser and the mortgagee is acting without power or in breach of duty.

In *McKean v Maloney*, McPherson J added that in his view *Forsyth v Blundell* also required knowledge of the impropriety of the mortgagee by the purchaser for an injunction or setting aside of the sale, which would clearly be provable here. The view that a purchaser could be protected from a mortgagee against a mortgagor, even when there was a breach of the s 85 PLA duty but the mortgagee is bona fide, is further supported by s 85(3) PLA, which attempts to state that the title of a purchaser is unimpeachable even if a mortgagee has breached its s 85 PLA duty.

Fraud or reckless disregard by Ryan, and knowledge of this by the purchaser, probably could arise on the facts as the following has occurred:

- no proper s 84 NCC or s 88 NCC notices, given acceleration clause did not provide for the required 30 days notice under the NCC;
- no formal independent valuation has been obtained on the facts provided;
- inadequate advertising and inappropriate date selected for auction;
- sale to Ryan or an associated entity is likely.

Sam could seek damages of only the difference between the sale price and what should have been received, that is the actual market value of the property, if the property had been correctly and more widely marketed: *Forsyth v Blundell*; *McKean v Maloney*.

If a sale actually occurs Sam might be able to seek to set aside the sale if it was fraudulent, but more likely due to Ryan's reckless disregard of the mortgagor's interests. The use of the high reserve, inadequate advertising and bad timing of the auction would all assist in making Sam's case: *Latec v Hotel Terrigal*. The possible relationship between Ryan and the purchaser would mean the knowledge of the fraud or reckless disregard would probably also not be difficult for Sam to prove.

The best advice for Ryan is to begin the entire process afresh; appoint an appropriate local agent; give proper notice; comply with the acceleration clause notice requirements; advertise properly; seek valuation evidence from two independent valuers to provide the basis of the reserve price; select a more appropriate auction date; and sell to an independent person, or have only a small interest in the purchaser and follow the required procedures properly.

 ## Examiner's Comments

7-33 This question addresses multiple issues and maintaining a clear order for arguments to follow logically is difficult. The student has done well in addressing such a large topic in a sensible, logical manner. There is some repetition but that is hard to avoid in this question. Appropriate emphasis has been given to the remedies available to Sam, an issue which was correctly identified in the plan and well executed in the answer. Ultimately this represents a fairly successful attempt at a very broad question.

 ## Keep in Mind

7-34 Students should keep in mind the following:

- Students should pay attention to the notice requirements under the National Credit Code, an area they often overlook.
- Remedies should be viewed as key part of the answer in a question like this, and not a throw away to be dealt with summarily in the conclusion.
- The mortgagee's breaches need to be assessed from a statutory and common law perspective; it is not enough to deal with them under only one regime.

Chapter 8

Licences and Leases

Key Issues

8-1 Core topics in property law are licences and leases, and the differences between them. The origin of the lease is usually traced by legal historians to the twelfth century and may be seen as one of the indices of the disintegration of feudalism. For hundreds of years, the leasehold interest was used in rural areas for agrarian purposes. By the late eighteenth century, with the advance of the industrial revolution, the leasehold was increasingly applied to urban circumstances. The law of landlord and tenant has, since that time, been closely linked with the law of contract, and thus the idea that parties to a lease are free to agree on its terms strongly reflects the assumptions of nineteenth century capitalism.

In more recent times, however, the general law of landlord and tenant has undergone extensive modification at the hands of the legislature. The states and territories have enacted comprehensive legislative schemes, particularly concerning residential tenancies, but increasingly also concerning smaller scale commercial tenancies.

While it is beyond the scope of this book to deal with the numerous statutory regimes governing leaseholds, it is important to note that the underlying agenda of legislative schemes has been to conceive of the leasehold in terms of consumerism. The concrete effects have been to provide for significantly more protection for the tenant.

This chapter focuses on the basic or general law of leases; the landlord–tenant relationship; and in particular, the distinction between leases and lesser forms of permissive occupancies (the various forms of licences).

8-2 Before attempting the following questions, please ensure you are familiar with the following:

✓ licences: definition, types, determination;

✓ the lease as an alternative to more permanent forms of property ownership: its practical advantages and disadvantages;

✓ legislative controls of residential tenancies: the rights and liabilities of tenants and landlords;

✓ the enforcement of specific lease covenants as against a lease's original parties, and also as against successors in title to both the tenant and the landlord;

✓ the courts' application of contractual principles to commercial leases;

✓ licences and leases:

- *Ashburn Anstalt v Arnold* [1988] 2 All ER 147;

- *Aussie Traveller Pty Ltd v Marklea Pty Ltd* [1988] 1 Qr R1;

- *Bahr v Nicolay (No 2)* (1988) 164 CLR 604;

- *Binions v Evans* [1972] Ch 359;

- *British Anzani (Felixstowe) Ltd v International Marine Management (UK) Ltd* [1980] QB 137;

- *Cowell v Rosehill Racecourse Co Ltd* (1937) 56 CLR 605;

- *Deventer Pty Ltd v BP Australia Ltd* (1983) ANZ Conv R 54-104;

- *Errington v Errington* [1952] 1 KB 290;

- *Friedman v Barrett* [1962] Qd R 498;

- *Graham v Market Hotels Ltd* [1943] HCA 8;

- *Hamilton Island Enterprises Ltd v Croycom Pty Ltd* (1998) Q Conv R 54-509;

- *Heidke v Sydney City Council* (1952) 52 SR (NSW) 143;

- *Houlder Brothers & Co Ltd v Gibbs* [1925] Ch 575;

- *JA McBeath Nominees Pty Ltd v Jenkins Development Corp Pty Ltd* (1992) 2 Qld Reports 121;

- *James v Registrar General* (1967) 69 SR (NSW) 361;

- *KJRR Pty Ltd v Commissioner of State Revenue* [1999] 2 VR 174;

- *Knockholt Pty Ltd v Graff* [1975] Qd R 88;

- *Laurinda Pty Ltd v Capalaba Park Shopping Centre Pty Ltd* (1989) 166 CLR 623;

- *Lewis v Bell* (1985) NSW LR 731;

- *Lister v Lane and Nesham* (1893) 2 QB 212;

- *Lurcott v Wakeley and Wheeler* [1911] 1 KB 905;

- *Masters v Cameron* (1950) 91 CLR 353;

- *Pimms Ltd v Tallow Chandlers Co* [1964] 2 QB 547;

- *Porter v Hannah Builders Pty Ltd* [1969] VR 673;

- *Progressive Mailing House Pty Ltd v Tabali Pty Ltd* (1985) 157 CLR 17;

- *Radaich v Smith* (1959) 101 CLR 209;

- *Ravenseft v Davstone* (1980) 1 QB 12;

- *Re De Jersey* [1989] 1 Qd R 133;

- *Re Eastdoro Pty Ltd (No 2)* [1990] 1 Qd R 424;

- *Rock v Todeschino* [1983] Qd R 356;

- *Shevill v The Builders Licensing Board* (1982) 149 CLR 620;

- *Tamsco Ltd v Franklins Ltd* [2001] NSWSC 1205;

- *Verral v Great Yarmouth Borough Council* [1980] 1 All ER 839,

✓ fraud

- *Assets Co Ltd v Mere Roihi* [1905] AC 176;

- *Bahr v Nicolay (No 2)* (1988) CLR 604;

- *Frazer v Walker* [1967] 1 AC 569;

- *Latec Investments Ltd v Hotel Terrigal Pty Ltd* (1965) 113 CLR 265;

- *Mills v Stokman* (1966) 116 CLR 61;

- *Tataurangi Tairuakena v Mua Carr* [1927] NZLR 688;

- *Valbirn v Powprop Pty Ltd* [1991] 1 Qd R 295;

- *Waimiha Sawmilling Co Ltd v Waione Timber Co Ltd* [1926] AC 101.

Question 1

8-3 In January 2011, the Mad Hatter Tea Party applied to Lauchlan Council in Queensland to hold a meeting at one of the council's halls. The meeting was to be the party's annual national conference, to be attended by private registered members only. The Mad Hatter Tea Party was highly controversial because of its support for a return to feudalism, and its view that land ownership should be limited to men over six-feet tall with a nett annual income of over $2.5 million. Lauchlan Council, which had a female mayor and was controlled by the Equality for All party, knew of the controversial nature of the Mad Hatter Tea Party but agreed to hire the hall to them for their meeting.

A booking was made for 2 December 2011, and the venue hire fee of $25,000 was agreed and paid to the council in full by the Mad Hatter Tea Party.

Equality for All's political rival, Outlanders Unite, became aware of the booking and used it as a core theme in their council election campaign. The minority Outlanders Unite party promised to cancel the meeting and ban the Mad Hatter Tea Party from gathering at any council venue in Lauchlan Shire, if they were elected.

At the July 2011 polls, the Equality for All party was voted out, and Outlanders Unite dominated the new council. Upon gaining office, Outlanders Unite held a council vote and won unanimous support to revoke the contract for the booking and to refund the Mad Hatter Tea Party their payment for the hall. The members of the Mad Hatter Tea Party are unhappy about this, and because the Council own most of the large affordable venues in Lauchlan Shire, they have been unable to find an alternative venue. Advise the Outlanders Unite Party whether they are bound to honour the agreement with the Mad Hatter Tea Party.

Time allowed: 45 mins

 Answer Plan

8-4 Identify and characterise the rights of the Mad Hatter Tea Party. Determine whether they have a lease or a licence, and what type of lease or licence. It is likely to be a contractual licence. Identify the characteristics of a contractual licence and distinguish it from the other types of licences: bare licences (mere permissions to do something on land, but not a proprietary right); a licence coupled with interest (permission to enter land and exercise some kind of proprietary interest, for example, *profit a prendre*), and a licence coupled with an equity (a proprietary interest usually under the doctrine of estoppel).

There are three cases which are similar to the fact scenario:

• *Verral v Great Yarmouth Borough Council* [1980] 1 All ER 839;
• *Cowell v Rosehill Racecourse Co Ltd* (1937) 56 CLR 605;
• *Heidke v Sydney City Council* (1952) 52 SR (NSW) 143.

Specifically, cases which have supported an order of specific performance as a remedy in situations such as this (*Verral v Great Yarmouth Borough Council* and *Heidke v Sydney City Council*) may be useful precedents for The Mad Hatter Tea Party's case.

Attempt to distinguish exceptions to the availability of the order of specific performance in *Cowell v Rosehill Racecourse*, and also in *Porter v Hannah Builders Pty Ltd* [1969] VR 673 and *Graham H Roberts v Maurbeth Investments* [1974] 1 NSWLR 93.

One might therefore conclude that, based on *Verral's* and *Heidke's* cases, it can be argued that the council is obliged to honour the agreement as damages are not sufficient.

Answer

8-5 The Mad Hatter Tea Party and the Lauchlan Shire Council have agreed, by contract, to allow the Mad Hatter Tea Party to hold its annual national conference in the Lauchlan Shire Council Hall. This cannot be a bare, gratuitous licence as the agreement has been formed under contract, and consideration has been given. No right in the land has been granted, merely permission to enter and use it for a stated purpose, so it cannot be a lease. The position of the Mad Hatter Tea Party, prima facie, is that of a contractual licensee.

A contractual licence gives the licensee (The Mad Hatter Tea Party) permission to enter and use land belonging to the council, an act which would otherwise be unlawful as a trespass. For this right the party has agreed to pay, and the council has agreed to accept, $25,000. After briefly surveying the basic legal propositions which govern the area of contractual licences, this advice will examine in greater detail some cases where the specific issue of councils, political associations and venue hiring has been considered. Council will be advised that there is a significant likelihood that the Mad Hatter Tea Party may obtain an order to enforce the contract and compel the council to make the shire hall available to the party on the agreed date.

Traditionally, there are three types of licences. The first, a bare licence, is a mere permission to do something on the lands. It is normally terminable at the will of the licensor, it therefore has no real commercial value and it is inalienable. Most crucially, such a licence is not a proprietary right. The second, a licence coupled with an interest, is permission to enter land to exercise some kind of proprietary interest. An example is a right to a *profit a prendre*. As this right is proprietary in nature, it confers on the licensee an interest in the land which can be transferred, and which will bind successors in the title to the licensor. It will not, however, bind a bona fide purchaser of the legal estate for value and without notice.

The third kind of licence is a licence coupled with an equity. This is also a proprietary interest, usually arising under the doctrine of estoppel. A contractual licence may fall into this last classification. At common law, contractual licences are revocable. The licensor would naturally be liable to pay damages for breach of contract. In *Cowell v Rosehill Racecourse Co Ltd* (1937) 56 CLR 605 it was held that the plaintiff could only claim damages ascertained with reference to the contractual breach, for the price of his admission ticket, and could not claim for assault, because once he was notified of the revocation he became a trespasser, and the defendant was entitled to use its right to self-help. This might seem to argue against the proprietary classification of a contractual licence, but the situation differs in equity. Where a contract (of licence) may be enforced in equity by an order of specific performance, it can be said that the contractual equity is coupled to the licence — thus rendering the licence irrevocable (for the agreed period) and in the nature of a proprietary right.

8-6 The facts of the present case are analogous to *Verral v Great Yarmouth Borough Council* [1980] 1 All ER 839, where Lord Denning held that damages were an inadequate remedy in such a purported termination of the contractual licence of the National Front, particularly as media attention made it impossible for the Neo-Nazi organisation to find an alternative venue. Instead, the court ordered specific performance of the contract. The precedential value of this English decision may depend, here, upon whether or not the Mad Hatter Tea Party has been subject to similar media scrutiny and whether it can demonstrate that such attention (or other factors beyond its own control) has resulted in the failure to obtain an alternative venue.

8-7 In New South Wales, *Heidke v Sydney City Council* (1952) 52 SR (NSW) 143 is an example of a more restrictive approach. In this case, a Communist youth organisation had agreed with the Sydney City Council to hire a number of halls and sporting facilities. The Supreme Court ordered specific performance of only a small proportion of a number of contractual licences, but significantly did so in those circumstances where damages were held to be an inadequate remedy. Thus, on the basis of *Verral's* case and *Heidke's* case, the Mad Hatter Tea Party is likely to argue that damages would be inadequate here to obtain an order of specific performance, to enable them to use the Lauchlan Shire Council Hall for their meeting.

The courts will usually only order specific performance as a discretionary order if damages are an inadequate remedy. The adequacy of damages will, as a matter of commonsense, be determined by the availability of suitable alternative conference facilities. Another discretionary consideration will be whether the order would place undue hardship on the licensor. On the facts, specific performance would not appear to place extreme hardship on the council. It would seem that, except perhaps for some unpopularity and a loss of support for the Outlanders Unite Party, the council will still obtain the $25,000 financial benefit under the contract. The council could possibly argue the principle expressed in *Porter v Hannah Builders Pty Ltd* [1969] VR 673, that the courts will not order specific performance of a contractual licence in a stalemate situation, where the parties are unhappy to maintain their relationship.

In building contracts especially, the courts are unwilling to force a licensor to keep his or her promise if he or she is unhappy with the builder. This approach was upheld in *Graham H Roberts v Maurbeth Investments* [1974] 1 NSWLR 93. It is submitted that the unique facts of building cases make the application of the rules associated with them inapplicable to other factual scenarios and that, as such, there should be no bar to the availability of an order for specific performance in the different circumstances in which the council has licensed its property.

Therefore, on the facts and using the principles laid down in *Verral v Great Yarmouth Borough Council* and *Heidke v Sydney City Council*, it would seem that the Mad Hatter Tea Party has an equitable interest in the hall, at least for 2 December 2011, and that the council would be obliged to honour the agreement. If the party can show that suitable alternative conference facilities are not obtainable, it is likely that they will be successful in any application for specific performance of the hiring contract because damages would be an inadequate remedy in the circumstances.

Examiner's Comments

8-8   There are two specific deficiencies in the sample answer:

- It is not stretching the given facts too far to suggest that The Mad Hatter Tea Party has a lease. It is possible for a 'term of years' leasehold to be for a period of as little as one day. There is detailed statutory regulation of the modes of creation of leases in all states and territories, and the facts given in the question do not contain enough detail to determine whether a lease was intended by the parties. Nevertheless, a good answer to a problem-style question must attempt to explore *every* possible legal avenue which a client may face. Although the possibility of a lease was summarily excluded, some attention could have been paid to this as a possibility.
- The answer might additionally consider what legal arguments might have been made on behalf of the council in an attempt to avoid the contract. Although the facts given are too scant to say, there may be legal arguments under the doctrines of mistake and contractual frustration which might (given more facts) enable the council to avoid the contract completely. Accordingly, some discussion of the remedies of rescission and restitution may also be required.

More generally, how does one deal with a question which seems to have a direct precedent, and which requires one to advise the party who 'lost'? Even a decision which might appear to favour strongly an opponent's argument might, ultimately, prove to be a strong weapon for your own client. For example, as this answer goes some way toward demonstrating, if the court could be persuaded that the *Verral* decision could be distinguished from the present case (perhaps in relation to the availability of alternative facilities, but perhaps even on the basis of media attention), it may be of little assistance to the party's claim to enforce the contract. Always try to find a point of factual difference between the hypothetical facts and that 'adverse precedent', attempt to demonstrate that this difference was crucial to the decision of the previous court, and therefore submit that the decision is by no means wholly advantageous to your opponent. Lastly, no mention has been made of how often political parties renege on agreements made by previous holders of an office from opposing parties. Granted this is at council level and not national, but there could still be some discussion on whether political parties have some kind of special status in not enforcing agreements made by their opposing predecessors, based on the justification they usually gain position by arguing they will not do as the previous party did so following the previous party's actions would negate the point of elections.

Keep in Mind

8-9   Students should keep in mind the following:

- In cases of a permissive occupancy of land do not focus on just one type of right — consider (if only briefly) every possible type of interest which an occupier may hold. Lease? Licence? Some right of an equitable nature arising, perhaps from the doctrine of estoppel, or perhaps as an ancillary right to a contract?
- Where rights are derived from contract, test the validity of the contract by asking some questions about its creation: Was there consideration? Are its terms sufficiently certain? Might the contract be avoided for mistake?
- 'Adverse' precedents must not be ignored or downplayed. Try to neutralise them, or turn them to your own advantage.

Question 2

8-10   Victor Vazine reached an agreement in writing in March 2011 with Bubb's Burgers Ltd, giving them permission to operate a small concession stand to sell burgers and snacks, and also to affix posters and other relevant advertisements, in a bowling alley scheduled for development on Vazine's land by a third party company due to be incorporated.

The agreement described Vazine as 'the licensor' and Bubb's Burgers as 'the licensee', and provided that the 'licence' was for a period of four years commencing either 1 July 2011, or the first day the bowling alley opened for business, at a rent of $20,000 per annum. The document also stated that Vazine agreed that while the licence remained in force, he would not permit any other person to sell snack foods or affix related posters, and that he would, upon request by Bubb's Burgers, take proceedings against any person who did so.

In May 2011, Vazine leased the land and assigned all his interest in the agreement with Bubb's Burgers to the newly formed company Bowling Blitzen Pty Ltd. The contract for the lease was stated as 'subject to' the rights of Bubb's Burgers; however, the lease itself contained no reference to the agreement between Vazine and Bubb's Burgers.

> The bowling alley has now been completed and is open for business, but Bowling Blitzen refuse to allow Bubb's Burgers to enter the property. Advise Bubb's Burgers as to its rights against both Vazine and Bowling Blitzen.
>
> **Time allowed: 45 mins**

Answer Plan

8-11   Introduce the answer by setting out a plan (as follows):

- a brief synopsis concerning the enforceability of licences generally;
- refer to the various types of licence, and their differing treatment according to their nature: bare licences; licences coupled with interests and equities; and contractual licences;
- rights and remedies arising from the contract;
- the basic principle of privity of contract, rights and remedies in contract, and the non-enforceability of contractual licences by non-parties: *King v David Allen and Sons Billposting Ltd* [1916] 2 AC 54;
- exceptional circumstances where the rights of contractual licensees may be upheld against third parties:
  - ♦ *Bahr v Nicolay (No 2)* (1988) 164 CLR 604;
  - ♦ *Errington v Errington* [1952] 1 KB 290;
  - ♦ *Binions v Evans* [1972] Ch 359;
  - ♦ *Ashburn Anstalt v Arnold* [1988] 2 All ER 147.

Conclude with a summary of the rights and remedies available to Bubb's Burgers as against both Victor Vazine and Bowling Blitzen.

Answer

8-12   This advice will commence with a summary regarding the enforceability of licences, by identifying the assorted types of licence and their differing treatment according to their qualities. It will proceed to a consideration of any rights and remedies arising from the contract, and then focus upon the exceptional circumstances where the rights of contractual licensees may be upheld against third parties.

Although a licence is not generally recognised as an interest in land, the question remains open as to whether third parties would be obliged to respect the rights of a licensee. Whether a licence is able to bind a successor in title to land will depend upon the character of the licence. The various kinds of licences: bare licences, licences coupled with an interest or licences coupled with an equity, and contractual licences, are dealt with by the courts in varied ways.

Bare licences will not bind successors in title: they are revocable at will by either the licensor or his or her successor, while licences coupled with an interest and licences coupled with an equity may bind third parties

— as was seen, for example, in *Inwards v Baker* [1965] 2 QB 29. Such licences are typically irrevocable by the licensor or any other person. Somewhere between these two positions lies the contractual licence, and the authorities concerning contractual licences and third parties are unfortunately divergent.

A contractual licence can ordinarily be terminated by a successor in title to the original licensor without that successor incurring liability for breach of contract, because the successor is not a party to the contract from which the licensee derives his or her rights. However, some uncertainty remains concerning 'irrevocable' contractual licences, particularly where (as here) there has been a recognition of the status of the licensee by the third party.

8-13 The fundamental rule of privity of contract, that only parties to contracts may be bound by them, is an impediment to the enforcement of the rights of contractual licensees against successors in title to their licensor. The House of Lords decision in *King v David Allen and Sons Billposting Ltd* [1916] 2 AC 54, promoted the principle that a contractual licence is incapable of enforcement against third parties. In that case King entered into a contract with David Allen and Sons Billposting Ltd, granting David Allen and Sons Billposting Ltd a licence to fasten posters to the walls of a cinema.

King later granted a lease of the cinema to a third party, but the lease itself did not refer to the earlier licence. When David Allen and Sons Billposting Ltd then sought to exercise its right to attach its posters to the walls of the cinema, it was thwarted by the lessee. The House of Lords held that King, by entering into the lease with the lessee, had cheated David Allen and Sons Billposting Ltd from the benefit of its licence. King was thus liable in damages for breach of contract. However, the licence did not bind the lessee. Even though it was acknowledged that the lessee actually had notice of David Allen and Sons Billposting Ltd's agreement with King, it was not bound. This was because, according to Lord Buckmaster LC, the agreement was purely a personal contract which did not give rise to an equity, let alone an interest, on the part of David Allen and Sons Billposting Ltd. The facts of *King v David Allen and Sons Billposting Ltd* are analogous to the problem posed, and therefore Bubb's Burgers is advised that it may sue Victor Vazine for his breach of the July contract. The licence granted to Bubb's Burgers does not in any way grant them an interest in the land, anymore than David Allen and Sons Billposting Ltd were granted a proprietary interest. It appears unlikely, on the basis of this decision alone, that Bubb's Burgers may either enforce its licence against Bowling Blitzen or sue that company for interfering with its licence.

There is one well accepted exception (to the privity rule that contractual licences cannot bind third parties), which may assist Bubb's Burgers. Where a purchaser of an interest in land actually contracts with a vendor that he or she will respect the rights of a licensee, he or she may be bound by the licence. This is along the lines of the personal equity exception under Torrens. In *Bahr v Nicolay (No 2)* (1988) 164 CLR 604 Mason CJ and Dawson J said:

> ... granted that an exception ... is to be made for fraud why should the exception not embrace fraudulent conduct arising from the dishonest repudiation of a prior interest which the [third party] has acknowledged or has agreed to recognise as a basis for obtaining title ...?

While the facts indicate that the lease to Bowling Blitzen did not refer to the rights of Bubb's Burgers, we are told that: 'In August 1999 Vazine leased his land and assigned all his interest in the agreement of July to the newly formed company Bowling Blitzen Ltd'. From this it may be taken that Bowling Blitzen had notice of Bubb's Burgers's licence and that it took its lease subject to the rights of Bubb's Burgers. On the basis of the decision of the High Court of Australia in *Bahr v Nicolay*, Bubb's Burgers may argue that Bowling Blitzen is bound to respect the licence of July 1999 because Bowling Blitzen, by its contract of August 1999, had knowledge of and had recognised the existence of the licence, and that it would be unconscionable for Bowling Blitzen to resile from that acknowledgment.

There are two English authorities which go even further than *Bahr v Nicolay*. In *Errington v Errington* [1952] 1 KB 290, the Court of Appeal upheld a contractual licence against a third party who took an interest under the will of a deceased licensor. The case was a competition between the licensor's widow (who took her interest under his will) and his son's estranged wife (who had lived in the disputed property). Lord Denning MR held that contractual licences bind all successors in title except bona fide purchasers for value without notice. In *Binions v Evans* [1972] Ch 359, Lord Denning MR confirmed his view that any party who purchases an interest in land with notice of an extant contractual licence is bound by it. In his Lordship's view the contractual licence gave rise to an equitable interest in the land. It is important to note, however, that the English Court of Appeal has since discredited Lord Denning's approach, in *Ashburn Anstalt v Arnold* [1988] 2 All ER 147.

Bubb's Burgers is therefore advised that its claim to enforce its licence against Bowling Blitzen may be countered, and that not all agreements for the transfer of an interest in land which acknowledge the rights of existing contractual licensees will oblige the successor to the licensor to respect those rights. In *Ashburn Anstalt v Arnold* the defendants were the sublessees of a shop which was part of a block which the landlords wished to redevelop. In 1973, the defendants entered into an agreement with the landlords for the sale of their interest. However, the agreement allowed the defendants to remain in occupation of the premises as licensees, rent-free, but to give up their occupation upon three months notice from the landlord. There was a further term which stated that the defendants would be granted a 21-year lease upon the completion of the redevelopment. In 1985, the plaintiffs purchased the freehold from the landlords, the purchase being expressly subject to the right of the defendant to be granted the 21-year lease. The plaintiffs then purported to terminate the defendants' occupancy.

It was held by the Court of Appeal, in which Fox LJ gave the leading judgment, that a mere contractual licence is not binding on a purchaser — even a purchaser with notice. In this case, the Court of Appeal held that the words 'subject to' were not intended by the parties to impose an obligation on the purchaser to respect the licence; rather the words were only intended to negative any question of the vendor's liability to the purchaser stemming from the licence. If this case were accepted as good law in Australia, then this distinction would amount to a significant qualification to the *Bahr v Nicolay* rule, and render the chances of Bubb's Burgers's success against Bowling Blitzen more doubtful.

8-14 Bubb's Burgers is advised that it may sue Victor Vazine for breach of contract. Vazine's breach appears to be evident in his actions in leasing the bowling alley property to Bowling Blitzen without incorporating the licence to Bubb's Burgers within the terms of the lease. He has effectively deprived Bubb's Burgers of the benefit of its contract. Success in such an action will result in an award of damages, but not in the enforcement of the company's licence to operate its kiosk to sell snacks, or to affix posters and other advertisements. There is, unfortunately, some doubt as to whether Bubb's Burgers may expect any success against Bowling Blitzen. No contractual remedies are available because Bubb's Burgers and Bowling Blitzen are not parties to any agreement inter se. Nor do the authorities necessarily provide Bubb's Burgers with a right to enforce its licence against Bowling Blitzen, even though Bowling Blitzen has acknowledged the existence of such rights. Any argument on behalf of Bubb's Burgers based on the decision of the High Court in *Bahr v Nicolay* risks failure, specifically if the court qualifies the exception to the general rule of non-enforceability by adopting reasoning similar to that currently endorsed in England as expressed in *Ashburn Anstalt v Arnold*.

Examiner's Comments

8-15 Contractual licences are sometimes referred to as the borderline between contract and property, with considerable justification. The issue of the enforceability of contractual licences against third parties highlights this marginal condition. This problem seeks to explore the interface between contractual and proprietary rights and remedies.

The basic (privity of contract) approach is exemplified by reference to *King v David Allen and Sons Billposting Ltd* in an extended example. The answer correctly notes that there are close similarities between the facts of the problem and this precedent. Some further reference may also have been made to another analogous case, *Clore v Theatrical Properties Ltd* [1936] 3 All ER 483, where it was held that a contractual licence to sell beverages and snacks at a theatre did not bind the successor in title to the licensor. The primary conclusion, that Bubb's Burgers may pursue a claim (in damages) for breach of contract against Victor Vazine, is arrived at expediently and supported by reference to an accepted authority.

The answer then proceeds to the more complex question of the rights of Bubb's Burgers against Bowling Blitzen, the third party. It squarely acknowledges that there can be no right or remedy against Bowling Blitzen in contract — owing to a lack of privity between the parties. From this point, the somewhat circumscribed exception to the general rule of non-enforceability of contractual licences against third parties is canvassed. The difficulties in precisely stating the law here are clearly expressed; however, the answer may have also explored (if only briefly) the remedies available to Bubb's Burgers if it was successful in showing that Bowling Blitzen is bound by the licence. It would appear that the constructive trust imposed by the High Court in *Bahr v Nicolay* may be inappropriate to the facts of a contractual licence situation. Would, for example, the recognition of the enforceability of the licence against Bowling Blitzen have the effect of elevating the contractual licence to the status of a licence coupled with an equity, along the lines suggested by Lord Denning in the cases cited?

Lastly, the student has assumed throughout there is no doubt this is a licence. A good answer should examine all the options, and while cases of contractual licences and licences with proprietary interests have been examined, the student has not addressed the possibility of this agreement representing a lease. The word licence in the agreement does not limit the agreement, as Denning LJ said in *Errington v Errington*, the primary test is the intention of the parties. Bubb's Burgers could be likened to *Radaich v Smith* (1959) 101 CLR 209 which deals with an exclusive licence granted to run a milk bar from premises, and which the court held to be a lease not a licence. This possibility should be examined, and if proven to be a successful option, would bind Bowling Blitzen under the *Bahr v Nicolay* equity exception.

Keep in Mind

8-16 Students should keep in mind the following:

- Never assume that just because something is called a licence or a lease in a question, that it is actually what it is purported to be. The legal tests are there for a reason. Apply the tests and identify the characteristics of the right in question and confirm which it is, and then look for the applicable precedents and remedies. Often you will find yourself applying solutions for both because the answer is not clear-cut or obvious do not be scared to do so.

- Contractual licences are first and foremost a creature of contract. It is to the law of contract which one should look first. The position upon breach of contract, an action resulting in an award of damages, is usually easy to make out. Do this first, before launching into the more complex proprietary issues.

- Do not be swayed by legends about the reputation of certain judges: just because Lord Denning said it, does not necessarily mean a proposition is wrong or right. Be critical and attempt to balance judicial statements, always with regard to the hypothetical 'facts' given in a problem and the real facts of the case you are referring to.

- Simply making out a legal right in a party is not enough. A good answer needs to address the kinds of remedies to which such a right gives access. No client will be satisfied with knowing that they have a 'right' — what they also want to know is how that 'right' can be translated into an order which is capable of alleviating the harm or problem with which they are faced. The common law provides damages; equity can provide a wide range of discretionary orders. In a problem-style question you should advise your 'client', in appropriate terms, what can be done to help him or her.

Question 3

8-17 On alternate Saturdays each month, Jeanne and Keith make part of the bottom field of their farm, 'Country JK', available as a market where local residents and businesses can hire stalls to sell their products.

Based on the following clauses of the terms of agreement, does this agreement create a licence or a lease?

Terms of Agreement Hire Agreement between Country JK (JK) and the Hirer:

1. The Hirer is entitled to exclusive occupation and use of stall number(s) [A1 and A2] for the period of one year from the date of this Hire Agreement. (A diagram is attached showing the number and location of each stall.)

2. If the Hirer does not use any of the stalls for a particular day or month, then JK may allow other persons to use those stalls.

3. The Hirer must pay rental to JK before the end of each month. The rental payable is calculated by the number of stalls actually used during each month.

4. The Hirer must keep the stalls in good repair and sanitary order. JK may enter and inspect the stalls at any time.

5. Either party may terminate this Hire Agreement at any time by giving one month's notice in writing. However, JK may terminate without notice if the Hirer fails to pay rental, or fails to repair any damage to the stalls, or otherwise misbehaves.

Time allowed: 30 mins

Answer Plan

8-18   Analyse the agreement using a clause-by-clause approach followed by overall assessment.

The test is whether the hire agreement grants the right to exclusive possession, having regard to the parties' intention and the nature of the rights granted: *Radaich v Smith* (1959) 101 CLR 209.

Each clause must be analysed to determine:

- the intention of the parties as demonstrated by a prima facie reading of the words in the agreement;
- the actual rights granted by the clause;
- a review of whether the actual rights granted match the apparent intention.

An overall conclusion should be reached by weighing all the factors identified in the analysis outlined above.

Answer

8-19   This answer will analyse the individual clauses of the agreement to identify the substantive rights actually granted by the words used, and then to compare those rights with the apparent intention of the parties (*Radaich v Smith* (1959) 101 CLR 209) without being unduly led by the words of the agreement: *KJRR Pty Ltd v Commissioner of State Revenue* [1999] 2 VR 174. The factors identified in each clause will then be weighed to determine an overall conclusion as to whether exclusive possession the general right to exclude all, including the lessor, from the premises (*Lewis v Bell* (1985) NSW LR 731) has been granted.

Title

'Hire Agreement' is neutral in meaning, though arguably more analogous with licence.

Clause 1: 'Exclusive occupation and use' does this phrase fall short of exclusive possession?

'Exclusive possession' generally means either the right to control the premises and persons entering the premises, as defined by McTiernan J in *Radaich v Smith*, or a general right to exclude others except under specific provisions for entry, as identified by Mahoney JA in *Lewis v Bell* at 735:

> Where the grant isn't expressed in terms of "possession" but instead, in terms of "use" or "occupation", then the court must determine "whether what is granted is mere occupation or use, or is possession in the relevant sense. And where what is granted is possession, it still, in principle, may remain to be decided whether what is granted is exclusive possession".

'Use' does not amount to possession, let alone exclusive possession (again Mahoney JA in *Lewis v Bell* at 737) and 'occupation' seems more akin to possession. The distinction between 'exclusive possession' and 'exclusive occupation' was not addressed in the *KJRR* case as the parties made no submissions on this point. It does seem likely here that exclusive occupation and use does not equate to exclusive possession.

The designation of specific stalls could arguably support a lease in that it conclusively identifies the area to be occupied by the hirer, and does not leave any leeway for Country JK (JK) to have the right to move the hirer within the premises, which is likely more indicative of a lease.

Clause 2: Use of designated stalls by others

The wording of this clause appears to directly counteract Clause 1, neutralising or diluting it by reverting the rights in the hired area back to JK in the event the hirer is absent from the premises. This suggests no substantive grant of exclusive possession has occurred. However, the alternative argument could be made that this clause would not be necessary unless JK intended to grant the hirer exclusive possession in the first place, thus making it necessary to contractually revert the ability to allocate those areas to JK in the hirer's absence.

Ultimately this clause is inconclusive, as its presence could be used to argue both for and against exclusive possession having been intended.

Clause 3: The word 'rental' itself is neutral

Mahoney JA in *Lewis v Bell* at 738–739 said that although terms such as 'rent' arguably support 'an inference of exclusive possession … such terms are not inconsistent with a relationship of licensor and licensee'. In the context of this document, the word 'rent' does not warrant an inference that the rights intended to be created were either those of possession or of exclusive possession. However, the calculation of rental based on actual use seems inconsistent with, or at least unusual for, a lease, and more indicative of a licence. The calculation lacks certainty and predictability compared with a normal rental, which is generally the same amount regardless of the hours a hirer spends inside or outside the property.

Clause 4: Repair and maintenance obligation with a right of inspection

The obligation to maintain and repair is a common obligation for a lease, but not necessarily inconsistent with a licence. However, JK's right to inspect at any time ensures a retention of control over the hired area which would ordinarily be deemed inconsistent with the hirer's exclusive possession of those stalls. This suggests that overall this clause tends to favour an interpretation of a licence and not a lease.

Clause 5: Right of termination

In and of itself, the right of termination is neutral. Although termination without notice in the event of a breach or misconduct is not uncommon in a lease, this clause again indicates a lack of exclusive possession, especially when read in light of the preceding clauses.

Conclusion

Ultimately, the important question is whether JK retains significant rights to interfere with the hirer's rights of occupation and use. If this can be answered in the affirmative then no substantive rights of exclusive possession have been given, regardless of the intention of the parties when they drew up the agreement: *Hamilton Island Enterprises Ltd v Croycom Pty Ltd* (1998) Q Conv R 54–509. Here it seems JK has retained fairly significant rights to access and reallocate the premises, suggesting exclusive possession has not been granted. On balance, the hire agreement is more likely to be construed as a licence rather than a lease.

 ## Examiner's Comments

8-20 This hire agreement illustrates the use of imprecise (if not inconsistent) language, which can be construed as either a licence or a lease. Unlike *Lewis v Bell* or the *KJRR* case, any issue about sham or pretence provisions is unlikely, or at least unintended. Thus, it is a relatively simple exercise for the student to ascertain the parties' intention by interpreting the express terms of an agreement. This has been clearly and succinctly done, recognising the inconsistencies in each clause and attempting to ultimately draw a conclusion. The conclusion is unlikely to be definitive and the agreement itself could be argued either way. However, in light of the student's arguments it is likely that is a conclusion that would find favour in the courts.

 ## Keep in Mind

8-21 Students should keep in mind the following:

- It is important that students should remember to analyse carefully the exact wording of individual clauses in this type of document, to determine precisely the specific substantive rights that have been granted, rather than take a high-level overview approach. Individual words or phrasing can noticeably change meaning.
- Students should not assume that the factual existence of exclusive possession means the hirer has been granted the right to exclusive possession. The agreement must always be examined to determine intention and the nature of the legal rights that have been granted.

 ## Question 4

8-22 James Joyce, a property developer, has big plans for Deadend Street, a commercial block of land on the Sunshine Coast. He wants to create 'Joyce's Junction', a high rise hotel with a retail complex on the ground floor. Deadend Street currently has a small retail shopping centre with three tenants. On 1 March 2011, James signs a contract to purchase Deadend Street from the current owner, Samuel. Settlement is set down for 1 May 2011. Clause 6 of the contract states: 'The purchaser's attention is directed to the leases as detailed in Schedule 3'.

Schedule 3 contains the following details:

Bakery: Under a three-year written lease held by Norman Nods, with six months remaining. Option to renew for a further three years.

Supermarket: Under a four-year written lease to Oscar Oswald with two months remaining. Option to renew for a further two years.

Chemist: Under a two-year written lease to Summer Soho with 12 months remaining. Two options to renew, each for a further two years.

Easement: Right of way used by neighbouring owner Barry Butz. Area specified in attached Deadend Street plan.

James checks the register and finds that only Norman's lease is registered. There is no mention of the other leases or the easement. In fact, the right of way was registered but when the property was transferred into Samuel's name, a clerk at the Titles Office (suffering from stress) failed to note it on Samuel's title.

Samuel informs his tenants that there will be a change of ownership. Summer is concerned that the new owner may not respect her rights under her lease. When she sees James walking through the shopping centre on 15 March, she asks him into her shop. Summer enquires: 'James, I'm concerned about the change of owners and I need security. Will you continue with the terms of my lease agreement with Samuel?' James responds: 'Don't be concerned. I have big plans for the future of this centre'. This conversation is recorded by the chemist's audio/visual security system.

On 27 March, pursuant to his lease, Oscar exercises his option. He notifies Samuel. At settlement, Samuel hands Oscar's notice to James saying: 'You'll look after Oscar, won't you?'. James remains silent, but takes the notice back to his office.

On 5 May, James sends the following circular to all tenants: 'Unfortunately your businesses are not compatible with the future tourist- focused profile of this centre. As the new owner of this complex, I hereby advise you that any options you may hold are not binding. All tenants are hereby given notice to vacate the premises at the expiry of the current terms'.

James reinforces the perimeter fence around Deadend Street, blocking Barry's right of way.

Norman, Oscar, Summer and Barry seek your advice. Advise them.

Time allowed: 45 mins

 Answer Plan

8-23 This question raises four main issues:

- fraud;
- *in personam* exception;

- registered leases;
- omitted easements.

The leases need to be considered first in terms of:

- registration:
  - ◆ if registered then registered term is binding;
  - ◆ if not registered, then must look to the short lease exception;
- if not covered by the short lease exception, look to alternative means to bind the new registered owner:
  - ◆ *in personam* or personal equity exception;
  - ◆ fraud exception.

The easement:

- if it is registered, it is binding;
- if it is not registered;
  - ◆ does it fall under an exception and can it be registered?
  - ◆ if it can't be registered it will not be binding.

 # Answer

Leases

8-24   The term 'short lease' is defined in s 4 of the Land Title Act (1994) Qld (LTA) as a lease for a term of three years or less; or a lease from year to year; or a shorter period. The leases here are unregistered but as short-term leases they are still protected by the LTA and still legal: *Deventer Pty Ltd v BP Australia Ltd* (1983) ANZ Conv R54-104. They are an exception to the usual provision that interests in Torrens title land are equitable unless registered.

When reviewing the leases in this question to determine if they are short leases, it must also be remembered that while the interests of a short-term lessee are protected as an exception to indefeasibility (s 185(1)(b) LTA), these rights do not include the right to acquire the fee simple or reversionary interest on or after the end of the short lease, or a right to renew or extend the term of the short lease beyond three years from the beginning of the original term: s 185(2) LTA.

Therefore, if a party has a fixed-term lease for a term of three years or less, with or without an option to renew, the sum of both being no longer than three years, or there is a periodic tenancy from year to year or for a lesser period (eg month to month, week to week), then that short lease does not have to be registered, and a person taking a registered interest in the property will be bound by the lease, notwithstanding that it is not registered.

If it is an unregistered lease of three years or less containing an option to renew where the option will take the total period to greater than three years, then the original term of three years or less is protected, but not the option: s 185(2) LTA; *Friedman v Barrett* [1962] Qd R 498. However, where the option to renew is also of three years or less and the option is exercised prior to the transfer of title then a new term is created and will be protected under s 185 LTA, which will be binding upon a purchaser registered after the creation of the new term: *Re De Jersey* [1989] 1 Qd R 133. This will not occur in relation to an option attached to an unregistered three-year lease if the option remains unexercised at the date of registration of the purchaser. The purchaser will be indefeasible on the basis of s 184(1) LTA as long as the purchaser does not become bound under the *in personam* exception.

The last permutation relevant under these facts would be a registered three-year lease with an option. As long as the option is specifically performable then registration of the lease will protect the option, as that interest is recognised as part of the landlord's estate: *Re Eastdoro Pty Ltd (No 2)* [1990] 1 Qd R 424. This also applies to leases greater than three years (*Mercantile Credit Ltd v Shell Co of Australia Ltd* (1976) 136 CLR 326), where Gibbs J (345–6) said:

> ... the right of renewal is so intimately connected with the term granted to the lessee, which it qualifies and defines, that it should be regarded as part of the estate or interest which the lessee obtains under the lease, and on registration is entitled to the same priority as the term itself.

Norman: Bakery

8-25 Norman has a registered three-year lease with six months remaining, and a further three-year option. The registration protects the option period (*Re Eastdoro*), as the option period is intimately connected to the original term. The current lease period is protected under s 185 LTA. Both Norman's current lease and option will be binding on James.

Oscar: Supermarket

8-26 The original four-year term of Oscar's lease is unregistered, making it an equitable lease. As it is for more than a three-year term, it will not fall under the short lease exception and will not be binding on the new owner. However, Oscar has exercised his right to renew by exercising his option prior to registration by the new purchaser. The option is for two years, therefore creating a term of less than three years and bringing it under the short lease exception (*Re De Jersey)* and making it protected and binding on the new purchaser: *Friedman v Barrett*.

Summer: Chemist

8-27 Summer holds an unregistered two-year lease which is less than a three-year short term lease and is thus protected by s 185 LTA. However, her first option of two years takes the combined sum of lease and option to greater than three years, so her first option will not be protected or binding under the short lease exception, and thus neither will the second, subject to any *in personam* exception: *Friedman v Barrett*.

Omitted easement

8-28 This is an express exception to indefeasibility of title under s 185(2) LTA. Here the easement was previously registered but we are told it has been left off the register due to an error. This would appear to come within the exception (*James v Registrar General* (1967) 69 SR (NSW) 361) where an easement was created over Torrens title land situated in New South Wales. The easement was registered against the title to the servient tenement, and subsequently a new certificate of title was issued for the servient tenement which, through some error in the Titles Office, failed to note the existence of the easement, that is the easement was 'omitted' from the title. The property underwent two further transfers of title, neither noting the existence of the easement.

The registrar then discovered the error and amended the current certificate of title by noting the easement on it. This action was argued against by the current owner of the servient tenement who was prejudiced by the addition and had no knowledge of the existence of the easement.

The New South Wales Court of Appeal held that the easement was omitted within the New South Wales equivalent of s 44 Real Property Act 1861, and was therefore binding against the servient tenement, notwithstanding two intervening transfers of bona fide purchasers for consideration. This case has been followed in Queensland: *Rock v Todeschino* [1983] Qd R 356. It is likely that *James v Registrar General* would be decided in the same way under s 185(1)(c) LTA.

The omission of the easement here arose as a result of an error in the Titles Office and would therefore fall within the wording of s 185(3)(b) LTA, and the registrar's power of correction under s 15(3) LTA would allow the amendment of the register. Even if that provision was not available, James's prior knowledge means that there would be no prejudice under s 15(8) LTA were the easement to be registered, as he knew the register was wrong, and how it was wrong.

Fraud

8-29 This is specifically set out as an exception to indefeasibility in s 184(3)(b) LTA. Fraud under Torrens means dishonesty of some sort: *Assets Co Ltd v Mere Roihi* [1905] AC 176. The fraud must be capable of being brought home to the purchaser or his or her agent as described in *Waimiha Sawmilling Co Ltd v Waione Timber Co Ltd* [1926] AC 101 where Lord Buckmaster said that '[i]f the designed object of a transfer be to cheat a [person] of a known existing right, that is fraudulent'. Kitto J in *Latec Investments Ltd v Hotel Terrigal Pty Ltd* (1965) 113 CLR 265 noted: 'Moral turpitude there must be; but a designed cheating of a registered proprietor out of his rights ... is ... clearly a fraud'. However, Kitto J declared in *Mills v Stokman* (1966) 116 CLR 61 that 'merely to take a transfer with notice or even actual knowledge that its registration will defeat an existing unregistered interest is not fraud', which concurs

— 183 —

with Wilson J and Toohey J in *Bahr v Nicolay (No 2)* (1988) CLR 604 who said:

> It is ... clear that to acquire land with notice of an unregistered interest such as a lease, to become the registered proprietor, and then to refuse to acknowledge the existence of the interest is not of itself fraud.

This mirrors the *Friedman v Barrett* approach. Therefore, despite the apparent unconscionability of James's action, he will not be caught by the fraud exception to indefeasibility and bound by the unregistered leases and options.

In personam exception

8-30   In this instance the contractual provision is quite weak, suggesting this scenario would not compare favourably with cases such as *Bahr v Nicolay* or *Valbirn v Powprop Pty Ltd* [1991] 1 Qd R 295. The conversation with Summer is not strong but could arguably form the basis of an *in personam* argument.

Under s 185(a) LTA, 'A registered proprietor of a lot does not obtain the benefit of s 184 namely the indefeasibility of title if there has been an equity arising from the act of the registered proprietor'. In *Tataurangi Tairuakena v Mua Carr* [1927] NZLR 688, the New Zealand Court of Appeal noted:

> The provisions of the [Torrens statutes] as to indefeasibility of title have no reference either to contracts entered into by the registered proprietor himself, or to obligations under trusts created by him, or arising out of fiduciary relations which spring from his own acts contemporaneously with, or subsequent to, the registration of his interest.

This principle was confirmed in *Frazer v Walker* [1967] 1 AC 569 where they stated the Torrens statute 'in no way denies the right of a plaintiff to bring against a registered proprietor a claim *in personam*, founded in law or in equity, for such relief as a court acting *in personam* may grant'.

Therefore if the courts were inclined to look favourably upon the verbal reassurances as successfully representing an *in personam* exception, the option would be binding on James: *Bahr v Nicolay*.

 # Examiner's Comments

8-31   This is a large question covering multiple areas. The answer is structured well, dealing clearly with one topic before moving to the next, and working through them in a logical order: first registered leases, then the short lease exception, then the easement and then using the *in personam* exception as a last resort to try and capture what could not be brought in successfully under the other options.

The student spent time at the beginning discussing the different kinds of lease scenarios and the answer could have been shortened had the discussion been applied to the facts in the question at the same time, rather than dealing with them separately below. This does not make the answer better or worse but would definitely have affected the time spent on the answer.

Good reference was made to common law and statute throughout. The *in personam* question could have had a bit more detail. Overall, a thorough and well structured answer.

Keep in Mind

8-32 Students should keep in mind the following:

- Students often misread whether a lease or any other interest is registered. In short lease questions such as this, it is important to be very careful about which leases are or are not registered before determining what is binding.
- Dates in these questions are important and it is recommended students make a timeline to work out exactly what occurs pre- and post-registration and exactly which terms are current and which ones are still pending exercising, and when terms expire.

Question 5

8-33 Angela and Blake are partners who enter into a lease agreement with Mr Wade to lease a downstairs office for their accounting firm, and purchase the upstairs living residence at Cairns Market. At the market there is already a Mexican restaurant, café, gym and fitness centre, newsagent, architect, a masseuse and a stall selling cushions outside the Mexican restaurant.

On 1 December 2010, the partners were given a draft lease agreement and disclosure statement by Mr Wade. All the parties then signed the lease on 4 December 2010, with the lease to be effective from 1 January 2011 to 1 January 2014. The lease contained the following clauses:

- Clause 1: Rent is $8,000 per month, to be paid monthly in advance. This is a fundamental clause of the lease.

- Clause 2: The premises shall be kept in good and tenantable repair by the tenant, and neither tenant nor lessor shall engage in activities that shall cause nuisance to other tenants or the lessor. The tenant specifically has the obligation to repair the interior of the premises.

- Clause 3: The lessee shall not sublet or assign this lease unless:

  (a) the assignee's or sub-assignee's financial viability and experience in the relevant industry are acceptable to the lessor; and

  (b) the lessee pays the lessor's expenses incurred in connection with the lease preparation and the assignment.

Angela and Blake seek your advice about the following situations:

(a) The downstairs office has a major leak in three places in the ceiling when it rains. Above the leak is the joint between the outside balcony and the main bedroom of the residential property. Angela and Blake have been told by other tenants that the leak has occurred in a number of other shops because the builder failed to properly seal the join where the balcony meets the wall. Mr Wade is insisting that Angela and Blake are responsible for repairing the leak in the leased offices.

(b) A new shop has opened in the shopping centre, a financial adviser who markets himself as 'Managing your money made easy!'. Angela and Blake believe that this business is in competition with theirs and that he is stealing their clients, so they wish to stop him trading.

(c) The relationship between Angela and Blake breaks down, ending their partnership. Angela is distraught, and brings in an old college friend, Danny, who was with a large corporate accounting firm but is looking for a change of pace. Blake is happy to transfer his part in the firm and the tenancy to Danny to be rid of everything, but Mr Wade refuses to allow the assignment since Danny is one of those 'office suit types, and just doesn't fit in with the neighbourhood vibe of the centre'.

(d) Given all of the issues facing Angela and Blake, they have not been able to open the shop for the past two weeks which has severely affected their income, and Angela was so distracted by the relationship breaking down that she has forgotten to pay the rent for the last three months.

Time allowed: 60 mins

Answer Plan

8-34 This question raises four main issues:

- Is there a valid lease?
- Is the lease enforceable?
- Does the Retail Shop Leases Act 1994 (Qld) (RSLA) apply?:
  - ◆ clause to remove RSLA valid?
  - ◆ application by looking at RSLA, Retail Shop Leases Regulation 2006 (RSLR), schedules, and number of shops;
  - ◆ considering each clause's validity.
- What is the 'issue'?
- Law and application (the clauses' meaning and the law applying to each clause).
- Consequence/conclusion for each clause (eg, can the lease be assigned?).
- Advise the client (conclusion).

Answer

Lease

8-35 The lease appears to be valid, as it does provide exclusive possession and is for a fixed term. It is for longer than three years and thus needs to be written, which it is, and therefore it satisfies the writing requirements of ss 10 and 11 of the Property Law Act 1974 (Qld) (PLA). The lease is not registered (s 181 of the Land Title Act 1994 (Qld) (LTA)) therefore, it is not enforceable at law but is still a valid lease: s 71 LTA. However, it is likely to be enforceable in equity as it fulfils the requirements to be final and binding: *Masters v Cameron* (1954) 91 CLR 353.

Retail Shop Leases Act 1994 (Qld) (RSLA)

8-36 Does the RSLA apply? The centre falls within the s 8 RSLA definition of a 'retail shopping centre' as it comprises at least five retail shops whose businesses are listed in the Schedule of the RSLR. The leases concerning the Mexican restaurant, café, gym and fitness centre, newsagent and masseuse are subject to the RSLA as they are used wholly or predominantly for the carrying on of retail business: Sch s 9(1) RSLR. However, the accountant and architect fall outside the RSLA as they provide services and are not retail businesses: Sch s 9(2) RSLR. The disclosure requirements seem to have been met (s 22 RSLA), but regardless it would be too late for the tenants to terminate as more than six months have passed.

Repairs

8-37 In the absence of any express covenant, both common law and s 105(1)(b) PLA would require Angela and Blake to keep the leased premises in 'good and tenantable repair'. However, the extent of this implied obligation is contentious as to whether they would be responsible for structural repairs and/or inherent defects.

Structural repair

8-38 Latham CJ in *Graham v Market Hotels* Ltd [1943] HCA 8 has noted the repair/renewal distinction is really a question of degree, as all repairs involve renewal to some extent. The duty to repair is confined to 'defective (subsidiary) parts' and does not extend to 'substantially the whole' of the leased premises: *Lurcott v Wakeley and Wheeler* [1911] 1 KB 905.

The *Lurcott* case is against Angela and Blake as the tenant in that case was responsible for the entire cost of replacing the front wall of a house. Here more facts are needed to distinguish this case, for example the age, size and condition of the shop at the commencement of the lease, and the cost of repairs.

Inherent defect

8-39 The status of the doctrine of inherent defect remains uncertain pending despite Latham CJ and Williams J's support in *Graham v Market Hotels* where Williams J gave inherent defect a slightly wider definition: '[defect] of such a kind that by its own inherent nature it will in course of time fall into a particular condition'. The issues of inherent defect and structural repairs may be interrelated in that both share the same basic view: the tenant is not obliged to 'make a new and different thing' (*Lister v Lane and Nesham* (1893 2 QB 212)) or give back to the landlord 'a wholly different thing': *Ravenseft v Davstone* (1980) 1 QB 12.

It could be said the difference between these two English cases is also one of degree. In other words the 'no obligation to repair any inherent defect' (*Lister* case) compared with 'no obligation to repair certain inherent defects where the repair of those defects would amount to structural repairs' (*Ravenseft* case).

Assuming that the doctrine is applicable in Angela and Blake's favour, they need to show that the leaks have been caused by an inherent defect, here the builder's non-compliance with the relevant standards and procedures by failing to properly seal the join, rather than by normal degenerative processes such as old age, which would make them liable rather than the landlord.

Derogation from grant — new shop

8-40 Mr Wade may have breached the common law implied covenants of quiet enjoyment and non-derogation from grant (that one cannot detract from what one originally granted), if he has failed to stop the shop by enforcing cl 2 of the agreement, regarding nuisance.

Aussie Traveller Pty Ltd v Marklea Pty Ltd [1988] 1 Qd R1 established that a landlord may be liable for others' conduct if he or she is 'in a position to correct or terminate such conduct', in addition to being liable where the landlord has given authorisation for or actively participated in the breach.

The landlord in *Aussie Traveller v Marklea* was held liable because of his awareness of the nuisance problems and his failure to control such problems by enforcing a nuisance clause in the lease similar to that here. The RSLA seems to support this approach, for example s 43(1)(c) RSLA says the landlord can be liable if he or she does not 'take all reasonable steps to prevent or stop significant interruption within the lessor's control'.

McPherson J seemed to suggest a general test that incorporates both implied covenants when he endorsed the trial judge's finding that 'substantial interference' with tenant's use of the leased premises rendered the leased premises 'substantially less fit' for the purposes of the lease. Indeed, the same conduct may, but doesn't necessarily, breach both covenants. Thus the two implied covenants remain separate but a breach of either would suffice, and a breach of both would strengthen the tenants' case.

The consequences if Mr Wade is found to have breached either or both of the covenants would be that Angela and Blake could get a court order requiring Mr Wade to remove the new tenant, or they could bring a claim for damages against Mr Wade if they could justify and quantify their losses.

Assignment to Danny

8-41 The current Australian approach seems to be that, in order to avoid s 121(1)(a)(i) PLA the statutory restriction that a landlord's consent cannot be unreasonably withheld the assignment clause needs to omit the word 'consent' completely and only set out the relevant objectively determinable and justifiable requirements. In the United Kingdom, cases such as *Moat v Martin* [1950] 1 KB 175 indicate that, despite reference to 'consent', a clause can still avoid the statutory proviso if it is clearly more favourable to the tenant (eg, there is no scope for a landlord's real or effective consent) and therefore the agreement would not need the statutory protection. The relevant wording in that case is 'such consent will not be withheld in the case of a respectable & responsible person'.

Here, cl 3(a) is similar to the clauses in both cases and is thus unlikely to avoid the s 121 PLA proviso. It follows that Mr Wade can still refuse consent even if Danny satisfies the criteria in cl 3, provided that it is reasonable for him to refuse consent. The issue then is whether he has unreasonably withheld his consent.

Assuming that the s 121 PLA proviso applies, the question is whether Angela and Blake can discharge their onus of showing that the refusal is unreasonable.

Lack of experience

8-42 This appears to be no reasonable basis for refusal as it concerns the proposed assignee's personality: *Houlder Brothers & Co Ltd v Gibbs* [1925] Ch 575 at 587. It is also one of the express requirements in clause 3(a) but there is no information about why Danny would not meet the requirements (*Tamsco Ltd v Franklins Ltd* [2001] NSWSC 1205), even if it was a valid consideration.

Administrative costs

8-43 This may be an unreasonable basis for refusal if it is regarded as 'independent of the lease relationship or entirely person to the lessor' (*Houlder Bros*), or a 'collateral purpose' (*Pimms Ltd v Tallow Chandlers Co* [1964] 2 QB 547), which is 'wholly unconnected with the terms of the lease': *JA McBeath Nominees Pty Ltd v Jenkins Development Corp Pty Ltd* (1992) 2 Qld Reports 121.

Section 121(1)(a)(i) PLA states that the proviso against unreasonable refusal 'does not preclude the right of the lessor to require payment of a reasonable sum in respect of any legal or other expenses incurred in connection with the ... consent'. However, this is a retail shop lease, and it is necessary to consider the RSLA regarding landlord's costs.

If just one of Mr Wade's reasons for refusal is reasonable, then Angela and Blake may have difficulty proving that such refusal is unreasonable.

If the refusal is reasonable and if Angela and Blake proceed with assignment of the lease regardless, then Mr Wade may be entitled to damages for breach and forfeiture. On the other hand, Angela and Blake may successfully obtain a court declaration that the refusal is unreasonable. This latter option is the safest.

Unable to pay the rent

8-44   The mutual breaches by Angela and Blake (not paying rent) and Mr Wade (repairs and derogation) may result in equitable set-off.

Rent in arrears can be set off under the common law but unliquidated sums, such as loss of business income, can only be set off in equity: *Knockholt Pty Ltd v Graff* [1975] Qd R 88; *British Anzani (Felixstowe) Ltd v International Marine Management (UK) Ltd* [1980] QB 137. In any event, Angela and Blake would need to give prior notice before claiming set-off as it cannot be done retrospectively.

Mr Wade has two alternatives: either keep the lease on foot and claim damages for breach against Angela and Blake (subject to set-off) or forfeit the lease.

The former option seems undesirable as Mr Wade may end up paying Angela and Blake rather than being paid by them (depending on the existence and assessment of the liability for compensation under s 43 RSLA). However, the latter option may not be any better unless Mr Wade can successfully forfeit the lease and claim future rent against Angela and Blake. There is no express right to forfeit in the agreement and one cannot exclude the requirements in s 124 PLA.

Mr Wade cannot exercise his right of forfeiture unless and until Angela and Blake fail to remedy the breach within a reasonable time after being served the default notice: s 124(1) PLA. Nor can Mr Wade forfeit if Angela and Blake are able to obtain relief against forfeiture under s 124(2) PLA. The court is likely to grant relief if Angela and Blake are able to pay the outstanding rent and they must be given the opportunity to do so. Angela and Blake may even seek to set off against such outstanding rent in the same court proceedings (plus compensation under s 43 RSLA) to enable Angela to remedy her breach of the rent clause, for example pay $3,000 after set-off.

If Mr Wade is able to forfeit the lease, then Angela and Blake can still claim contractual damages against him for the breach of implied covenant of quiet enjoyment and/or non-derogation from grant.

However, the question must be addressed whether Mr Wade can offset or reduce liability by claiming future rent against Angela and Blake.

If clause 1 concerning the rent as a fundamental clause is effective as a Shevill's clause, then it may entitle Mr Wade to recover future rent: *Shevill v The Builders Licensing Board* (1982) 149 CLR 620. The issue is whether merely stating that the clause is an essential or fundamental term would suffice as a Shevill's clause, or whether there needs to be a further statement that breach of such term would entitle the lessor to claim future rent or losses on termination of the lease.

If this were not an option, Mr Wade would have a heavy onus in proving repudiation or fundamental breach by Angela and Blake; *Progressive Mailing House Pty Ltd v Tabali Pty Ltd* (1985) 157 CLR 17; *Laurinda Pty Ltd v Capalaba Park Shopping Centre Pty Ltd* (1989) 166 CLR 623. He would need to show that Angela and Blake intend to 'no longer to be bound by the contract' or 'to fulfil the contract only in a manner substantially inconsistent with obligations & not in any other way'.

Progressive Mailing House v Tabali is quite a serious case involving multiple and prolonged breaches by the tenant, where it was held absolute repudiation could be demonstrated by a failure to pay rent coupled with abandonment of the premises. It seems unlikely that Angela and Blake's closure for two weeks and current inclination against re-opening could be stretched to abandonment.

 ## Examiner's Comments

8-45 This is a good effort for a large, complex question. While all the main issues are discussed, the student has failed to close each topic properly by failing to reach a conclusion on many of the issues. While much of it is grey, the arguments should be drawn to some kind of conclusion in order to be able to do as the question asks: advise the client. There is good breadth in the answer, and good reference to precedents from other jurisdictions, and the arguments appear well-researched. It is let down by its failure to summarise and conclude the arguments.

 ## Keep in Mind

8-46 Students should keep in mind the following:

- Often when the issues or arguments are complex, or there are multiple judgments on either side of an issue, students fail to reach a conclusion on a point. They will review both sides of the argument and then leave it hanging, without drawing it together at the end. If the question requires advising a client, some kind of determination must be drawn at the end, in order to inform a client of their chances of success. At the least the student should be able to say whether the facts are more analogous to one precedent or another, and draw a conclusion as to which side the judgment is likely to go, if there is no definitive answer. Strong arguments become weak without some closure.

 # Question 6

8-47 Now that common law principles of contract are applicable to commercial leases, what are the ramifications for the development of the doctrine of 'lease repudiation'?

Time allowed: 45 mins

 # Answer Plan

8-48 This is an essay-style question, and it requires some thought as to how it should be approached. The area of 'lease repudiation' is one of the most complicated recent developments in property law.

Much has been written by academic authors about the issues and questions raised by the application of contractual principles to the law of leases. Note that the question begins with a given proposition: 'that common law principles of contract are applicable to commercial leases'. The question does not require an explanation of how this change in judicial approach came about. It does not require a detailed survey of the lineages of the development so far. The question asks the student to consider what implications the development (so far) suggests. As such, it is appropriate to identify some of the more complex and unanswered issues concerning lease repudiation and focus upon these.

Consider the general commercial flavour of the relationship between parties to non-residential leases, and address the following specific issues:

- the (contractual) liability of the lessee-assignor;
- the (contractual) liability of the lessor-assignor;
- damages for forfeiture;
- the doctrine of implied surrender;
- practical considerations — drafting damages clauses.

 # Answer

8-49 In recent times, the law of leases has been the subject of significant modification via the introduction of contractual principles. In a string of decisions, commencing with *Shevill v Builders' Licensing Board* (1982) 149 CLR 620 and culminating in *Progressive Mailing House Pty Ltd v Tabali Pty Ltd* (1985) 157 CLR 17, the High Court of Australia has given recognition to the commercial aspect of leases by permitting plaintiffs contractual damages attendant upon rescission for repudiation — an approach previously regarded as inapplicable to the relationship of lessor and lessee.

While it seems appropriate, in the commercial context at least, to accept the business orientation of the leasehold relationship, there remain some difficulties in the precise articulation of the positive elements of contract law within the doctrines of leases. This essay will focus upon some of these difficulties, namely the residual (contractual) liability of the lessee-assignor, the (contractual) liability of the lessor–assignor, the issue of damages for forfeiture and the implications for the doctrine of implied surrender. It will be seen that there are inconsistencies and inequities, highlighted by these examples, which are yet to be resolved by the courts.

8-50 The application of contractual principles to leases may affect the positions of the parties after an assignment of a lease occurs. An assignment of a lease is a transfer of the whole of the tenant's interest in the lease (the whole of the unexpired term of the lease). Under the principles established by the High Court (in *Shevill* and *Tabali)*, a lessee–assignor will remain contractually bound to the lessor for the remainder of the term, notwithstanding that the lease has been assigned.

The contractual relationship can be seen as separate from the estate assigned, and thus the assignment of the leasehold estate to an assignee will not end the contractual obligations of the lessee-assignor to the lessor. In a sense, the lessee-assignor becomes his or her landlord's guarantee that the assignee will perform all covenants and other obligations imposed by the lease. This result may appear to be very attractive for lessors, but one must question whether this is an appropriate or desirable consequence of the courts' new approach to leases. Of course, it would always be possible to draft the head lease or contract with a term which provides for the termination of the contractual relationship between lessor and lessee upon an assignment of the leasehold by the lessee to a third party. However, it would appear that there is now a strong incentive for landlords to insist that no such term be incorporated into contracts for leases and that, to the contrary, a term specifically maintaining a lessee's obligations be incorporated. As the law currently stands, it would appear that even without such a clause the lessee-assignor remains contractually liable to his or her lessor in the post-assignment phase.

8-51 Does the converse apply? Where the lessor assigns his or her (reversionary) interest, may the lessee nonetheless maintain an action in contract against the original landlord? In New South Wales, s 118 of the Conveyancing Act 1919 appears to preclude this possibility. If this is the case, and as yet there has been no judicial opinion on the question, it seems to be unfair that the introduction of contractual principles to the law of leases should operate for the benefit of lessors only. If the law, as it stands, leaves the lessee-assignor as the guarantor of his or her assignee, then why should it not equally impose a similar responsibility upon the lessor reversion assignor in respect of his or her original tenant?

8-52 The previous law, for centuries, was that damages were not payable to a landlord who forfeited a lease; only liabilities arising before the forfeiture could be claimed as damages by a forfeiting landlord:

Buchanan v Byrnes (1906) 3 CLR 704. The doctrinal basis of this rule was that forfeiture, being a proprietary remedy, operated so as to terminate the leasehold estate and (with it) all the obligations of the tenant. As a matter of pragmatic commercial reality it was understood that the forfeiting landlord should take the responsibility for his or her decision.

After *Shevill* and *Tabali* all that has changed. Beyond the traditional landlords' remedy of forfeiture, damages are now available for the landlord's reliance on, and the court's application of, the contractual doctrine of rescission for repudiation. However, it should be noted that the new principles of lease repudiation do not in every case give rise to a claim for damages. The new position is that a landlord who has forfeited may claim damages where the forfeiture is for conduct amounting to a repudiation of the lease. The availability of damages is thus dependent upon the contractual rights attendant upon the landlord's conduct in response to the tenant's default. It should also be noted that the contractual doctrine of mitigation of damages applies to lease repudiation, and thus a landlord who claims damages must be able to show that he or she has attempted to find another tenant. All the same, the availability of damages in the forfeiture context is a momentous enlargement of landlords' remedies.

8-53 The lease repudiation doctrine may also signify the effective abolition of the doctrine of implied surrender. The conventional circumstances where a surrender of a lease by a tenant was implied was where a landlord re-entered abandoned premises (and/or re-let the premises). In such circumstances, the landlord may have been deemed to have accepted the residue of the tenant's term. The surrender ('implied' from the conduct of the landlord) operates to terminate the leasehold estate and effectively precludes the landlord from claiming damages: *Buchanan v Byrnes*.

Under the new rules, such conduct (by a landlord) can now be characterised as an election to terminate the lease contract by rescinding the lease in response to the tenant's abandonment or repudiation. As such, the landlord's rescission would give rise to a claim in damages. We are left with a situation whereby the same set of facts (abandonment and re-entry) may give rise to two legal resolutions, either implied surrender (which does not give rise to a claim in damages), or lease repudiation (which does). In *Wood Factory Pty Ltd v Kiritos Pty Ltd* (1985) 2 NSWLR 105, McHugh and Priestley JJA favoured the availability of damages, while Samuels JA did not. Unless and until there is a definitive statement by the courts in relation to the status of implied surrender, then this area of the law remains dangerously uncertain.

8-54 Aside from the academic difficulties associated with the collision of proprietary and contractual doctrines, there are practical matters which need to be considered. If it is accepted that the doctrine of contractual repudiation is now generally applicable to leases, lessors will naturally wish to protect and enhance their opportunities to claim damages. How should leases be drafted so as to provide express rights to damages in circumstances (such as surrender and forfeiture) where hitherto damages would not have been available? In particular, may a clause be drafted so as to stipulate that the rent covenant is to be deemed 'essential' in the sense that a breach is to be regarded as repudiation which entitles the lessor to forfeit *and* claim damages? Despite the fact that Gibbs CJ in *Shevill* (at 796) held that such a practice would be 'inequitable', this type of clause is now quite common in many modern commercial leases.

To a certain extent, the law of leases has now come full circle. The lease began, in the dying days of feudalism, as a contract. Eventually, it became recognised as an interest in land, and proprietary rather than contractual principles governed its development. In more recent times, the law of leases has been reintroduced to contractual principles, and recognition has been given to the commercial aspect of leases. In the commercial context, it has been held to be legitimate to acknowledge the mercantile nature of the leasehold relationship. However, there continues to be some problems in the fair application of contract law to the doctrines of leases. This essay has attempted to demonstrate that there are still inconsistencies and inequities, exemplified above, which require further consideration by our lawmakers.

Examiner's Comments

8-55 The answer makes a laudable attempt to identify and discuss some of the most important consequences of the recent developments in the law of leases concerning the importation of contract law principles. It adopts an analytical approach which is highly appropriate to an essay-style question such as this. No effort is wasted in surveying the details of *Shevill, Tabali* or the numerous other cases which are part of the lineage of recent developments. All the same, some reference to *Marshall v Snowy River Shire Council* (1995) NSW Conv R 155-719, as probably the most contemporary expression of the emergence of the lease repudiation doctrine, may have been apt.

The case is especially pertinent to the question as to whether a landlord may choose repudiation as an alternative to forfeiture (and thus avoid the formalities required by statute in respect of forfeiture). On the whole, the answer is well structured, critical, and displays a firm command of the intricacies of the law. The historical reference in the conclusion is helpful, but may have been introduced at an earlier stage.

More specifically, in respect of the rights of tenants to sue their original landlords (in New South Wales, apparently precluded by s 118 of the Conveyancing Act 1919), note that similar legislation exists in other states: s 118 Property Law Act 1974 (Qld); s 11 Conveyancing and Law of Property Act 1884 (Tas); s 142 Property Law Act 1958 (Vic); s 78 Property Law Act 1969 (WA). These legislative provisions have a common forebear in the Grantees of Reversions Act 1540 which evidently still applies in South Australia.

Further references

- Cases:
  - ◆ *Highways Properties Ltd v Kelly, Douglas & Co Ltd* (1971) 17 DLR (3d) 710;
  - ◆ *J & C Reid Pty Ltd v Abau Holdings Ltd* [1988] NSW Conv R 55-416;
  - ◆ *Laurinda Pty Ltd v Capalaba Park Shopping Centre Pty Ltd* (1989) 166 CLR 625;
  - ◆ *National Carriers Ltd v Panalpina (Northern) Ltd* [1981] AC 675;
  - ◆ *Ripka Pty Ltd v Maggiore Bakeries Pty Ltd* [1984] VR 629.
- Articles:
  - ◆ P Butt, 'The Contractualisation of Leases: A Further Step?' (1996) *ALJ* 97;
  - ◆ C Chew, 'Leases Repudiated: The Application of the Contractual Doctrine of Repudiation to Real Property Leases' (1990) 20 *UWALawRw Western Australia LR* 86;
  - ◆ W Duncan, 'Of Straws and Camels' Backs Fundamental Breach of Lease' (1986) 2 *QITLJ* 31;
  - ◆ J Effron, 'The Contractualisation of the Law of Leasehold: Pitfalls and Opportunities' (1988) *Monash ULawRw* 3;
  - ◆ G Teh, 'Rescission: A Landlord's Alternative to Forfeiture?' (1994) 68 *Law Inst J* 512.

Keep in Mind

8-56 Students should keep in mind the following:

- The question commences with a given premise: 'that common law principles of contract are applicable to commercial leases'. Do not recapitulate the premise, or narrate the history of the development of the law. Accept the given and focus on the question.
- Do not forget the formalities associated with the assignment of leasehold interests. Under old system title, an assignment must be by deed to be effective at law. Under the Torrens system, and if the lease is registered, a transfer of the lease in the approved form should be executed and registered. Where a lease in respect of Torrens land is not itself registered, then an assignment of the lease must be by deed: see P Tebbutt, 'Surrenders and Assignments of Leases — Is a Deed Necessary?' (1961) *ALJ* 353.
- Even though ultimately predicated in contract, the ability of landlords (and reversion assignees) to enforce covenants against tenant–assignors is not dependent upon the courts' new contract-based approach.

Chapter 9

Servitudes: Easements and Restrictive Covenants

Key Issues

9-1 Easements and restrictive covenants are, broadly, rights that govern how people may use the land of another, by some private agreement, for a planning purpose.

Easements run with the land and are not personal to the owners. At law, the burden of restrictive covenants did not run with the land. It was only the intervention of equity (*Tulk v Moxhay* (1848) 2 Ph 774; 41 ER 1143) in the mid-nineteenth century that brought that about.

There are similarities between easements and restrictive covenants: they both require a dominant and servient tenement, and they must both 'touch and concern' the land to pass with the land. However, they are conceptually different: a restrictive covenant must be negative in substance, while an easement may be positive or negative; restrictive covenants have their source in equity (if they are to run with the land). A further difference is that easements could be acquired by prescription under old system land, while restrictive covenants cannot; and easements are recognised both at law and equity.

Easements

9-2 Before attempting the questions on easements in this chapter, students should be familiar with the following:

✓ nature of easements: *Re Ellenborough Park* [1956] Ch 131;

✓ method of creation of easements:

  - *British Railways Board v Glass* [1965] 1 Ch 538;
  - *City Developments Pty Ltd v Registrar General of Northern Territory* (2000) 135 NTR;
  - *Clos Farming Estates Pty Ltd v Easton* [2001] NSWSC 525;
  - *Codelfa Construction Pty Ltd v State Rail Authority (NSW)* (1982) 149 CLR 337;

- *Delohery v Permanent Trustees Co (New South Wales)* (1904) 1 CLR 283;

- *Elliot v Renner* [1923] St R Qd 172;

- *Gallagher v Rainbow* [1993-1994] 179 CLR 624;

- *Hoy v Allerton* (2002) Q Conv R 54-559;

- *Jelbert v Davis* [1968] 1 WLR 589;

- *London Corp v Riggs* [1880] 13 Ch D 798;

- *Mercantile General Life Reassurance Co (Aust) Ltd v Permanent Trustee Australia Ltd* (1988) 4 BPR 9534;

- *Re Ellenborough Park* [1956] Ch 131;

- *Weigall v Toman* [2006] QSC 349;

- *Westfield Management Ltd v Perpetual Trustee Company Ltd* [2007] 233 CLR 528;

- *Wheeldon v Burrows* [1879] 12 Ch D 31;

- *White v Grand Hotel Eastbourne Ltd* [1913] 1 Ch 113;

✓ extinguishment of easements:

- *Australian Hi-Fi Publications Pty Ltd v Gehl* [1979] 2 NSWLR 618;

- *Dobbie v Davidson* (1991) 23 NSWLR 625;

- *Pieper v Edwards* [1982] 1 NSWLR 336;

- *Post Investments Pty Ltd v Wilson* (1990) 26 NSWLR 598;

- *Treweeke v 36 Wolseley Road Pty Ltd* (1973) 128 CLR 274;

- section 89 of the Conveyancing Act 1919 (NSW);

- sections 88(1) and 88B of the Conveyancing Act 1919 (NSW);

- section 42(1)(a1) of the Real Property Act 1900 (NSW).

Restrictive covenants

9-3 Before attempting the questions on restrictive covenants students should be aware of the following matters:

- burden and benefit of covenants:
  - ◆ *Austeberry v Corporation of Oldham* (1885) 29 Ch D 750;
  - ◆ *Bourseguin v Stannard Bros Holdings Pty Ltd* [1994] 1 QD R 231;
  - ◆ *Norton v Kilduff* (1974) Qd R 47;
  - ◆ *Re Ballard's Conveyance* [1937] Ch 473;
  - ◆ *Roger v Hosegood* [1900] 2 Ch 388;
  - ◆ *Ryan v Brain* (1994) 1 Qd R 681;
  - ◆ *Tulk v Moxhay* (1848) 2 Ph 774; 41 ER 1143;
  - ◆ *Tweddle v Atkinson* [1861] EWHC QB J57,

- schemes of development:
  - ♦ *Elliston v Reacher* [1908] 2 Ch 374;
  - ♦ *Re Lows and the Conveyancing Act* [1971] 1 NSWLR 164,
- negativity of covenants:
  - ♦ *Frater v Finlay* (1968) 91 WN (NSW) 730;
  - ♦ *Haywood v Brunswick Permanent Benefit Building Society* (1881) 8 QBD 403.

Question 1

9-4   Monza and Domus are two adjoining allotments under common law title situated in New South Wales. There is a narrow fenced right of way over Domus for the benefit of Monza, giving the latter access to a public road. A residential dwelling is erected on Domus. The improvements on Monza consist of a dwelling and large shed. The original owner of Monza (with the consent of the local council), used the shed for a motor vehicle repair business at weekends. During the week, the right of way was used mainly for residential access, but at weekends it was also used by the customers of the mechanical repair business. This was the use carried out on Monza by the original owner when the right of way came into existence.

The ownership of Monza and Domus has changed a number of times since the easement came into existence. The current owner of Monza now seeks the consent of the local council to demolish the improvements on Monza and erect a large commercial building. The building is to be a new and used motor vehicle showroom, and includes a facility for the service and repair of motor vehicles. Access to the site is planned via the existing right of way.

The owner of Domus objects to the plans for Monza, particularly on the basis that the new development will generate increased traffic. What advice would you give?

Time allowed: 1 hour

Answer Plan

9-5   This question is concerned with the extent of the rights conferred by an easement and the principles applicable in defining those rights. A definition of the rights will require an examination of the way the easement was created. Was it created expressly, impliedly or by prescription? Different principles emerge regarding the extent of the rights of an easement depending upon its method of creation. There may be broader scope for enlargement of rights in an easement expressly created (depending on the construction given to the instrument creating the rights), than where an easement is created by implication (eg by necessity). There will also be a difference between the extent of rights for an easement created by prescription, compared with an expressly created easement (or even one created by implication). Accordingly, this question should be approached on the following basis:

- The nature of easements (a brief introduction).
- Expressly created easements:
  - ◆ method of creation;
  - ◆ principles governing extent of rights;
  - ◆ application of principles,
- Implicitly created easements:
  - ◆ method of creation;
  - ◆ principles governing extent of rights;
  - ◆ application of principles,
- Prescriptive easements:
  - ◆ method of creation;
  - ◆ principles governing extent of rights;
  - ◆ application of principles.

 # Answer

9-6 *Halsbury's Laws of England*, 3rd ed, vol 12, p 519 defines an easement as:

> ... a right annexed to land to utilise other land of different ownership in a particular manner (not involving the taking of any part of the natural produce of that land or any part of its soil) or to prevent the owner of the land from utilising his land in a particular manner.

Nature of easements

9-7 There are four characteristics essential to an easement (*Re Ellenborough Park* [1956] Ch 131) that have received judicial approval:

- There must be a dominant and servient tenement. The benefit of an easement is attached (appurtenant) to land referred to as the 'dominant tenement'. The land benefiting from the right and burdened with the right must be clearly identified.
- An easement must accommodate the dominant tenement: a benefit must be conferred on the dominant tenement as such. The benefit must relate to the user of the dominant tenement, contributing to its full enjoyment. There must be sufficient proximity between the two tenements to enable a practical benefit to be conferred on the dominant tenement:

  > ... it is not essential that the dominant and servient tenement be contiguous, and an easement in the nature of a right of way may sufficiently 'touch and concern' or 'accommodate' the dominant tenement if, although it does not abut on the servient tenement, it is sufficiently close to it for the owner of the dominant tenement, if he can acquire permission to pass over any intervening land, to use the servient tenement as a means of access to, or egress from, the dominant tenement. (*Dewhirst v Edwards* [1983] 1 NSWLR 34)

- The ownership of the dominant and servient tenement must not exist in the one person. An easement is:

  ... some right which a person has over land which is not his own, but if the land is his own, if he has an interest in it, then his right is not an easement. You cannot have an easement over your own land. (*Metropolitan Railway Co v Fowler* [1892] 1 QB 165 at 171)

  There is an exception made to this characteristic by s 88B of the Conveyancing Act 1919 (NSW). This section allows common ownership of dominant and servient tenements in respect of easements created under this section. Practicably, a tenant can also be granted an equitable easement to land under lease, while the owner owns both parcels of land.
- An easement must be capable of forming the subject matter of a grant. This requires that the rights granted fall within the general nature of rights capable of creation as easements. The rights created require precise definition. They cannot be too vague or uncertain if they are to constitute an easement. They also require a grantor capable of making the grant of easement and a grantee capable of receiving that grant. The issue of an easement being capable of forming the subject matter of a grant was addressed in *Re Ellenborough Park* [1956] Ch 131. It was argued that the grant for the dominant tenements of the right to full enjoyment to the use the servient tenement as a park was too wide and vague. The rights granted, it was argued, were of mere recreation and amusement, lacking utility. The court held the rights were properly defined and understood.

  In *Mercantile General Life Reassurance Co (Aust) Ltd v Permanent Trustee Australia Ltd* (1988) 4 BPR 9534 at 9537–8, Powell J questioned the view commonly accepted that the right of exclusive or unrestricted use of land cannot constitute an easement being a grant of property in the servient tenement, citing *Bursell Enterprises Pty Ltd v Berger Bros Trading Co Pty Ltd* (1971) 124 CLR 73 and *Wright v McAdam* [1949] 2 KB 744. However, the point remains that if the rights granted are too vague, they will not be ascertainable, and if too wide, they may go further than a grant of easement to an actual grant of property in the servient tenement.

Creation of easements

9-8 An easement may be created by express grant or reservation. At common law, such a grant is made by deed: s 23B(1) Conveyancing Act 1919 (NSW). Equity will, of course, recognise an agreement in writing (or part performance) to create an easement: *Talga Investments Pty Ltd v Tweed Canal Estates Pty Ltd* (1974) 1 BPR 9675 at 9681. For land under the Real Property Act 1900 (NSW), an easement may be created by registration of a transfer and grant of easement; Also, after 1964, by application of s 88B of the Conveyancing Act 1919 (NSW) for both common law and Torrens title.

Where an easement is expressly created or reserved, the extent and mode of the easement is a matter of constructing the instrument of creation:

> ... it is legitimate to have regard to the circumstances existing at the time of its execution for the purpose of determining what was the intention of the parties. In particular, when one is concerned with a right of way, one must "consider (1) the locus in quo over which the way is granted, (2) the nature of the terminus ad quem; and (3) the purpose for which the way is to be used". (*Mercantile General Life Reassurance Co (Aust) Ltd v Permanent Trustee Australia Ltd* (1988) 4 BPR 9534 at 9539 per Powell J)

It seems that the exception or reservation distinction is important, particularly when it comes to ambiguity of expression. In an exception, any ambiguity is construed against the grantor. On the other hand, in a reservation, any ambiguity is construed against the conveyee up to the time of the passing of s 45A of the Conveyancing Act 1919 (NSW). Since the passing of that section, the ambiguity is construed against the grantor (in the case of reservation): *Mercantile General Life Reassurance Co (Aust) Ltd v Permanent Trustee Australia Ltd* per Powell J (at 9539).

In *White v Grant Hotel Eastbourne Ltd* [1913] 1 Ch 113, the use of the dominant tenement changed from a private dwelling house to a hotel. The grant was in general terms 'at all times and for all purposes'. Cozens-Hardy MR stated (at 116):

> ... unless there is some limitation to be found in the grant, in the nature of the width of the road or something of that kind, full effect must be given to the grant, and we cannot consider the subsequent user as in any way sufficient to cut down the generality of the grant.

However, a general grant 'at all times and for all purposes' might raise the issue of excessive user. In this regard, a general grant is subject to the proposition:

> ... that no one of those entitled to the right of way must use it to an extent which is beyond anything which was contemplated at the time of the grant. (*Jelbert v Davis* [1968] 1 WLR 589 at 595 per Lord Denning MR)

While a general grant might open up a wide use, it does not invite excessive user. What constitutes excessive user will go to the intention of the parties at the time of grant. In that regard, the court held in *Todrick v Western National Omnibus Co* [1934] Ch 190, that the quality of user was limited by the physical nature of the right of way. The right of way was seven feet, nine inches wide and clearly was not intended for omnibuses seven feet, six inches wide.

In *Jelbert v Davis* [1968] 1 WLR 589, the general grant of right of way was made to the dominant tenement when it was used for agriculture purposes. The contemplated use was a camping area of 200 sites with the potential number of people making use of the right of way being 600. The court held the proposed use excessive and far beyond that contemplated by the parties at the time of grant.

Referring to the question, the first matter to consider is whether the easement has been made by grant or reservation and the terms of the easement. Whether the owner of Domus could object to the usage would depend on what construction could be given to the instrument of creation.

The facts indicate that the right of way is narrow. It was used originally for residential use five days a week, and commercial use two days a week. It is now proposed to use it for commercial use. *White v Grant Hotel Eastbourne Ltd* tells us that full effect must be given to a general grant unless something like the width of the path limits the grant. Further, in *Jelbert v Davis,* Lord Denning MR indicated that even with a general grant, the right of way cannot be used beyond anything contemplated by the parties at the time of the grant. Both these elements of (1) physical inhibition of the right of way and (2) intention beyond original contemplation seem to be present in the facts before us. On this basis, it would seem the owner of Domus would have solid grounds for objection. However, it would depend on the construction of the grant. It might well be the terms of the grant are so unambiguous that any limitation arising from the physical nature of the easement or the use of the dominant tenant at the date of the creation of the easement will have no effect.

Easements, by implication, arise when one of two parcels of land with unity of ownership and possession is disposed. Rights may be implied in favour of the purchase for enjoyment of the parcel disposed. Rights may also be excepted or reserved, by way of implication, by the vendor, for the enjoyment of the parcel retained. The rights implied for the vendor are limited to easements of necessity and those of common intention (intended by both parties). The rights implied for the purchaser include easements of necessity and common intention. They also include all those easements necessary to enable the land transferred to be enjoyed and used at the time of conveyance that are continuous and apparent: *Wheeldon v Burrows* [1879] 12 Ch D 31. *Wheeldon v Burrows* limited the nature and use of easements to that exercised immediately before severance. Where an easement arises by necessity, the extent of use is limited by the necessity which led to its creation: *London Corp v Riggs* [1880] 13 Ch D 798.

Applying these principles to the question in hand it is not clear whether the two allotments were in common ownership and possession for the easement to rise by implication. On the basis the easement was created by implication, the intention of the parties at the time of creation will require consideration. Whether the proposed use was within contemplation seems unlikely. If the easement arose out of necessity, then *London Corp v Rigg* tells us that the necessity is limited to the purpose at the time the right arose. Again, it would seem the proposed use would be beyond the original necessity — arguably, at least on the basis of excessive user and on the basis of change of user. Any argument on the basis of continuous and apparent use based on the *Wheeldon v Burrows* principle would also seem to fail, if for no other reason than the narrowness of the right of way leading to excessive user.

Finally, an easement may be created by prescription, by virtue of application of *Delohery v Permanent Trustees Co (NSW)* (1904) 1 CLR 283. This means that an easement will arise from use over a 20-year period. This use must be continuous, in the sense that it is of sufficient frequency to demonstrate an assertion of a right. There must be no force or secrecy in respect of the use. The use must be of right, as by a claim of entitlement to which the servient owner succumbs or acquiesces in, rather than permits: see *Delohery v Permanent Trustee Co of New South Wales* (1904) 1 CLR 283 at 300–1.

The difficulty that arises in matters relating to the extent of user in prescriptive easements is the continuity of the use and variance in user. In *Ballard v Dyson* (1808) 1 Taunt 279, it was held that a right to drive carts did not include a right to drive cattle. It was held the degree of inconvenience occasioned by the movement of the cattle was an argument against the probability of the grant including the more expansive use. In *Finch v Great Western Railway* (1879) 5 Ex D 254 at 258, it was stated:

> ... where there is a right of way proved by user, the extent of the right must be measured by the extent of the user.

In *Wimbledon and Putney Commons Conservators v Dixon* (1875) 1 Ch D 362, a user for farming purposes was held not to include the carting of building materials for a new house. The court would not imply a right of way for all purposes. In *British Railways Board v Glass* [1965] 1 Ch 538, the court held that a prescriptive right to use a level crossing for the purposes of a caravan site encompassed an increase of 30 caravans from a presumed user for six. The court said there was an increase in user, not excessive user; and that there had been no change in the character of the right of way.

In the question before us, and based on whether the right of way arose by prescription, the issue to be decided is whether the proposal of Monza amounts to a change in character of the usage of the right of way. If there is no change in the character of the usage then the next consideration is whether there is merely an increase in user or excessive user. In all probability, the proposal will bring about a change of character of the use. If it does not, it would be strongly argued that the traffic from the proposal would constitute excessive user.

 # Examiner's Comments

9-9 The answer began by describing the nature of easements. It then examined the way easements might be created, setting out the principles defining the extent of the rights of an easement. These rights varied according to the method of creation. Having defined the principles involved, they were then applied to the problem at hand.

The introduction describing the nature of easements and their essential characteristic was longer than necessary. It might even be argued that it might have been omitted in a question of this nature. It remained in the answer to be instructive. However, it is suggested that some introduction relating to the nature of easements generally is required before the topic of their creation can be dealt with.

The method of creation of easements was set out. The principles regarding the extent of the rights of easements emerging from their method of creation were summarised. Relevant case law analysing these matters was referred to. The application of the principles to the facts seemed to lack precision in places, but this is explainable in terms of the generality of the facts in the question.

Keep in Mind

9-10   Students should keep in mind the following:

- It is important to deal with the method of creation of an easement. In this question, the method of creation was not revealed. Accordingly, the answer requires that each method of creation is explained. Depending on the method of creation, the extent of rights of a particular easement will be affected. In defining the extent of the rights, it is essential to refer to the case law, although the case law is unclear at times. In an answer of this nature, the principles applicable must be discussed in terms of the facts of the question and connected with the facts.

Question 2

9-11   Greenland and Westland are two adjoining allotments registered under the Real Property Act 1900 (NSW). Behind both allotments is a large nature reserve. The rear boundary of Greenland forms a common boundary with the nature reserve. A right of way over Greenland for the benefit of Westland gives Westland access to the nature reserve. This right of way was for many years the only access Westland had to the nature reserve. However, for some time now, Westland has enjoyed access to the nature reserve by means of a public walkway which is a more convenient and direct route to the reserve than the right of way. The right of way across Greenland has now fallen into disuse. In places it has become overgrown with vegetation. A fence has been erected across the path of the right of way.

The current owner, Graham, has erected a number of large pens on Greenland where he keeps injured animals before releasing them into the wild when they are healed. These pens impinge on the path of the

> right of way making passage across it difficult. Maurice, the current proprietor of Westland, seeks your advice regarding his rights in respect of the right of way. Advise him.
>
> **Time allowed: 1 hour, 15 mins**

Answer Plan

9-12   This question raises the issue of extinguishment of easements. It calls for a discussion of the various methods an easement might be extinguished with particular focus on abandonment. It will also call for some discussion of s 89 of the Conveyancing Act 1919 (NSW) when dealing with extinguishment by court order. An answer would take the following outline:

- extinguishment of easements by operation of the law;
- extinguishment of easements by express release;
- extinguishment of easements by implied release:
  - ♦ abandonment;
  - ♦ principles emerging from *Treweeke v 36 Wolseley Road Pty Ltd* (1973) 128 CLR 274,
- extinguishment by court order:
  - ♦ section 89 of the Conveyancing Act 1919 (NSW) — terms of the section;
  - ♦ discussion of *Pieper v Edwards* [1982] 1 NSWLR 336;
  - ♦ discussion of key words in s 89 in light of case law,
- application of principles to the facts of the question.

Answer

9-13   This question raises the issue of extinguishment of easements. Easements may be expressly released by deed, for land under common law title, and by transfer, for land under the Torrens system. They will be extinguished by operation of the law where there is common ownership and possession of the dominant and servient tenement. Both common ownership and possession are required. In *Richardson v Graham* [1908] 1 KB 39, the Court of Appeal unanimously rejected a proposition that unity of ownership sufficed in itself for extinguishment of an easement for ancient light. However, this principle has been altered in New South Wales by the effect of s 47(7) of the Real Property Act 1900 (NSW) and s 88B of the Conveyancing Act 1919 (NSW).

Easements may also be extinguished by implied release, and in New South Wales, by s 89 of the Conveyancing Act 1919 (NSW). It is these two modes of extinguishment that are raised in the question.

Implied release

9-14   Implied release may be established by evidence of intention of owner of the dominant tenement to release the right. Abandonment establishes implied release, but what constitutes abandonment is not always clear. Mere non-user will not constitute abandonment, this principle being made clear by *Treweeke v 36 Wolseley Road Pty Ltd* (1973) 128 CLR 274 and by Alderson B in *Ward v Ward* (1852) 7 Ex 838; 155 ER 1189 at 1190:

> The prescription of abandonment cannot be made from the mere fact of non-user. There must be other circumstances in the case to raise that prescription.

However, it was the view of Walsh J (in dissent) in *Treweeke v 36 Wolseley Road* (at 288):

> ... that the longer it [non-user] continues the more readily will the conclusion be reached that the person entitled to benefit of the easement may be deemed to have abandoned it, unless of course, there is proof of facts or circumstances which provide a satisfactory explanation for the non-user and which negative any intention of abandonment.

In *Treweeke v 36 Wolseley Road*, the appellant was the registered proprietor of the servient tenement, subject to a right of way in favour of the dominant tenement of which the respondent was the registered proprietor. The right of way in contention was in a 'precipitous condition at places' which McTiernan J found was one reason for its non-use: at 284. It was also impassable due to a number of obstructions: a plantation of bamboo impeded passage; there were three fences affecting the right of way (one of iron and one of chainwire ran across it at intervals), a further fence at the boundary of the respondent's land ran across it, a fence the construction of which had been contributed to by the parties' respective predecessors in title; and there was thick vegetation growing in the right of way.

The respondent and its predecessors in title had not attempted to make the path suitable for pedestrian use, although some parts of the site had been made for pedestrian use by the appellant. There was evidence that persons from the respondent's land had used a nearby path and part of the right of way made passable by the appellant to obtain access to Double Bay. Finally, although the obstructions referred to previously were easily removed, there was also part of a swimming pool extending onto the right of way near the high watermark of Double Bay.

In his judgment, Mason J stated (at 302):

> Non-user may be referable to the absence of a need to use the right of way and the use of an alternative and more attractive means of access; then it may be thought that the non-user indicates not so much an intention to abandon the right of way as a preference for the alternative means of access so long as it remains available.

His Honour also stated (at 303):

> Acquiescence in, and failure to object to, the placing by the owner of the servient tenement of obstructions on the site of the right of way which are inconsistent with the exercise of rights by persons having the benefit of the right of way may lead to the inference that they intend to abandon it.

The court took the view that there had been no abandonment. So long as an alternative method of access to the bay existed, the respondent and its predecessors in title had not objected to the appellant's use of the right of way. Apart from the swimming pool (of permanent construction), the court found the obstructions of the right of way were not necessarily consistent with abandonment, and the respondent had objected on ascertaining the location of the swimming pool was in the path of the right of way.

Conveyancing Act 1919 (NSW)

9-15 Section 89 provides a statutory form of extinguishment of easements and restrictive covenants. The basis of the exercise of the court's power under the section is that the court deems the easement obsolete, or finds that continued existence of the easement impedes reasonable use without securing practical benefit to the persons entitled to the easement; that the persons entitled to the easement have agreed to the extinguishment of the easement, or by their acts or omissions indicated their abandonment of it. The court must also be satisfied that extinguishment or modification will not cause substantial injury to those entitled to the benefit of the easement.

The section has wider application to covenants rather than easements; however, factors relevant to the exercise of the court's discretion in *Pieper v Edwards* [1982] 1 NSWLR 336 were: (1) the conduct of the owners of both tenements; (2) the acts of prior registered proprietors (a factor which affected the High Court's decision in *Treweeke v 36 Wolseley Road*; (3) the state of the Real Property register. This latter matter loomed large in *Pieper v Edwards,* as the appellant (dominant tenement) argued that he purchased on the faith of the register.

In *Pieper v Edwards* the owner of the servient tenement had sought a release from the easement (a right of way) from the appellant/dominant tenement's owner-predecessor. This release had been prepared, but not signed. The appellant had inquired from his predecessor in relation to the matter and was assured no release had been signed.

The easement had been obstructed by a fence, gully pit and concrete works. The appellant particularly wanted the easement for vehicular access (it gave his property two accesses). The respondent's predecessor had successfully negotiated the release of the easement. The respondent thought the release would be registered, and left it in his solicitor's hands who failed to attend to it. The court upheld the trial judge's decision in favour of the proprietor of the servient tenement releasing the servient tenement from the easement. In doing so, the court had regard to the conduct of the predecessors in title. Their conduct was evidence of abandonment and this was relevant to the exercise of the court's discretion, having regard to *Treweeke v 36 Wolseley Road.*

In respect of the argument regarding dealing on the faith of the register, Samuel JA said (at 342):

> Section 89 necessarily assumes that, at the time of application and hence when the discretion for which it provides comes to be exercised, the land will be subject to an easement which the application seeks to modify or extinguish. If the state of the register were conclusive the scope and purpose of the legislation which contemplates encroachment upon indefeasibility would be destroyed.

In any case, Samuels JA found (at 343), that the appellant was on notice regarding the extinguishment of the easement before he exchanged contracts to purchase the dominant tenement.

In respect of the question before us, Graham could argue that the easement had been abandoned and based on that evidence seek an order under s 89 of the Conveyancing Act 1919 (NSW).

One of the matters that would need to be clarified is the length of time there had been non-user. However, this is only:

> ... one element from which the dominant owners intention to retain or abandon his easement may be inferred. (*Treweeke v 36 Woseley Road Pty Ltd* 1973 128 CLR 274 at 284 per McTiernan J)

There has been no attempt by Maurice to use the easement. Maurice has preferred the easier public route. Does this constitute renunciation? Maurice might argue that:

> Non user may be referable to the absence of a need to use the right of way and the use of an alternative and more attractive means of access. (*Treweeke v 36 Wolseley Road Pty Ltd* (1973) 128 CLR 274 at 302 per Mason J)

Another factor for consideration is the rather permanent construction of the pens. In *Treweeke v 36 Wolseley Road* (at 303) Mason J commented on the cost and permanency of the construction of the swimming pool. He discounted this as a consideration in the appellant's favour, because it affected only a small portion of the right of way, and because the respondent objected when he ascertained that it was located on the right of way. In the question before us, the cost of construction of the pens (apparently without objection) would be a consideration, as would be the degree of their permanence. More than likely, Maurice would argue that he did not acquiesce in their construction or object to them because, like the respondent in *Treweeke v 36 Wolseley Road*, he had alternative access.

However, Graham would argue that, unlike the occupants of the respondent's tenement in *Treweeke v 36 Wolseley Road Pty Ltd*, there had been available a legitimate legal access and that the right of way was now 'obsolete', and its 'impeding use without securing practical benefit' was an argument that extinguishment would cause 'no substantial injury' (all further grounds under s 89 as alternatives to abandonment).

'Obsolescence' was referred to in *Re Truman Hanbury, Buxton & Co Ltd's* application (in respect of covenants [1956] 1 QB 261 at 272) in the context that 'their original purpose can no longer be served'. Again, 'impeding user' would seem to require that the land could not be put to reasonable use, unless the easement was extinguished: *Scannard v Issa* [1987] 2 WLR 188. Further, 'no substantial injury' would require that there was no substantial interference with the amenities of the dominant tenement of Maurice, if the easement were extinguished: *Heaton v Loblay* (1960) 77 WN (NSW) 140. In this instance, value is not relevant.

Whether Graham would be successful in an application under these heads of s 89 would again depend on evidence. Certainly, Maurice might have difficulty with the 'no substantial injury' argument as there is now superior access. The other matters of 'obsolescence' and 'impeding user' might be difficult for Graham to maintain. It would seem the only impediment to the original purpose being served are matters in Graham's hands. Further, Graham might have difficulty maintaining the land could not be put to reasonable use unless extinguishment takes place.

Examiner's Comments

9-16 The answer generally followed the answer plan, although it varied the order of the application of the principles to the facts at the completion of the answer. In itself, this variation had a neutral affect on the answer. The answer dealt briefly with extinguishment by express method and operation of law and then went on to deal with implied release and release by court order.

In respect of implied release by abandonment, it discussed this method by reference to the decision of the High Court in *Treweeke v 36 Wolseley Road*. It dealt with the facts of that case (which was relevant in view of some similarity of those facts with the facts raised in the question), discussing the principles applied to those facts. The answer then went on to deal with the discussion in *Pieper v Edwards* [1982] 1 NSWLR 336, setting out the factors relevant to the court's exercise of discretion in that case. In dealing with *Pieper v Edwards*, the answer also raised the issue of land under the Real Property Act 1900 (NSW) and the applicability of s 89 of the Conveyancing Act 1919 (NSW) to that land. The answer then applied the principles of abandonment to the facts. It discussed the facts of the question, referring to the similarity of the facts in *Treweeke v 36 Wolseley Road*, applying the relevant principles and addressing the issues. It went on to discuss key words in s 89 of the Conveyancing Act 1919 (NSW) and their relevance to the facts in the light of case law.

The answer might have made more of the issue of conduct of prior registered proprietors. Such conduct is relevant to any consideration of abandonment as the High Court indicated in *Treweeke v 36 Wolseley Road*. The issue was also of some concern in *Pieper v Edwards*.

Keep in Mind

9-17 Students should keep in mind the following:

- It is common to answer the question in terms of implied release and abandonment and to disregard the necessity to deal with s 89 of the Conveyancing Act 1919 (NSW) and court order. It is also necessary when dealing with abandonment to discuss *Treweeke v 36 Wolseley Road* in terms of the facts of the case. The interpretation of the facts in that case had bearing on the manner the relevant principles were applied. Further, the facts of that case should be linked to the facts in the question, so that the application of the principles is made clear.
- In dealing with s 89 of the Conveyancing Act 1919 (NSW), its interpretation in *Pieper v Edwards* should be addressed. It is also necessary to have regard to judicial interpretation to key words in the section. This judicial interpretation should be applied to the facts of the question.

Question 3

9-18 Simon owns Lot 3, a large tree-filled lot on a river near Cairns. On one side is his neighbour William, who owns Lot 4, and on the other is Roxanne, who owns Lot 2. The three lots were originally developed as part of an exclusive residential development 30 years ago when the area was virtually undeveloped. Cairns is now a thriving metropolis and the river is a well-developed tourist area and busy every weekend and holidays. The original purchasers of the three lots, Simon, William and Veronica (the prior owner of Lot 2), entered into identical mutual covenants with each other to develop their land in specific ways. No document was registered on the freehold land register reflecting these covenants. The covenants included the following clauses:

- Any dwelling house built must be built predominantly in brick.
- If a lot owner sells their land they will obtain a deed of covenant in similar terms from any purchaser in favour of the other two lot owners.

Veronica sold her vacant land eight years ago to Roxanne who is now the registered owner of Lot 2. Veronica gave Roxanne a copy of the mutual covenant prior to signing the contracts, but Roxanne did not sign any covenant. At the contract signing, Roxanne pointed out the covenants and reassured Veronica, saying "Don't worry, I understand the conditions; it's fine, I know how things have to be done".

Late last year Roxanne began to build a wooden cottage on Lot 2. Simon is concerned that having this next door will substantially devalue his property.

Advise Simon.

Time allowed: 45 mins

Answer Plan

9-19 This question calls for a discussion of the enforceability of covenants in Queensland.

The following must be determined: can William or Simon enforce the covenant against Roxanne?

- Is the covenant binding? If yes, then it can be breached and therefore enforced against the breach:
  - ◆ privity of contract?
  - ◆ registration of the interest?
- Is it an exception to indefeasibility?:
  - ◆ personal equity exception?
- Is there a building scheme?
- Conclusion.

Answer

9-20 This question raises the issue of the enforceability of covenants in Queensland and can be summarised as whether Simon and/or William can enforce the covenant against Roxanne under the current circumstances.

The first issue is that Simon and William have no privity of contract with Roxanne, whose only agreement was with Veronica. As they are not parties to the contract they cannot enforce Veronica's agreement with Roxanne: *Tweddle v Atkinson* [1861] EWHC QB J 57.

Roxanne would use that argument herself, relying upon *Norton v Kilduff* 1974 Qld Reports 47 and *Ryan v Brain* [1994] 1 Qd R 681 to confirm that as there is no privity of contract between her and the other lot owners she is not bound by the covenant, and is indefeasible under s 184 of the Land Title Act 1994 (Qld) (LTA).

In *Norton v Kilduff* at 53 Hart J acknowledged that restrictive covenants are equitable interests in land and not on the register. However, there is no provision in the LTA for registration of a restrictive covenant and s 4(2) of the Property Law Act 1974 (Qld) (PLA) makes it clear that nothing in the act confers a right to registration of a restrictive covenant.

In *Norton v Kilduff* Hart J was asked to consider an action by a purchaser against another purchaser of a lot in a residential development. The original developer had sold the land to the defendant subject to a covenant that included a limitation on the height that a floor was built above the ground level. The owner then tried to build a Cape Cod house which was outside the guidelines of the covenant. The plaintiff, who was another lot owner in the development, sought an injunction to restrain the defendant, on the basis that the covenants comprised a building scheme. The plaintiff relied on English precedent to enforce a building scheme against the defendant.

The judge held that if the covenant was binding against the defendant then there had been a breach of the covenant. He also assumed for the purpose of the discussion that a "building scheme' had come into existence, and that this scheme would, in theory, allow the plaintiff to enforce the building scheme by stopping the construction of the house.

However, since the land was under the LTA the defendant argued he could only be liable if there was some notation of the covenant on the title, which there was not, as there was no privity of contract between the plaintiff and the defendant.

Hart J confirmed that restrictive covenants are not within the exception to indefeasibility under s 185 LTA for omitted easements. As equitable interests in land they are not enforceable without privity of contract. Had the action been brought by the original developer, it may well have been a different conclusion. As in the facts here, there might have been a much more straightforward case had the action been brought by Veronica and not Simon, as Veronica had privity of contract. Under this authority it seems unlikely a building scheme can be enforced without privity of contract.

There is also the possibility that *Norton v Kilduff* would be decided differently today on the basis of the personal equity exception. It could be argued that Roxanne's statements to Veronica represent an acknowledgement and acceptance of the covenant pre-registration, and that it would be unconscionable for her to change her mind post-registration and try to renege on the agreement. As in the short lease exception, there is pre-registration notice of the covenant in writing, and a verbal acknowledgement of the obligation, akin to *Bahr v Nicolay (No 2)* (1988) 164 CLR 604. There that was seen as enough to make the unregistered interest binding on the defendant. An even lower standard for acknowledgement of the interest by the transferee was set in *Bourseguin v Stannard Bros Holdings Pty Ltd* [1994] 1 QD R 231, where the purchaser's response to the seller's request for acknowledgement of the unregistered interest was silence, which the court held to be 'patent cheating' and therefore found the unregistered interest binding on the purchaser. Clearly Roxanne's reassurances to Veronica constitute more than the silence in *Bourseguin v Stannard Bros* and likely are enough to make the covenant binding on Roxanne. As a party directly affected by the unregistered interest, Simon could try and enforce the covenant against Roxanne on the basis of the personal equity exception. Simon's actions would be supported statutorily by ss 13(1)(b) and 13(2) PLA, which allow Simon to take the benefit of the covenant, regardless of privity of contract, and to sue and be entitled to all rights of said covenant as if he had been a party to the original contract. Further, under s 55 PLA it could be argued that Roxanne's acknowledgement and verbal acceptance of the covenant represent a promise which can be enforced by Simon, a beneficiary to that promise, who was identified and in existence at the time the promise was made.

This view was supported in *Ryan v Brain* by the Court of Appeal.

There the applicant had brought from the developer under a particular covenant, and sought to enforce that covenant against a later purchaser, the defendant, who had also purchased from the developer, but under a less strict covenant.

The court held that on the facts the defendants, at best, had notice of the existence of the stricter building covenant, but in no way had they at any point acknowledged or accepted the stricter covenant. Without some kind of acceptance or acknowledgement this could not fall within Torrens system fraud, nor could it raise a personal equity obligation.

Macrossan J did suggest that if the purchasers had purchased, not only with knowledge of the standard covenants but had also given some kind of undertaking to be bound by them, that is had they agreed to accept or entered into similar covenants with the developer, then they may have been bound under the personal equity exception relative to Torrens title as applied under *Bahr v Nicolay*.

Here Roxanne had clear knowledge of the covenant when she purchased the property. She has verbally acknowledged and recognised its existence and seems to have agreed to its terms. One would assume from her words that she had read the covenant and was aware of its conditions. This could be interpreted as an undertaking to abide by the covenant and that her later decision to renege could be viewed as unconscionable. Here Simon would also be trying to rely on ss 13 and 55 PLA as explained above.

The other issue to ensure enforcement of the potential liability requires establishing that there is a building scheme, which would make the covenants enforceable between all who are parties to the scheme. In equity the benefit of a restrictive covenant — as here — could pass where:

- the restrictive covenant was expressly annexed to the land by the appropriate formulae;
- by express assignment; or
- if it was part of a scheme of development where the restrictive covenant was inherent in the way the residential development was planned, and purchasers purchased their lot on the basis of the restrictive covenants. Such a scheme is deemed to occur when:
  - there is one common vendor;
  - there are covenants that are the same or similar;

♦ the development is intended to be part of a planned scheme.

This exclusive residential development into which Simon, William and Veronica initially purchased, seems to be a planned scheme of development where all parties purchased from one vendor and entered into agreements with the same covenant, supporting the argument that this is a scheme.

It will all depend on whether the *in personam* exception can apply. It seems likely that under the personal equity exception, with the help of ss 13 and 55 PLA, Simon will be able to enforce the scheme against Roxanne. Of course there is always the option that the original developer could bring an action for breach of contract against Veronica for not obtaining the required covenant when she sold to Roxanne.

Examiner's Comments

9-21 The answer covers all the issues outlined in the answer plan. The issue of whether there is a building scheme is handled quite briefly and perhaps could be explored a little more. The student has not addressed the issue of remedies, should Simon win in his application to enforce the covenant against Roxanne, which needs to be included. The relevant historic case law and development into statute, and the personal equity exception has been reasonably handled, but the arguments there could have been streamlined a little further. They get a little vague and over-detailed a times. However, all the key information is there and generally the question discusses the issues and options quite well.

Keep in Mind

9-22 Students should keep in mind the following:

• It is important not to forget remedies in a question. Although the rights have been established as valid and enforceable, they are no use unless the client knows how they will be enforced and what the client can get.

• Often students forget either the personal equity exception or the statutory options under the PLA, or they find they can successfully make a case under one and then do not bother to address the other. All the options should always be addressed. Not only does it ensure an answer that covers the full breadth of the topic, but students should remember it is often the cumulative weight of evidence that wins a case, and there is seldom a death knell blow where one rule will annihilate any opposing argument. If that were the case there could be no opposing argument!

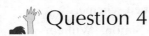

Question 4

9-23 Harold Horatio purchased a six-hectare Torrens title property in Brisbane, and subdivided it into three 2-hectare lots: Lots 1–3 Registered Plan 5552968. The development is designed and advertised as an exclusive residential estate. The three lots are shaped round Nelson Court, a tarred area providing vehicle access. Each lot has a narrow strip in the front providing access to Nelson Court, and acting as a reciprocal easement for the other two lots. The resultant area is just big enough for vehicles to pass through and turn around.

The lots and easements are all correctly registered on the relevant certificates of title. Each easement has identical covenants including those outlined in the Annexure below. Harold then sells each allotment to the following purchasers:

Lot 1 – Napoleon; Lot 2 – Elizabeth; Lot 3 – Drake

Drake obtains local authority consent to rezone his area from a residential zone to commercial zone, builds a commercial three-shop complex on Lot 3, and registers it as 'Golden Fleece Community Title Plan No 45890' (Golden Fleece), subject to a community titles scheme. Drake includes the original easement as part of the common property of Golden Fleece. There are no special by-laws denoted in the community management statement at the time of registration.

Drake then transfers the lots as follows:

- Lot A is transferred to Francis, who sells organic teas and coffees;
- Lot B is transferred to Sultan, who opens a newsagent;
- Lot C is transferred to Meg, who opens a cafe.

All of the body corporate tenants require business hours access through Nelson Court for their customers and suppliers.

Napoleon and Elizabeth do not think the easement area should be available to the lessees in Golden Fleece as the easement only applied to the original Lot 3 in RP 5552968. Napoleon and Elizabeth also complain about the more intensive use of the easement caused by the registration of the community title scheme.

Napoleon and Elizabeth complain that Francis often uses the easement area for loading and unloading of stock. Francis has to use the easement area for this purpose because the way the building is placed, his premises do not have access to any other loading area. Sometimes the delivery trucks remain there for up to 30 minutes, but they have never actually blocked access to another lot. Napoleon and Elizabeth want to completely stop access to the easement by the Golden Fleece tenants, but if they cannot achieve that, their goal is to at least prevent the loading and unloading on the easement area.

Sultan has put in a complaint to the body corporate manager that Meg has cordoned off part of the common property for tables and chairs for her coffee shop. Meg has told Sultan that as she is part owner of the common property, she is fully entitled to use a portion.

Advise Napoleon, Elizabeth, Meg and Sultan on their legal entitlements on the matters raised above.

Annexure

Easement covenants — rights granted

1. The right of way for the registered proprietors and occupiers of the dominant tenement and all persons authorised by them, together with all others having the same rights as the grantee but in common with the grantor, and every other person who is for the time being the registered proprietor of the servient tenement, at all times, day or night, and for all purposes ordinarily incidental to or connected with the use and enjoyment of the dominant tenement, with or without animals, carriages, wagons, motor vehicles and all vehicles of any other description whatsoever, laden or unladen, to pass and repass over along or across the servient tenement.

Parties

2. The term 'the grantor' shall, where the context so admits or requires, be the registered proprietor or proprietors or owners (or their respective successors, executors, administrators and assigns) of the servient tenement. The expression 'the grantee' shall, where the context so admits or requires, include the registered proprietor or proprietors or owners (or their respective successors, executors, administrators and assigns) of the dominant tenement.

Maintenance of easement area

3. The grantor and grantee covenant, and it is a condition of this easement, that the costs of maintenance and repair of the servient tenement shall be borne by the registered proprietors of Lots 1–3 of Registered Plan 5552968 as to one-third respectively.

Time allowed: 1 hour, 15 mins

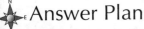

Answer Plan

9-24 A number of issues need addressing in this question:

- Lot 3: do the holders of the subdivided tenement, that is the body corporate tenants, have the same rights to use the easement as the original dominant tenement holder Drake?
- Is using the easement for loading and unloading outside the permitted uses in the Annexure?
- Can the common property be cordoned off for tables and chairs?
- Conclusion.

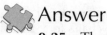

Answer

9-25 There are a number of issues raised in the question which must be addressed before advice can be given to the relevant parties.

Rights of holders of subdivided tenement

9-26 The first one concerns the subdivision of Lot 3 and whether the body corporate tenants are entitled to use the easement.

In *Gallagher v Rainbow* [1994] HCA 24 the High Court confirmed there is a rebuttable presumption that each division of a subdivided dominant tenement has the same rights to an easement over a servient tenement that the original whole dominant tenement enjoyed. The facts in that case were similar to those in the current scenario. Therefore, after the division, Meg, Francis and Sultan could still use the easement in the way Drake could, unless the terms of the easement suggested otherwise. The question is then whether there is anything in the language of the easement that might rebut the presumption. The language of the easement does allow for more than one grantee, while the maintenance provision implies there was no contemplation of subdivision. On balance, it seems unlikely the provisions exclude the presumption from applying here.

A further issue is whether the additional burden created by the increased traffic represents a use not contemplated by, or included within, the scope of the easement, suggesting the body corporate owners cannot use the easement. The High Court did raise but did not resolve the possibility that the subdivision of a dominant tenement could take the usage so far outside what was contemplated by the easement that it would rebut the presumption. One could consider *Jelbert v Davis* (1968) 1 WLR 589 where agricultural land was entitled to access via an easement, but when that land was developed for 200 caravan sites the increased traffic was held to be outside the terms of what was contemplated originally and was therefore not enforceable. It seems unlikely the increase in traffic here is of the same scale, but the possibility that the court could refuse the body corporate tenants use of the easement should be considered, given the small space of the easement.

Use of easement for loading and unloading

9-27 The nature of easements which are granted at one time and which continue for many years, means the purposes of the easement may need to be considered in the light of modern forms of traffic and technology. For example, should a right of way granted 150 years ago be limited to allow only persons on foot, or does it include access by motor vehicles, not in contemplation at the time but certainly the currently accepted means of accessing a right of way?

It used to be held that a court could look to extrinsic evidence at the time to determine what the parties had in contemplation so that meaning could be extrapolated from that. However, the current authority

Westfield Management Ltd v Perpetual Trustee Company Ltd [2007] 233 CLR 528 no longer permits the court to consider extrinsic evidence as to the intentions of the parties at the relevant time about what was intended in the easement, as it has been held this would be disruptive of the Torrens system of title by registration.

Therefore the primary focus must be on the words used in the registered document, and the nature of the land over which the easement has been granted.

It can be stated that based upon *Westfield* that:

- The court must look to the express terms of the registered easement, the deposited plans and folio identifiers. The principles derived from the *Codelfa Construction Pty Ltd v State Rail Authority* (NSW) (1982) 149 CLR 337 case should not be applied for the interpretation of a registered easement.
- Extrinsic evidence about what the parties contemplated can no longer be acknowledged as being included as part of the easement covenants.
- Evidence about the physical make-up of the dominant and servient tenements at the time the easement was created, and the nature and dimensions of the easement area, is probably admissible evidence, but this is not specifically stated.
- One might consider the circumstances surrounding the execution of the instrument and the nature of the surface over which the easement is granted for bare easements only but this is obiter.

With that background the following might be a way to deal with these issues. In *St Edmundsbury and Ipswich Diocesan Board of Finance v Clark (No. 2)* [1975] 1 All ER 772, the issue was whether a right of way easement included a right to drive vehicles over the easement. The court held a narrow interpretation was preferred, because of the narrowness of the easement area which suggested that use by vehicles was not intended.

The court can also give consideration to the purpose of the right of way. In *Elliot v Renner* [1923] St R Qd 172 the court considered the intended purpose of a right of way over a laneway. The lane provided access to a pastry cook's business and the court held that access to the business impliedly included the right to stop to allow loading and unloading of goods.

However, assessing the construction of easements can lead to difficulty as in *SS and M Ceramics Pty Ltd v Yeung Yau Kin Neville Lee* (Unreported Appeal No 39 of 1995 Supreme Court of Appeal).

In this case the easement, registered approximately 40 years earlier, gave a standard right of way to the rear of a grocery store in Innisfail. At that time the rear of the store allowed room for trucks to load and unload on the dominant tenement. Since then the store had expanded and due to the extension, trucks were forced to load and unload on part of the easement area on the servient tenement.

The owner of the servient tenement sought an injunction to stop the loading and unloading on the servient tenement. The court had to determine whether the right to pass and repass included the right to load and unload for the purposes of the dominant tenement.

Derrington J in the Supreme Court acknowledged that normally loading and unloading would be considered as part of a right of way, although precedent did not directly address a circumstance where the physical layout of the land had changed, as had occurred here, which necessitated the change in use. Derrington J concluded that the easement did allow loading and unloading, determining the easement should be viewed in its broad context and not limited to the physical layout at the time the easement was created.

Derrington J was overturned on appeal where Macrossan CJ and McPherson J held that precedent which did concede a right to load and reload, only dealt with circumstances where there was no area on the dominant tenement for parking at the time of the grant, and implying the right to park and unload was based upon a necessity to allow the easement to work properly.

They considered the question of whether a grant of a right to pass and repass would be rendered impossible to use if it did not include a right to pass and repass, and held that it depends on the circumstances prevailing at the time of the grant. They held that as there was plenty of space available in 1955 when the easement was created, and there were no plans then to extend the premises, there was no need to imply a right to load and reload in order for the easement to work properly.

The easement originally gave access and its use has changed because the current building is different. However, the original easement did not, at any point, include loading and unloading.

Use of part of common property for tables and chairs

9-28 Lot owners are joint owners of common property as tenants in common in shares proportional to their interest schedule lot entitlement. This means that all lot owners are joint owners of the common property and all have access to it. However, here there appears to be an attempt to use the area exclusively. This is not contemplated by joint ownership. As no by-laws are specified in the community titles scheme, the by-laws in Sch 4 of the Body Corporate and Community Management Act 1997(Qld) (BCCMA) will apply, and this action would presumably be a breach of those, potentially opening the door to an action for occupation rent by the excluded joint owners.

Meg should seek exclusive use of the area under ss 170–178 of the BCCMA. This will require a resolution without dissent of the body corporate with the consent of the lot owner, and may require a new community management statement to incorporate the new by-law, and registration of a new plan demarcating the exclusive use area within the common property area: s 172 BCCMA.

Examiner's Comments

9-29 Although this answer addressed the key issues in the question and those noted in the answer plan, the student has failed to properly relate the information back to the question provided. There is much relevant discussion on the issues, but the question specifically sought advice for particular parties and that is lacking in the conclusion. The issues were well identified and the authorities relevantly discussed but the information should have been related back to the parties and facts in the scenario provided. The conclusion also lacks a proper discussion of the remedies available to each of the parties.

Keep in Mind

9-30 Students should keep in mind the following:

- Remedies: students often discuss the rights of the parties but then forget how these can be enforced and what remedies are available.
- Although discussion of precedent and authorities is necessary, students should always remember to relate the information back to the question provided. The discussion should always be taken back to the parties and facts in the scenario.
- A conclusion should always deal directly with what the question asked. For example, if the student is supposed to advise a particular party then the answer should close with the advice for that particular party, and a remedy explaining how it can be enforced.

Question 5

9-31 Zak recently bought a farm at Jimboomba in Queensland comprising a large farm house and eight acres of land behind the house. Ronald owns and occupies the acreage backing onto the river behind Zak's property. When Zak bought the farm, the estate agent told him he could draw water from the river by using water pipes that cross Ronald's land.

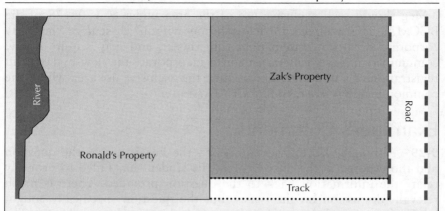

Soon after moving in, Zak saw Ronald walking along the narrow track across the field to the main road. When he asked him about it, Ronald said that this was the only way to reach his cottage and he and his visitors had been using the track since he bought the cottage twenty-five years earlier. It was the only way to reach the main road from his land.

Zak was due to go away on a business trip shortly thereafter, so he took no further action until his return three months later. When he got back he discovered that Ronald was running a small accommodation business, comprising an eight-bedroom guesthouse and two stand-alone villas, on his land. Ronald has also laid tar over the track to make it easier for guests and suppliers' deliveries to reach the guesthouse.

Advise Zak.

Time allowed: 40 mins

 Answer Plan

9-32 This question simply requires an overview of how easements are created, the requirements of an easement, and whether it can be varied. Appropriate subheadings to cover all the material would be:

- Is it an easement to cross the land?:
  - ◆ How was the easement created?
- Are all of the general characteristics of an easement present?:
  - ◆ There must be a dominant and a servient tenement.
  - ◆ Easement must benefit the dominant land.
  - ◆ Dominant and servient tenements cannot be owned and occupied by the same person.
  - ◆ The right in question must be capable of forming the subject matter of a grant.
  - ◆ Has the easement been interfered with, extinguished or modified?
- Remedies.
- Access to the river.

Answer

9-33   The key issue here is whether the track is an easement and whether Ronald is entitled to use it.

Is it an easement to cross the land?

9-34   An easement exists where a right is held by one person that either entitles them to make specific, limited use of land owned by another person, or to prevent the owner of the land from using it in a particular manner (*Halsbury's Laws of England* 4th ed, vol 14, p 4).

An easement is not a licence as one party receives benefit while the other is burdened, and an easement can be registered and is a recognised interest in land, although it does not grant a general right to occupy the neighbouring land.

Here it appears that Ronald receives the benefit of a right of way, burdening Zak's land, allowing Ronald and his visitors to pass to and from his guesthouse and the main road. As a right of way it does not extend in height and is limited to only a right to access the road.

How was the easement created?

9-35   Given Ronald's use of the easement appears to be limited to travelling over it, and does not in any way imply a grant of exclusive possession, it would appear the use bears the characteristics of an easement. What is then in issue is how this easement was created. There are various possible methods, including:

- **Implied grant through necessity:** this would justify the granting of an easement to Ronald on the basis that he has no other means of accessing the road from his land.
- **Express grant:** for this easement to be created under an express grant there would need to be some evidence documenting the granting of the right of easement to Ronald. It seems there is none here, otherwise presumably Ronald would have referred to it in his discussions with Zak, and Zak would have been aware of the grant.
- **Prescription:** this is similar to adverse possession and requires that the owner of the dominant tenement use the prescribed area in an open, continuous, hostile manner for the prescribed number of years, which is 20 years in Queensland. Ronald claims he has been using the easement, not in secret, not obtained by threats or force, and without the owner's consent. If Ronald had the owner's consent then really he has just been exercising a licence from the previous owner which would have no binding effect on Zak.

To determine which might be applicable, it is necessary to consider various factors:

- Intention: was Ronald's intention to pass over the land to gain access to and from his property and the road?

- Nature and purpose of the easement: was the intention to grant a right of way or was the easement for some other purpose?
- Nature of the dominant and servient tenements: in this instance both are domestic residences.
- Circumstances at time of grant: in *Hoy v Allerton* (2002) Q Conv R 54-559 it was held that an examination of the facts and circumstances existing at the time of the grant could be used as an aid to interpret the meaning of the grant, bearing in mind that a grantee is limited to what has been granted, and a grantor cannot derogate from grant. Here the conclusion would be one of necessity of access on the basis that the circumstances are such that Ronald has no alternative but to cross over Zak's land.

Are all of the general characteristics of an easement present?

There must be a dominant and a servient tenement

9-36 An easement involves the exercise of a right annexed to the land over another piece of land; therefore, it is necessary for two pieces of land to be involved: a dominant tenement gaining the benefit of the easement, and a servient tenement, burdened by the easement: *Harada v Registrar of Titles* [1981] VR 743. Here Ronald's land benefits from the easement as it gives him access to the road, and is thus the dominant tenement. Zak's land is burdened by the alleged easement and is therefore a servient tenement. The dominant and servient tenements do not need to be contiguous, although in this instance they are: *Re Ellenborough Park* [1956] Ch 131.

Easement must benefit the dominant land

9-37 The easement needs to accommodate or benefit the dominant tenement and make it a better and more convenient property: *Re Ellenborough Park*. Here the easement is necessary for Ronald and his dominant tenement land, as without the easement he and his visitors are unable to access the road from his property, and vice versa.

The big issue is whether the right has a connection with the land in the sense of being reasonably necessary: *Re Ellenborough Park*. There must be a natural connection between the dominant and servient tenements, and the right must be reasonably necessary for the enjoyment of the dominant tenement. There must be a nexus between the land and the right in a real and intelligible way, and it is not enough for the land to be a convenient incident to the right: *Clos Farming Estates Pty Ltd v Easton* [2001] NSWSC 525. Necessity is an element here as there is no other access to Ronald's property as it is bordered by a river.

However, Ronald has now changed his use of the easement to using it for business conducted on the land. As long as the original right granted accommodates a business on the land he can use it accordingly, as the grantor cannot derogate from grant, and an easement right may be created: *Copeland v Greenhalf* [1952] Ch 488; *Harada v Registrar of Titles*[1981] VR 743. The crucial matter is whether the right has a connection with the land in the sense of being reasonably necessary for the better enjoyment of the parcel of land: *Re Ellenborough Park*. Here it would appear the right is connected with the land and can accommodate the business and therefore the easement benefits the land.

Dominant and servient tenements cannot be owned and occupied by the same person

9-38   The dominant and servient tenements cannot be owned and occupied by the same person: *Re Finlayson Ltd v Elder Smith and Co* [1936] SASR 20. The very nature of an easement is the exercise of rights by one landowner against another, which would be invalid if both parcels of the land were owned by the same person. Here the dominant tenement is owned by Ronald and the servient tenement by Zak. They are two separate people and therefore this is not an issue.

The right in question must be capable of forming the subject matter of a grant

The granted right will not be recognised where it is too general or vague (*Re Ellenborough Park*), such as rights granting access for recreation only. This right of way has been granted since there is no other way that Ronald can access the road without the access through Zak's property. Thus this is capable of forming the subject of a grant, as is the right to enjoy a park (*Riley v Penttila* [1974] VR 547), unlike other rights such as a mere right of recreation (*Re Ellenborough Park*); protection from the weather (*Phipps v Pears* [1965] QB 76); privacy (*Browne v Flower* [1911] 1 Ch 219).

Has the easement been interfered with, extinguished or modified?

9-39   No extinguishment has been demonstrated here but Ronald has modified the easement by covering the surface with tar. However, it could be argued this was still done for necessity. If the increased traffic is permitted under the easement then covering the surface is merely protecting the easement and making it more usable under the increased usage.

Remedies

9-40   There may be abatement allowing Zak to remove the hard surface if it is interfering with his land, but only if it is positively necessary. It would appear that it is not necessary, and therefore abatement may not be available.

Access to the river

9-41   The same issues occur here as to how the easement has been created and whether it is necessary. It is unlikely Zak needs to draw the water from the river, unless it is as a water supply for his farming. However, unless he has changed the use of the farm from the way the previous owner used it, it is likely this would either be a case of easement by prescription on the basis he would be using the farm and water the same way as the previous owner did, or necessity if there was no other water access. The issue to avoid here is that raised in *Hoy v Allerton,* where Atkinson J determined that an easement for laying pipes could not be extended to include the right to draw water, as this would involve varying the express terms of the easement. There do not seem to be express terms here, so Zak would be relying on much the same criteria as Ronald to enforce an easement.

 ## Examiner's Comments

9-42 The answer follows exactly the outline in the answer plan. While it covers the necessary information clearly and reasonably concisely for the ascertainment of Ronald's easement, the answer peters out when it comes to the access to the river for Zak. This part of the answer could have done with more discussion concerning the likely establishment of the original right and how this may or may not have included the right to the water, with more detail. Generally the answer was thorough in what it presented, but the same detail should have been applied to the second main issue, despite the clearly repetitive nature of the answer.

 ## Keep in Mind

9-43 Students should keep in mind the following:

- It is important to explore all the authorities and to discuss the different elements that can affect an easement.
- Students should be careful not to overlook the issue of extending or changing the use of an easement and how this may impact the enforceability of the grant.

Chapter 10

Possession and 'Adverse' Possession

Key Issues

10-1 It is difficult to understate the importance which the common law accords to the concept of possession. Ownership of, or entitlement to, material things often forms the basis of wealth in modern western society, and much of property law focuses on the exercise of an individual's rights in an item against third parties. The successful enforcement of those rights depends on the success of the concept of possession. A number of theories have been put forward justifying why the concept of private property exists, including occupation theory, labour theory, personality theory and economic theory. The weight that the law places on the possession of material things can therefore, at least in part, be explained by examining the issues raised by those theories. Even though society has radically changed in many crucial ways over the centuries, the importance of the concept of the possession of land and goods remains virtually undisturbed and the law reflects this stasis. However, there is no 'unified theory' of possession.

Possession, in law, is made up of two complementary elements: the mental and the physical. To be in possession (of either land or goods), a person must demonstrate an intention to exercise both mental and physical control over an item. This does not require having actual physical possession, merely demonstration of the intention to do so.

Some of the remedies for infringements of possession are best dealt with under the law of torts, such as the remedies for trespass, conversion and detinue. From this point, at least in so far as goods are concerned, the law of bailment is an important reference point, because some possessor's rights may be limited by the terms of a bailment. Under the recent implementation of the new personal property legislation which addresses bailment quite extensively, students should find bailment is now clearly personalty and not in their real property courses. However, this chapter does look at finders keepers, where the common law has remained stable.

Equally, in matters concerning land, the doctrine of tenure means that all titles are relative in the final analysis anyway. In limited circumstances (in matters concerning either land or goods), a defendant to an action may claim the benefit of the *jus tertii* — and rely upon the title of a third party to defend against the plaintiff's suit — but these instances are rare.

This chapter also deals with the impact of the limitation of actions legislation upon possessory titles. Each state and territory has its own legislative regime. The area is generally known as 'adverse possession', and the basic idea is that if a possessory title can be maintained for so long that the true owner's right to sue the wrongful possessor is barred by statute, then the law operates to effectively recognise a non-consensual transfer of ownership. By extinguishing the true owner's title, the possessor becomes the person with the 'best' interest. The primary rationale behind the legislation is that people should not be allowed to rest upon their rights without exercising them forever: that the law should protect the vigilant and not the tardy. Secondary justifications for the statutory rules include the practical considerations of the availability of evidence, the productive usage of scarce resources and the legal recognition of the reality of possession.

Adverse possession of land can sometimes give rise to a dispute which captures public attention. Media organisations have been known to latch onto a court's decision to recognise the statutory limitation which bars an owner's title to land and effectively vests title in a squatter. Sometimes, quite wrongly, the law is portrayed as rewarding the 'theft' of land. Most media organisations will report only the more sensational elements of the facts. They will usually fail to explain the legislative basis of the limitations rules or the sound reasons for their existence.

10-2   Before attempting the following questions, please ensure you are familiar with the following:

✓	the law of trespass to goods, conversion and detinue;
✓	the law regarding lost and abandoned goods;
✓	the doctrine of *jus tertii*;
✓	the operation of limitation of actions legislation with respect to the possession of land;
✓	adverse possession:

- *Asher v Whitlock* (1865) LR 1 QB 1;
- *Buckinghamshire County Council v Moran* [1989] 2 All ER 225;
- *Bligh v Martin* [1968] 1 All ER 1157;
- *George Wimpey & Co Ltd v Sohn* [1967] Ch 487;
- *Monash City Council v Melville* [2000] VSC 55;
- *Mulcahy v Curramore Pty Ltd* [1974] 2 NSWLR 464;
- *Nicholas v Andrew* (1920) 20 SR (NSW) 178;

- *Quach v Marrickville Municipal Council* (1990) 22 NSWLR 55;
- *Re Johnson* [1999] QSC 197;
- *Riley v Pentilla* [1974] VR 547;
- *Whittlesea City Council v Abbatangelo* [2009] VSCA 188;

✓ Finders keepers:

- *Armory v Delamirie* (1722) 93 ER 664;
- *Bird v Town of Fort Francis* [1949] OR 292;
- *Button v Cooper* (1947) SASR 286;
- *Byrne v Hoare* [1965] Qd R 135;
- *Elwes v Brigg Gas Co* (1886) 33 Ch D 562;
- *Hannah v Peel* [1945] 2 All ER 288;
- *Moorhouse v Angus & Robertson (No 1) Pty Ltd* [1981] 1 NSWLR 700;
- *Parker v British Airways Board* (1982) 1 QB 1004;
- *Ranger v Giffin* (1968) 87 WN (NSW) (Pt 1) 531;
- *Re Jigrose Pty Ltd* (1994) 1 Qd 382;
- *South Staffordshire Water Co v Sharman* (1896) 2 QB 44;
- *Tamworth Industries Ltd v Attorney-General* (1991) 3 NZLR 616;
- *The Tubantia* [1924] 18 Lloyd's LR 158;
- *Waverley Borough Council v Fletcher* [1995] 4 All ER 756.

Question 1

10-3 Derwent is considering renovating his house on the Gold Coast, Queensland, to accommodate his growing family. He moved into the house on 5 November 2001, having inherited it from his uncle, Garth, who came across the abandoned house in January 1998. Garth's journal indicated he had maintained the garden and constructed a large outdoor patio on the property, in addition to using the property as a residence before his death in 2001.

From 20 March 2002 to 15 August 2002, Derwent vacated the Southport house to live with his then-girlfriend and returned to the house only twice during that period. Derwent has always paid rates and, in 2008, erected a stone fence to match the exterior of the house. Since 2009 he has hosted bi-weekly neighbourhood barbeques on the large outdoor patio.

In January 2012 Derwent lodged an application to become the registered owner of the Southport house. Kane, who was released from jail in

2011 after serving a 15-year jail sentence, recognised the image of the Southport house in the newspaper. Kane was certain the house belonged to his grandfather, who died in a car crash along with his wife Alice in October 1997.

On 19 March 2012 Kane travelled to the Southport house and confronted Derwent, demanding the keys to the house. Kane handed Derwent a copy of Kane's grandfather's will, which stated the Southport house was left 'to my wife Alice for life, then to my grandson Kane in fee simple'. Kane also told Derwent that he had lodged a caveat against Derwent's application.

Advise Derwent with respect to the Southport house. (Assume you are advising him of his position as at 20 March 2012.)

Time allowed: 45 mins

Answer Plan

10-4   The question is about adverse possession. The answer must:

- provide an explanation and definition of adverse possession;
- identify the relevant legislative sections and how they operate in relation to the facts given;
- identify the different factors provided that could indicate the start of the adverse possession timeframe and apply the relevant case authorities;
- take note of both sides of the argument and identify factors for and against adverse possession, and address any potential breaks in continuous possession;
- conclude whether an adverse possession claim could be successful;
- identify the relevant remedies.

Answer

10-5   Derwent lodged his application under s 99 of the Land Title Act 1994 (Qld) (LTA) and Kane caveated against Derwent's application under s 104 LTA.

Mini brain teaser for doctrine of estates

10-6   Alice: life estate in possession (which ended upon her death in October 1997).

Kane: vested fee simple remainder (which vested in possession upon Alice's death in October 1997).

If it is assumed that the will under which Kane inherited is registered, then prima facie he has indefeasibility under s 84(1) LTA. Thus Derwent will need to invoke s 185(1)(d) LTA in accordance with the Sch 2 definition of 'adverse possessor' in order to have any success in his claim to become the new registered owner.

If Derwent is to make an adverse possessor's application under s 99 LTA; he has to meet the criteria for the definition of adverse possession under Sch 2. Adverse possession is an exception to indefeasibility: s 185(1)(d) LTA. The two caveats have been lodged under s 104 LTA.

Limitation period

10-7 The 12-year limitation period applies as Kane is the known true owner and would expire if adverse possession began before 2000: s 13 Limitation of Actions Act 1974 (Qld) (LAA) and *Re Johnson* [1999] QSC 197. Imprisonment is not a legal disability for LAA purposes, which would otherwise extend the period for up to 30 years. The limitation period would commence against Kane upon Garth or Derwent's commencement of adverse possession: s 19(1) LAA and *Re Johnson*. Note: the limitation period must start afresh if adverse possession is not continuous: s 19(2) LAA.

General law elements of adverse possession

10-8 In order to determine the start of adverse possession, it must be established if Garth and Derwent have demonstrated the requisite degree of physical control and intention to exclude everyone, including the owner, since January 1998. Periods of successive possession by Garth and Derwent can be aggregated if there has been no abandonment: *Mulcahy v Curramore Pty Ltd* [1974] 2 NSWLR 464.

Section 13 LAA says adverse possession must last 12 years, and s 19(1) LAA defines when adverse possession starts: *Re Johnson*. The elements that qualify as the start of adverse possession can depend on the purpose of the land, for example *Monash City Council v Melville* [2000] VSC 55, where it was confirmed that adverse possession of a private road does not require full occupation or possession by full enclosure, but that practical considerations such as the purpose of the land can be considered.

Under the ss 98–108 LTA, possession must be open, peaceful and not secret (*Mulcahy v Curramore*) and continuous: s 19(2) LAA. The start of adverse possession can be shown by: paying rates (*Quach v Marrickville Municipal Council* (1990) 22 NSWLR 55); cultivation or agistment (*Buckinghamshire County Council v Moran* [1989] 2 All ER 225); complete enclosure of the space by fencing (*Buckinghamshire County Council v Moran*), bearing in mind that having an unlocked gate has been deemed insufficient as it still allows access by third parties (*George Wimpey & Co Ltd v Sohn* [1967] Ch 487). The key factor is demonstration of an intention to exclude the whole world including the true owner. Any breaks in continuity of possession will restart the clock unless it is a temporary break where the land is unworkable (*Nicholas v Andrew* (1920) 20 SR (NSW) 178); or where farming land is not used for a practical reason such as it is a non-growing season: *Bligh v Martin* [1968] 1 All ER 1157.

1998–2000 (Garth Derwent's uncle)

- Possession was 'adverse' as it was without Kane's consent.
- It is not clear on the facts whether rates have been paid continuously since 1998.
- Cultivation, agistment, repairs and other improvements have occurred, indicating that Garth used the land as a normal landowner would: *Buckinghamshire County Council v Moran*.
- Grass mowing is insufficient by itself.

It could be tentatively concluded that Garth possessed the property adversely from 1998–2000, which could be aggregated with Derwent's period if his conduct is also found to satisfy the elements of adverse possession. This would mean that the 12-year limitation period for Kane to object will have expired.

2000–March 2012 (Derwent)

- Rates payments-strong indicator of adverse possession: *Re Johnson/ Quach v Marrickville*.
- Holding social gatherings (BBQs and social cricket matches) are additional, albeit weaker, acts of adverse possession: *Whittlesea City Council v Abbatangelo* [2009] VSCA 188.
- No fencing until 2008, but it appears the fence was constructed to fit the decor of the house rather than exclude others. If the purpose of the fencing was decorative and not exclusionary, then the fencing would not be indicative of adverse possession. Derwent could try and rely on *Buckinghamshire County Council v Moran* where fencing off the only access to the land with a locked gate was sufficient but his intention of putting in fencing for decorative purposes is likely to go against him.

In contrast, Kane could rely on *George Wimpey & Co Ltd v Sohn* [1966] 1 All ER 232 at 240 where fencing of a hotel garden was insufficient because certain people retained access as easement holders, or *Riley v Pentilla* [1974] VR 547 where fencing of a communal park was insufficient as its purpose was not to preclude others from using the recreational facilities.

If it is determined that Derwent ceased or discontinued adverse possession in 2002 when he moved in with his ex-girlfriend, then the 12-year limitation period would start afresh when Derwent resumed adverse possession after the end of the six months in 2002: s 19(2) LAA:

- A temporary relocation instead of permanent departure or abandonment will not break adverse possession, as evidenced by the four-year gap of residency in *Whittlesea City Council v Abbatangelo*.
- Adverse possession need not be continuous from day to day: *Re Johnson*.

- The fact that Derwent visited the property twice in that six-month period may indicate that he did not intend to abandon the property, although the facts are ambiguous.

Therefore there are three possible conclusions:

- Adverse possession began in 1998 upon Garth taking possession, and continued uninterrupted until March 2012 with no break in continuity. Kane's time will then have expired under the LAA to make a claim (1998 + 12 = 2010).
- Adverse possession began on 5 November 2001 when Derwent took possession. This relies on the conclusion that Garth did not meet the elements of adverse possession. Kane would be within time to contest the application under the Limitation of Actions Act (2001 + 12 = 4 November 2013).
- Adverse possession began in 1998 upon Garth taking possession, but was discontinued in 2002 when Derwent moved out. This would mean the limitation period started again in 2002 and Kane will be within time to enforce his ownership (2002 + 12 = 2014).

This last is the most likely scenario, but the other two are possible as adverse possession is not always clear-cut.

If conclusion 2 or 3 is followed, then the Registrar of Titles may reject Derwent's application under s 107(1)(a) LTA.

If conclusion 1 is made, then the registrar may register Derwent as the new registered owner of Kane's land under s 108 LTA. This is subject to s 108B LTA which will require (1) the registrar to cancel Kane's registration and (2) create an indefeasible title in Derwent's name.

There is always the possibility the registrar will decide to grant Derwent a lesser interest, under s 107(b) LTA.

Examiner's Comments

10-9 This answer is very typical of a student exam answer. Although it covers the issues, it is quite haphazard in its approach and lacks structure and cohesive arguments. It also lacks grammar and sentence structure. Adverse possession is a tricky area as both common law and legislation should be referenced in the answer, and there are a number of factors to be considered when determining conclusions. This kind of question can often produce answers that turn into a bullet list of check points, particularly under exam conditions.

This student has successfully grasped the idea that each situation must be considered on its merits. While there are some factors that can be strongly persuasive towards establishing adverse possession, such as paying rates, generally it is the cumulative weight of evidence that will tip the scales towards starting the clock to determine adverse possession.

This means students need to identify and consider all the probative factors and clearly establish all the possible starting points for the clock; and all the possible breaks in possession as well. When all the factors are considered together, it is not uncommon for there to be more than one possible conclusion to a question, depending on how the court reads each factor. Students should always play the 'if game', as this student did in the conclusion. For example, if the court determines this is continuous possession then ..., but if the court determines it is not continuous possession, then ...

More detailed arguments could have been provided concerning the application of different cases to each factor in the question. A more cohesive structure outlining the issues and then discussing the various factors should have been used, and would have resulted in the presentation of an argument rather than a check list. However, the student's structure was clear and reasonable for an exam scenario. Under non-exam conditions this answer would have required complete restructuring into an essay form, rather than bullet points. Grammar and sentence structure are again typical of an exam answer here, but clearly not sufficient for non-exam conditions. Overall the content was thorough and dealt quite comprehensively with the issues in the question.

Keep in Mind

10-10   Students should keep in mind the following:

- Students have a tendency to miss how grey this area is and are tempted to focus on one or two key factors to reach a determinative conclusion, rather than realise the concept of cumulative weight of evidence often results in multiple possible conclusions.
- Students often forget in this type of question to examine an issue or factor from the perspective of both parties. Even if a question says to advise one party, the options to both should be considered, as Party A's options undoubtedly shape Party B's options in response.
- Students should remember cases can be used not just to apply the ruling to similar facts, but also to distinguish from a scenario if a client needs the opposing conclusion.

Question 2

> **10-11**   Hamish Hamilton and Lulu Lacey both owned seaside cottages on the Gold Coast, which were separated by a vacant block of land owned by Archie Alfred. A wide tree-lined registered easement ran down the back of Archie and Hamish's properties which Lulu could walk along to access the small bay with a little beach overlooked by the cottages, and where she worked as a waitress at a beach cafe. Lulu walked along

the easement every morning and evening on her way to and from work. Hamish and Lulu both built their cottages and began living there in May 1980. In June 1982 Archie moved back to Italy without building on his land. In January 1992 Hamish started paying the rates on Archie's land and mowing the grass, and when he had guests for BBQs they often sat or played cricket on the vacant block. Hamish worked as an architect and in May 1998 he started a contract in Sydney. For two years during the contract Hamish lived in Sydney and only came back to the cottage for one week every four months or so. In July 2000 he moved back into the cottage permanently.

In August 2006 there was a large storm and one of the trees on the easement at the bottom of Archie's garden was uprooted. As Lulu walked past the next day she saw the corner of a metal box sticking up from the ground between the tree's raised roots. Using her hands she dug the soft soil around it and finally managed to pull up a heavily engraved silver box. Opening it she found it filled with old gold coins with strange markings and foreign writing. As she was examining her find Hamish arrived to look at the uprooted tree. 'Look what I found embedded in the soil under the tree on my way to work!', exclaimed Lulu. Upon seeing the box in her hands and the pile of gold coins Hamish immediately said 'Hey! That's my property! That tree's on my land! Give me the box, it's mine!' Lulu refused to hand the box over and replied 'I am allowed to walk on this path; I've used it every day for the last 26 years, as you well know'.

'Huh! That's what you think! Well, we'll soon see about that!', replied Hamish. Scooping the coins into the box Lulu grabbed her things from the ground and made her way to the cafe for work.

After work Lulu took the box and coins to the local police, and lodged a claim with them for the box and coins if they could not find the true owner. The police put notices in the paper looking for the owner. When Lulu returned home that evening she found that Hamish had put a fence up along the bottom of his property and the vacant block enclosing the trees and easement, and Lulu had to go back and walk along the main road to get to her cottage. Lulu immediately went home and emailed Archie, with whom she had remained in contact. One week later Lulu received a visit from the local police advising her that her employer, Mrs Stafford, had lodged a claim for the engraved box and coins, and so had Hamish Hamilton.

Two weeks later Hamish lodged an application under s 99 of the Land Title Act 1994 (Qld) over the vacant block. The Land Registry Office then advised him that two caveats had already been lodged against his application, one by Archie Alfred and one by Lulu Lacey.

Advise Hamish of his status concerning the vacant block and the engraved box and coins.

Time allowed: 45 mins

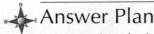

Answer Plan

10-12 Identify the issues: finders keepers and adverse possession.

- Finders keepers:
  - ◆ Identify the parties and their roles:
    - True owner: abandoned?
  - ◆ Finders prior possessor/subsequent possessor:
    - Prove possession — mental and physical intent;
    - Disentitlement — any dishonest intent?
  - ◆ Employer:
    - Employee? Item found in course of employment?
  - ◆ Land owner/occupier:
    - Item embedded? Knowledge of item? Control over space?
- Adverse possession:
  - ◆ Entitlement to claim: timeframe, factors, caveats.

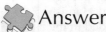

Answer

10-13 Finders keepers: The main objective of finders keepers is to reunite the item with its true owner: *Tamworth Industries Ltd v Attorney-General* (1991) 3 NZLR 616. Here the true owner of the valuable is unknown.

True owner: Proof of ownership would be needed to make the claim. If it could be shown the true owner had abandoned the item, then they would lose all rights to the item: *Re Jigrose Pty Ltd* (1994) 1 Qd 382. However, unless and until abandonment can be proven, the true owner's rights will always be superior to those of any other claimant: *Armory v Delamirie* (1722) 93 ER 664. Mere inactivity will not cause the true owner to lose priority: *Moorhouse v Angus & Robertson (No 1) Pty Ltd* [1981] 1 NSWLR 700.

Finder Lulu: Lulu is making a claim as prior possessor. In order to establish her right to claim she must demonstrate the mental and physical intention to possess: *Button v Cooper* (1947) SASR 286; *The Tubantia* [1924] 18 Lloyd's L. R. 158. Lulu demonstrates this by refusing to hand the box to Hamish, by taking it with her, and by asking the police to return it to her if it is not claimed. Lulu has demonstrated a lack of dishonest intent by asking the police to find the true owner (*Parker v British Airways Board* (1982) 1 QB 1004), and was entitled to be on the land when she found the item: *Bird v Town of Fort Francis* [1949] OR 292.

Subsequent possessor: Hamish does not meet the criteria to make a successful claim as finder. He demonstrated a mental intention to try and possess by trying to take the box from Lulu, but never actually obtained any kind of physical control over the box, nor did he succeed in excluding anyone.

Employer: It is recognised that generally employees find things for their employers: *Hannah v Peel* [1945] 2 All ER 288. Mrs Stafford has made a claim as Lulu's employer. For this to be successful, Lulu must first be proven to be employed as an employee and not as an independent contractor, and it seems as a waitress she is likely to be an employee. Secondly, her employment must be the effective cause of her finding: *Byrne v Hoare* [1965] Qd R 135. Given she found the item along the path while she was walking to work, it is more likely her work was incidental to her finding, as opposed to the effective cause of her finding. If that is the case, Mrs Stafford's claim as Lulu's employer will fail.

Occupiers and land owners: The item was found embedded in the easement. *South Staffordshire Water Co v Sharman* (1896) 2 QB 44, *Elwes v Brigg Gas Co* (1886) 33 Ch D 562; *Waverley Borough Council v Fletcher* [1995] 4 All ER 756 all suggest that when an item is embedded, the land owner will have priority over occupier and finder, regardless of their knowledge of the item.

True owner of land: Archie Alfred has not put in a claim as true owner of the land on which the item was found, and so is not a party to the dispute and cannot be entitled to the item.

Occupiers: Arguably both Lulu and Hamish are equal occupiers of the land by virtue of their easements. Comparatively Lulu's claim would take priority over Hamish's, as she successfully established herself as a finder and she has displayed a lack of dishonest intent. It could be argued Hamish failed to establish himself as a finder and that his attempt to block Lulu from the easement is a sign of dishonest behaviour, by blocking her from her entitled access. Even if Hamish succeeded in his adverse possession claim over Archie's land, Hamish would still be bound by the easement and would have to allow Lulu access; so blocking her is unjustifiable. Comparatively it seems likely Lulu has better entitlement and cleaner hands.

Ultimately it seems Lulu has the most successful claim as finder and occupier.

Adverse possession

The application was made as an adverse possessor under s 99 Land Title Act (Qld) 1994 (LTA) as an exception to indefeasibility under s 185(1)(d) LTA. Schedule 2 defines adverse possession as starting when the adverse possessor meets the legal criteria of adverse possession under s 19(1) Limitation of Actions Act and *Re Johnson*.

The caveats were lodged under s 104 LTA. The caveators had caveatable interests in the land under s 36(b) of the Acts Interpretation Act 1954 (Qld) which would be affected by the adverse possession application, Archie as registered land owner and Lulu as easement holder, and were entitled to lodge caveats against Hamish's application.

True owner: The true owner is known and is without legal disability, so the limitation period would expire after 12 (not 30) years of adverse possession: *Re Johnson*; s 13 Limitation of Actions Act 1974 (Qld) (LAA). The limitation period would start afresh if adverse possession was not continuous: s 19(2) LAA. Hamish's adverse possession must meet the definition of adverse possession under ss 98–108 LTA: it must be not secret, open, peaceful, without owner's consent: *Mulcahy v Curramore*.

The test of the adverse possessor's actions is that they must demonstrate an intention to exclude all, including the true owner. The table below shows the dates of the action, the relevant authority, and whether the action is an indicator of adverse possession (AP).

January 1992		
Paying rates	*Quach v Marrickville*	Strong AP indicator
Mowing	*Buckinghamshire County Council v Moran*	Positive AP indicator
Hosting guests	*Abbatangelo v Whittlesea City Council*	Positive AP indicator
1998		
Sydney for 2 years, back 4 weekly	*Abbatangelo v Whittlesea City Council*	Not abandonment
July 2000 permanent move back		
August 2006		
Fence	*Buckinghamshire County Council v Moran; George Wimpey & Co Ltd v Sohn; Riley v Pentilla*	Not AP indicator as below

Fencing: Both the extent and purpose of fencing are relevant. Here the adverse possessor, Hamish, fenced off the easement primarily to annoy Lulu, the other easement holder, because she refused to hand over the treasure box, not because he was trying to exclude others.

Remedies: The registrar may refuse Hamish's application under s 107(1)(a) LTA.

Easement: The adverse possessor is likely to be bound by the registered easement if they become the registered owner: s 184(1) LTA.

Conclusion: If the adverse possession clock runs continuously from 1992–2010 then it has run for 18 years and Hamish's adverse possession claim will succeed and Hamish will be the registered owner.

If the clock stops in 1998 and starts again in 2000, then only 10 years have passed and Hamish's adverse possession claim would fail, and Archie would remain the registered owner.

Examiner's Comments

10-14 The student has made a good attempt at unravelling the two issues. The answer has been presented clearly and logically in an easy-to-follow format. All the relevant facts in the question have been acknowledged and addressed.

Under the finders keepers part of the question the student made a good effort at not just identifying the legal tests but also applying them to the facts in the question. The table was a nice clear way of laying out information in the adverse possession section, but it would have been better with more information on the cases and more detail about the facts pulled from the question in relation to the authorities. It lacked the detail of which rule from the case was applied and why it was appropriate to apply that case in this scenario. Citing cases is not enough; it should be accompanied by an explanation of why the case is being applied in this instance. The conclusion of the adverse possession part of the question was also a bit light on remedies available to the registrar under statute and more reference should have been made to the Act.

Overall a good attempt. The finders keepers portion of the answer was more thorough with more explanation and application to the facts in the question, while the adverse possession section of the answer was not at the same level.

Keep in Mind

10-15 Students should keep in mind the following:

- Always address issues chronologically, not based on which one you think you know better. This student managed to avoid falling into the trap of addressing the adverse possession question first, which could have resulted in successfully establishing Hamish's adverse possession claim and then resolving the finders keepers claim with Hamish in the position of land owner, and thus successful winner of the item, which would have been clearly incorrect.
- All problem-style questions are exercises in application. All too frequently, examiners are presented with answers which purport to 'advise' the hypothetical client, but which, in fact, do little more than recite abstract legal propositions.
- Never report cases as if they have equal precedential value where they do not. Evaluate any precedent, both in terms of its factual similarity to the hypothetical and in terms of its curial source.

Question 3

10-16 In 1969 Waratah Municipal Council acquired a parcel of land (the parcel) with a view to carrying out a road widening project. It was envisaged by the council that the project would not require commencement, nor would funds be available, for several years and accordingly the land was left vacant.

The parcel adjoined Tony's land, and although the council fenced the roadside boundary of the parcel, no fence was erected between the parcel and Tony's garden. The only means of access to the parcel was thus through Tony's land.

Tony maintained the parcel and treated it as part of his garden. In 1983, Tony sold his land to Elizabeth. She knew that the parcel belonged to the council, but continued to maintain the parcel as if it was part of the garden.

In December 1987, the council wrote to Elizabeth asking her on what basis she exercised rights over the parcel. In January 1988, Elizabeth replied by letter stating that she understood that she was entitled to use the parcel until the road widening project was undertaken. Elizabeth's letter was expressed to be 'without prejudice'. In February 1988, the council replied by letter, and disclaimed Elizabeth's right to use the land. Nothing more was done by the council.

The council now wishes to know whether it may commence proceedings to recover the parcel and what are its chances of success. Advise the council.

Time allowed: 45 mins

Answer Plan

10-17 The plan for approaching a problem such as this is relatively straightforward:

* The doctrine of implied licence — is it good law in Australia?

  Refer to *Buckinghamshire County Council v Moran* [1989] 2 All ER 225; *Leigh v Jack* (1879) 5 Ex D 264; *Clement v Jones* (1909) 8 CLR 133; and *Wallis Cayton Bay Holiday Camp Ltd v Shell-Mex and BP Ltd* [1974] 3 All ER 575.

* The facts of Tony and Elizabeth's occupation of the parcel:

  What is in evidence about the facts and circumstances of Tony and Elizabeth's occupation of the land in question? Do the facts evidence an intention on their part to treat the land as their own, to the exclusion of all others (including the council)?

* Successive adverse possession:

  If Tony has not (by himself) statute-barred the council, might Elizabeth 'tack on' her own time in possession to make a cumulate period of adverse possession sufficient to bar the council? What is the effect of Elizabeth's letter?

Refer to *Asher v Whitlock* (1865) LR 1 QB 1; *Allen v Roughly* (1955) 94 CLR 98.

 # Answer

10-18 The advice given to council is largely based upon the English case *Buckinghamshire County Council v Moran* [1989] 2 All ER 225, as there has not yet been any clear Australian authority on such a fact scenario at appellate level. The facts present a number of related issues, all concerning the doctrine of adverse possession. First, it must be determined whether the possession of the parcel of land by Tony and Elizabeth could be under the council's implied licence. Second, it must be determined whether Tony could have been considered to be in adverse possession of the land in question. Finally, it must be determined whether Elizabeth succeeded to Tony's possessory interest (if any) and whether she continued in adverse possession.

Possession cannot be 'adverse' where it is taken under a permission or licence from the lawful owner of the land. There have been some instances where the courts have been prepared to imply such a licence. In particular, the courts have been prepared to imply a licence where a purported adverse possessor's possession of the land was not inconsistent with its true owner's current use of, or future plans for, the land. This rule appears to have developed from the English case of *Leigh v Jack* (1879) 5 Ex D 264 and was mentioned with approval by Griffith CJ of the High Court of Australia in *Clement v Jones* (1909) 8 CLR 133. The 'implied licence doctrine' reached its zenith in the judgment of Lord Denning MR in *Wallis Cayton Bay Holiday Camp Ltd v Shell-Mex and BP Ltd* [1974] 3 All ER 575. In more recent years, however, the doctrine has been discredited, and in particular Slade LJ in *Buckinghamshire County Council v Moran* held that the doctrine was not good law because its practical effect is to abrogate the legislature's limitation of actions legislation.

In the United Kingdom, parliament has confirmed its opposition to judicial interference with the limitation of actions legislation and abolished any remnant of the doctrine of implied licence. Criticism of the doctrine has been endorsed in Australia, but only by single judges. As yet there is no higher Australian authority upon the implied licence rule, and the possibility that the council might rely upon the doctrine remains open — with some hint of support from Griffith CJ in *Clement v Jones*. Therefore, council may attempt to argue that at all material times any purported possession by either Elizabeth or Tony is not inconsistent with council's future plans for road development, so that time does not run in their favour, and therefore no adverse possession will arise. Given the recent criticism of this approach its chances of success must be considered slim.

The second issue raised by the facts concerns whether Tony may have acquired the rights of a possessor. A person who enters into and maintains possession of land for the 12-year period specified by the Limitation Act 1969 (NSW) gains a title to the land which is good against the rest of the world. Council could, without question, have recovered the land before the 12-year period expired, but upon the expiry of this period council's title to land and right of action are extinguished.

Time runs from the date of Tony's trespass, which from the facts may have been as early as 1969. Whether possession was in fact assumed by Tony can be determined from evidence of the normal physical and mental elements of possession. The facts suggest that Tony had fulfilled the normal requirements of assuming possession: he had the only means of access to the parcel of land and had incorporated the parcel as part of his own land. Where a trespasser took similar actions in the *Buckinghamshire* case, Slade LJ held that there was little more which could have been done to complete the physical control of the land in question.

So far as the *animus possidendi,* the mental element of possession, is concerned, a trespasser must intend to exclude the world at large, including the true owner, from the use and enjoyment of the land and to treat the land as his or her own. To make out the relevant intention it would be necessary to demonstrate that an intention to possess the land, on the part of Tony (and later Elizabeth), could be inferred from acts such as the enclosure of the land and its maintenance as a garden. It should be noted that while these two actions have clear probative value (going to intention), neither Tony nor Elizabeth placed a lock on the land as was done in the *Buckinghamshire* case. Nevertheless, it would appear that both Tony, and later Elizabeth, would at least be able to put forward a strong argument that council was dispossessed in 1969 and that, therefore, their right of action and title to the parcel has now been extinguished.

Third, Elizabeth's purchase of Tony's land and her continuation of Tony's use of the parcel must be considered. If it can be shown that Elizabeth continued Tony's trespassory acts, with the requisite intention, then it is possible for her to 'tack on' Tony's period of adverse possession to her own and thus bar the council: *Asher v Whitlock* (1865) LR 1 QB 1 and *Allen v Roughly* (1955) 94 CLR 98. It appears that there was no material difference between Elizabeth and Tony's use and enjoyment of the parcel of land in question so, prima facie, the council will be barred by statute from asserting its title. Thus, council could not prevent Elizabeth's possession, simply because at the time of their letter to Elizabeth she had only utilised the parcel for four years. While time would cease to run against the council upon any admission of the council's title by Elizabeth, her letter of January 1988 comes after the sufficient time period has already elapsed (assuming she has continued Tony's adverse possession and that the council is already barred), and thus is of no effect. Alternatively, assuming she has not continued Tony's adverse possession, it must be noted that Elizabeth's letter was expressed to be 'without prejudice', so it will not be available to the council as evidence of an admission on Elizabeth's part that the council had title. All the same, even if Elizabeth did not continue Tony's adverse possession, it is possible that she may be able to make out her own sufficient period of adverse possession. Although the facts do not disclose any material difference between Tony and Elizabeth's possession of the land in question, it may be open to the council (if further facts were available) to argue that Elizabeth did not manifest either the requisite physical or mental elements of possession or that she did not do so until after her letter of 1988.

If this last alternative is available (ie if further facts reveal that Elizabeth's possession of the parcel did not *commence* until 1988), council is advised to initiate legal proceedings for the recovery of the parcel of land immediately. Otherwise, council will have to rely upon the implied licence doctrine which, as indicated, does not offer strong hopes of success.

Examiner's Comments

10-19   The answer states, accurately, that there is no appellate authority for the rejection of the implied licence doctrine in Australia. There is also evident in the answer some recognition that the doctrine has been criticised by a single judge (or judges), but this line is not pursued. This is something of a conspicuous omission, and some reference should have been made to *Woodward v Wesley Hazell Pty Ltd* [1994] ANZ ConvR 632 and *Shaw v Garbutt* (1996) 7 BPR 14,816 per Young J at least. Justice Young had occasion to reiterate his resistance to the doctrine in *Re North Sydney Council* (SC(NSW), No 3838 of 1996, 17 September 1997, unreported). Other recent cases dealing with adverse possession (more generally) include: *Malter v Procopets* [1998] VSC 79 (23 September 1998) per Smith J and *Re Johnson* [1999] QSC 197 (19 August 1999) per Wilson J. The answer, in this respect, may have been further augmented by the citation of dicta from some of the more important cases, although under exam conditions it is acknowledged that this may be an over-ambitious requirement.

The answer is a little flimsy in its consideration of the effect of Elizabeth's letter. Is this an admission of the council's title? Is it sufficient to say that her use of a 'no prejudice' rubric avoids any possible admission? Commenting upon an English case, *Edgington v Clark* [1964] 1 QB 367, Bryson J in *Cawthorne v Thomas* (1993) 6 BPR 13,840 stated in relation to an offer to purchase disputed land that:

> ... there was not in their Lordships' view a general principle that an offer to purchase freehold property is an acknowledgment that the offeree has a better title than the offeror. Their Lordships' judgment shows the need for consideration of the whole terms of the supposed acknowledgment in its circumstances.

There are some important academic articles which are worthy of consideration: D Jackson, 'The Legal Effects of the Passing of Time' (1970) 7 *MULR* 407; M Goodman, 'Adverse Possession of Land — Morality and Motive' (1970) 33 *Mod LR* 281; and D Irving, 'Should the Law Recognise the Acquisition of Title by Adverse Possession?' (1994) *APLJ* 112. In an assignment, as opposed to a formal exam, a student would be expected to tease out some of the theoretical issues raised by the concept of adverse possession, such as the morality of the law as it now stands. As part of a more detailed consideration one might also be expected to consider other issues not directly raised by the hypothetical facts, such as the effect of the payment of council rates: see *Quach v Marrickville Municipal Council (No 2)* (1990) 22 NSWLR 55.

Keep in Mind

10-20 Students should keep in mind the following:

- In adverse possession problems, always examine the dates carefully. If the limitation period has expired the plaintiff's action is barred. The critical time, therefore, is when time starts to run against the plaintiff. At what stage can it be said that the squatter has dispossessed the plaintiff (and thus given rise to an action)? One must be able to point to facts which are capable of demonstrating that the intruder held the relevant intention to treat the land as his or her own, to the exclusion of the true owner.

- Be aware of the current legislation in your state: Limitation Act 1985 (ACT); Limitation Act 1969 (NSW); Limitation of Actions Act 1974 (Qld); Limitation of Actions Act 1936 (SA); Limitation Act 1974 (Tas); Limitation of Actions Act 1958 (Vic); Limitation Act 1935 (WA). In New South Wales, Queensland, Western Australia and Tasmania, the limitation period (for land) is 12 years. In Victoria and South Australia the period is 15 years.

- The implied licence doctrine may have been criticised by single justices of state Supreme Courts, but there has not yet been similar criticism at the state appellate level or by the High Court of Australia. It therefore remains an option for a plaintiff to argue that an adverse possessor's alleged possession of land has not been sufficiently 'adverse' to his or her intended uses of the property and, accordingly, does not amount to possession in law. A plaintiff might therefore argue that the squatter is merely a persistent trespasser, but not a 'possessor' in the legal sense. We await higher authority before consigning the implied licence to the annals of legal history.

Question 4

> **10-21**   Othello entered into a contract with Iago Pools Ltd (IPL) to design and construct a swimming pool in the backyard of his Brisbane house.
>
> Troy and Cassius are the employees of IPL involved in the construction of the pool. While excavating the soil from Othello's house and shovelling into a truck, Troy struck a large wooden box. At that time Cassius was four metres away shovelling into the other side of the truck. Troy pulled the box out and examined it with Cassius. Inside the box was a rare and valuable leather-bound copy of Makepeace's famous book, *Shakspire's Singles*.
>
> Troy and Cassius then jointly re-buried the large box (with the book inside) and informed their employer. The next morning, the managing director of IPL dug up the box and handed the book to the police.
>
> After a series of newspaper announcements, Othello, Troy, Cassius and IPL all lodged claims to the book with the police.
>
> Who is entitled to the rare and valuable copy of *Shakspire's Singles*?
>
> **Time allowed: 45 mins**

Answer Plan

10-22   The plan is as follows:

- True owner — unknown: proof of ownership, abandonment;
- Finder: Prior possessor — Troy;
- Finder: Subsequent possessor;
- Employer;
- Occupier;
- Priority: True owner finder — Troy; IPL — employer: yes; occupier: no;
- Go through for each claimant:
    ♦ identify their alleged entitlement and whether they can support their claim;
    ♦ test-proof of their entitlement;
    ♦ lose rights: have they anything to disentitle them from their claim?
    ♦ final position under *Armory v Delamirie* (1722) 93 ER 664,
- Approach it from all perspectives: identify all parties:
    ♦ finder versus true owner: Troy versus unknown;
    ♦ finder versus occupier: Troy versus Othello;
    ♦ finder versus employer: Troy versus IPL.

If 'finding' was in the course of employment it is likely that the employer has better priority than the finder; however, as the item was embedded in the land then it is likely that the occupier has better priority.

The true owner will always have best priority unless it can be argued that they abandoned it and gave up mental possession (in this case it is unsure who is the true owner or their intention).

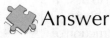 Answer

Is othello the true owner?

10-23 The objective of the finder's law is to reunite the lost item with its true owner: *Tamworth Industries Ltd v Attorney-General* (1993) 3 NZLR 616.

Proof of ownership: Othello would most likely argue he is the true owner as the owner/occupier of the property. However, there is no proof he had any knowledge of the book's location and, given the book's age, it is more likely that the book was heavily embedded in the ground long before his arrival.

Abandonment: Even if Othello could prove he is the true owner, has he abandoned the book? The test in *Re Jigrose Pty Ltd* (1994) 1 Qd 382: did the true owner intend to relinquish his or her proprietary interest in the book when the book first went missing in the park? Mere inactivity (mere failure to dig up the book) is not abandonment *Moorhouse v Angus Robertson Pty Ltd (No 1) Pty Ltd* [1981] 1 NSWLR 700.

It would be difficult for Othello to argue he is the true owner as he has no proof of ownership; therefore, his claim may be stronger if he makes the argument on the basis of being the *owner/occupier* of the land where the object was found.

Finder — Troy

In order to be a finder he needs to demonstrate the physical and mental elements of possession: *Button v Cooper* (1947) SASR 286; *The Tubantia* [1924] 18 Lloyd's L. R. 158. Troy did have physical control of the box, but did he ever intend to keep the book permanently? The fact that he shared the find with Cassius indicates perhaps not, as well as the fact he reburied the box. However, reburying the box could also be viewed as a demonstration of a lack of dishonest intent, as he then reported the find to his employer. There is no issue of trespass as he is entitled to be on Othello's land, and is carrying out a legitimate activity when he finds the box: *Bird v Town of Fort Frances* [1949] OR 292. If he can prove his prior possession then his claim as the finder may succeed against all except the true owner: *Armory v Delamirie* (1722) 93 ER 664. The most significant competing issue here is that of the employer, which was fatal to the finder in *Ranger v Giffin* (1968) 87 WN (NSW) (Pt 1) 531.

Finder/subsequent possessor — Cassius?

Cassius did not find the book so he would have a very poor claim if *Ranger v Giffin* is followed. Even if Cassius could make a claim as subsequent possessor, Troy's prior possession would prevail (*Asher v Whitlock* (1865) LR 1 QB 1), and his claim would also be subject to IPL's claim as Troy's employer.

Employer/occupier — IPL

As employer: No information is provided about the employment contract between IPL and Troy and Cassius, so the presumption is that Troy is not contractually bound to hand over property. IPL may raise the general rule in *Hannah v Peel* [1945] 1 KB 509, that is employees finding things during the course of employment generally find them for their employers, but this is always subject to the test in *Byrne v Hoare* [1965] Qd R 135: is Troy's employment the effective cause of the finding? *Byrne v Hoare* is distinguishable here as Troy was on duty and performing the tasks for which he was employed when the book was found, so his employment would be the effective cause of his finding. Arguably IPL have quite a good case to suggest they have a better claim than Troy.

As occupier: IPL may argue that they had constructive possession of, and control over, the portion of Othello's land where the box and book were found. However, such right of occupation was derived from the contract with Othello, and was temporary in nature and for limited purposes, as in *Ranger v Giffin*, it was merely a licence to perform a contract. Unless the purpose for which they occupied the space as stated in the terms of the contract, allowed IPL to retain everything they excavated, it is unlikely their remit would include salvage rights to valuable items. Generally such contracts allow for the removal of soil or debris, which would not include this item. It is unlikely they would have a successful claim as an occupier.

IPL displayed no dishonest intent either, as they handed the book to the police. It seems possible they may have a case as employer, but not one as occupier.

Owner/occupier — Othello

As the owner of fee simple he has the strongest claim to ownership: *Bridges v Hawkesworth* (1851) 21 LJQB 75; *Ranger v Giffin*. However, his entitlement is impacted by whether the book was found on or in the land, and whether it was partially or completely buried.

If the box were embedded in the land, then Othello's actual possession of the land would constitute constructive possession of the book. If it were unattached to the land (not the likely scenario here as it was found during excavation) then Othello would need to demonstrate either knowledge of the item or control over the area: *Parker v British Airways Board* (1982) 1 QB 1004; *Bridges v Hawkesworth* (1851) 21 LJQB 75. If Othello could not prove he had control over the area, he would need to show he knew the item was there, although as it is a private dwelling he could argue his position is more akin to *National Crime Authority v Flack* (1998) 86 FCR 16 than *Hannah v Peel* so having no knowledge of the item may not be fatal to his claim.

As the item was embedded, Othello would raise such cases as *South Staffordshire Water Co v Sharman* (1896) 2 QB 44 (rings in swimming pool); *Elwes v Brigg Gas Co* (1886) 33 Ch D 562 (boat embedded below surface); and *Waverley Borough Council v Fletcher* [1995] 4 All ER 756 (use of metal detector in park). Othello would need to distinguish his position from those cases where the item was not attached: *Bridges v Hawkesworth; Parker v British Airways.*

Although it is debatable, it is most likely Othello has the best claim, assuming judgment was made along the same lines as *Ranger v Giffin.*

Conclusion: Cassius does not satisfy the first test as he is not a finder and thus has no entitlement to ownership of the item. Although Troy could make a successful claim as finder, his claim is likely to be beaten by IPL's claim as his employer, despite their failure to establish a claim as occupier. However, based on the balance of probabilities, it seems Othello satisfies the test as land owner, and is therefore the most likely to be entitled to the rare and valuable copy of *Shakspire's Singles* as the item was embedded in the land. Othello's claim will win against all but the true owner: *Armory v Delamirie.*

 ## Examiner's Comments

10-24 The answer is correct to point out, from the outset, that there is often a true owner to consider. The rights of the true owner, unless he or she has abandoned the goods, will always be paramount to those of a finder or those of a person upon whose land objects are found. In *Moffat v Kazana* [1969] 2 QB 152, Wrangham J considered whether a vendor of a house who had forgotten that he had hidden an old biscuit box full of money in his chimney had abandoned it. His Honour held that more than a flawed memory was required to evidence an intention to relinquish possession.

The answer also quite rightly recognises that the objective of the law is to balance the interests of claimants, and this student attempts to weigh up and identify the competing interests of each party. Again there are issues of structure and layout here. The student has attempted to be clear in their answer but there are too many disjointed sentences for it to read well.

Much like the earlier answer, this is clearly in the style of an exam answer. However, in most instances this answer does a better job of explaining which cases are being used and why. There is still a lack of fluidity and structure, but the use of headings to separate and clarify the relationships under discussion is always a good idea.

Ultimately, the issues are clearly grasped and identified and it is a good attempt to clearly address all the issues raised by each party in the question.

Keep in Mind

10-25   Students should keep in mind the following:

- Do not forget to do both parts of the test for each party: not only does each party have to prove their entitlement to their claim, but you should always check a party has not lost their entitlement through other actions. For example, finders must prove their entitlement to a claim as finder by proving possession, but they lose their entitlement if they do not demonstrate a lack of dishonest intent.
- If it is established that an item is not attached to the land, it is important to thoroughly examine the occupier/landowner's knowledge of the item and control over the area, rather than skim over those issues, as they are determinative in forming a conclusion.
- Remember to use authorities to justify statements; this area is primarily common law and any conclusion must be borne out of precedent.

Question 5

10-26   Clarke Properties Pty Ltd is a large company in the business of developing rural properties. The company has recently purchased an old system property known as Mortimer's Edge for the purpose of developing it as a 'farmstay' tourist venture. The southern boundary of Mortimer's Edge, according to the survey plan (which is incorporated into the contract of sale, the deeds and other documentation relating to Mortimer's Edge) extends along a line 500 metres (more or less) to the south of, and parallel to, a creek known as Scrubby Creek. To the south of Mortimer's Edge lies another old system property, Itylldoo. Itylldoo is owned by Patrick Carroll, who runs about 300 sheep on the property.

The previous owner of Mortimer's Edge, Clive Roebuck, was a friend of Patrick Carroll's. When Patrick bought Itylldoo in 1977, he asked Clive whether he could remove a section of the fence which separated their properties. Patrick explained that he wanted to be able to take some of his sheep down to drink at Scrubby Creek from time to time. Clive agreed, a bit reluctantly, but stipulated that Patrick would have to put in a gate, keep the whole of the fence in good repair, and not use the land on the southern bank of the creek for grazing sheep. Shortly after, Clive had a heart attack and did not visit the area south of the creek again. Clive's son took over the management of Mortimer's Edge, but was so busy on the rest of the property that he did not visit the land south of the creek either. Clive remained the owner of the property until his death in 1995; then his son inherited Mortimer's Edge. Clarke Properties Pty Ltd purchased the property from Clive's son in 1998.

In 1979, Patrick had become tired of opening and closing the gate, and in fact he removed it and also a large section of the fence which separated the properties. He allowed his sheep to wander freely and graze over the strip of land near the creek. By 1981, all of the fence had completely fallen down. Now that Clarke Properties Pty Ltd have bought Mortimer's Edge, the company wishes to use the creek as an important part of the 'farmstay' experience it will offer its guests. The company plans barbecue, swimming and fishing activities for which the creek will be ideal. To this end, the company has prepared plans to erect a cabin on the south side of the creek, the northern side being unsuitable for construction. But when Clarke Properties' builders arrive on the site Patrick warns them off and says that the strip of land south of the creek is now his.

Does Patrick have a good claim to the 500-metre-wide strip of land next to the creek on the southern side?

How would your answer differ if the titles to the two properties were registered under the Torrens system?

Time allowed: 45 mins

 Answer Plan

10-27   The basic question: has Patrick dispossessed Clive, his son and/or Clarke Properties of the disputed land?

- the issue of permission;
- Patrick's acts and his *animus possidendi*;
- if Patrick has taken possession of the land, when did time start to run against Clive?
- Clive's heart attack: is there an extension of the limitation period?

Note that all states have provisions to extend the limitation where the person to whom an action accrues suffers a disability:

- examples — New South Wales and Victoria;
- what is a 'disability'?
- how might Clive's disability (if he suffers one) affect the running of time?

What if the properties were subject to the Torrens system of title registration?

- Summarise the various relationships between possessory titles and systems of title registration in the states.
- Note in particular that the disputed 500-metre strip does not constitute a 'whole parcel' or a 'lot', and in which jurisdictions this may be significant.

 Answer

10-28   Patrick's claim to the disputed land will depend upon whether his possession of the land has had the effect of dispossessing Clive (and his successors), and whether any action for recovery of the land which may have arisen in favour of Clive (or his successors) is now statute-barred. Whether Patrick has effectively dispossessed Clive, his son and Clarke Properties, will turn on (firstly) the issue of Clive's permission to use the land, and (secondly) on Patrick's acts and his *animus possidendi* in relation to the disputed land. It is also important to note that Clive's heart attack may result in an extension of the limitation period. If the properties were subject to the Torrens system of title registration, then the various relationships between possessory titles and the systems of title registration in the various states must be examined. It is significant (in some jurisdictions) that the disputed 500-metre strip does not constitute a 'whole parcel' or a 'lot'.

It is well established that to dispossess the owner of land there must be actual possession of the land without licence or permission. That possession must consist of: an appropriate degree of exclusive physical control of the land in question coupled with an intention to possess that land to the exclusion of all others (including the true owner). Patrick's first occupation of the disputed land in 1977 was with the permission of Clive. His initial possession, therefore, cannot amount to adverse possession. It may be argued by Patrick that the nature of his possession changed, and that (perhaps in 1979) he formed the intention to dispossess Clive and thereafter he treated the land as his own. Since the land was rural in character, Patrick's use of the disputed strip for grazing (as opposed to mere watering) may be held to be consistent with exclusive possession. Whether there has been an adequate degree of exclusive control will depend upon the nature of the property, its character and location, and the ordinary use to which a proprietor might be expected to put the land. In *Kirby v Cowderoy* (1912) AC 599 Lord Shaw of Dunfermline said:

> Possession must be considered in every case with reference to the peculiar circumstances ... the character and value of the property, the suitable and natural mode of using it, the course of conduct which the proprietor might reasonably be expected to follow with a due regard to his own interests; all these things, greatly varying as they must under various conditions, are to be taken into account in determining the sufficiency of a possession.

Patrick's use of the property for grazing is not consistent with the terms of the licence given to him by Clive. It is also significant that the other terms of the licence (the keeping of the gate and fence) were disregarded by Patrick. It is arguable that in 1979 (and perhaps by 1981 at the latest) Patrick may be able to demonstrate, by reference to his overt acts, that he had assumed exclusive control of the disputed land, and done so with the intention of dispossessing Clive. If this can be made out, for the purposes of the limitation period, time would therefore have commenced to run against Clive not later than in 1981. The result would be that Clive (and his successors) would have been statute-barred (at the latest) in 1993 (in New South Wales, Queensland, Tasmania or Western Australia) or in 1996 (in South Australia or Victoria). All other factors aside, it could be argued by Patrick that he has a possessory title to the disputed land which cannot be challenged by Clarke Properties Pty Ltd because the company is statute-barred.

It is important to note that, shortly after the agreement between Patrick and Clive, Clive suffered a heart attack. Extensions of the limitation period are available where a person to whom a cause of action has accrued suffers a disability. If Clive was under such a 'disability' as a result of his heart attack then, even if Patrick is able to demonstrate his dispossession of Clive, Clive (and his successors in title — his son and Clarke Properties Pty Ltd) may not yet be statute-barred. The rules in relation to the extensions vary according to the jurisdiction where the land is located.

In New South Wales, the limitation period against a person who is under a disability is suspended while he or she remains under the disability: s 52(1) Limitation Act 1969 (NSW). If he or she dies while still under the disability, his or her estate is allowed three years in which to commence the action. In New South Wales, a person is under a disability if he or she is, inter alia, unable to manage his or her affairs in relation to the cause of action for at least 28 days by reason of mental or physical disease: s 11(3) Limitation Act 1969 (NSW). The effect of the extension of the limitation period, if the land is in New South Wales, and if Clive was 'disabled' in the sense designated by the legislation, and (of course) if Patrick in fact dispossessed Clive not later than in 1980, is that Patrick's estate in the 500-metre strip was complete in 1998 (notwithstanding the inheritance of Clive's son and the conveyance to Clarke Properties Pty Ltd). By contrast, in Victoria (where the base period is 15 years), the extensions (in cases of both continuing disability and death under disability) are six years.

The definition of 'disability', for these purposes, in Victoria is where a person is for reasons of mental or physical incompetence unable to make reasonable judgments with respect to his or her estate: ss 3 and 23 Limitation of Actions Act 1958 (Vic). However, in Victoria, a person must suffer the relevant disability at the time of the accrual of the action: a subsequent disability will not attract the extension. On the facts it is possible that there could be no extension of the limitation period if the land is in Victoria, and thus if Patrick is able to demonstrate his possession for 15 years, Clarke Properties Pty Ltd will be barred from bringing its action. Other jurisdictions have similar provisions to extend the statutory limitation period where the landowner suffers a disability.

If the titles to the two properties were registered under the Torrens system then the preceding advice may need to be significantly modified. The effects of the Torrens system on the general law rules of adverse possession are also highly dependent upon the applicable jurisdiction. In the Australian Capital Territory there is no provision for the acquisition of title by adverse possessors: no procedure exists for squatters to obtain title and no registered proprietor's title can be extinguished by operation of limitations rules: s 69 Real Property Act 1925 (ACT). Patrick would certainly fail if the disputed land was in the Australian Capital Territory. In New South Wales, it is possible, by virtue of Pt VIA of the Real Property

Act 1900, for an adverse possessor who can demonstrate possession for the statutory period to obtain registration of a 'whole parcel of land'.

Even if all other aspects of adverse possession could be made out, Patrick has not dispossessed the owners of Mortimer's Edge of their 'whole parcel' and thus, in New South Wales, his claim to adverse possession would also fail. The position in Queensland is similar to that in New South Wales. In Queensland, adverse possession may be acquired against the owner of a 'lot': ss 98 and 99 Land Title Act 1994 (Qld). Again, Patrick's claim would fail if the disputed land was situated in Queensland.

In South Australia, the position is somewhat unclear, with the potential for adverse possession of portions of Torrens land existing under ss 251 and 80A–80I of the Real Property Act 1886 (SA), but with that 'right' of the squatter apparently subject to a caveat by the registered proprietor. In South Australia, the registrar is required to refuse applications by persons such as Patrick where he or she is satisfied that a counterclaim (by way of caveat) is made by the registered proprietor: s 80f. It would appear, therefore, that Patrick's claim (even if all other factors of adverse possession were made out) could be easily defeated in South Australia upon the lodgment of a caveat by Clarke Properties Pty Ltd, in response to any application by Patrick for registration. In Victoria, Tasmania and Western Australia, there is no effective distinction between adverse possession of general law land and Torrens system land: s 42(2)(b) Transfer of Land Act 1958 (Vic); s 117 Land Titles Act 1980 (Tas); and s 68 Transfer of Land Act 1893 (WA). All other tests being satisfied, Patrick may (in theory) obtain a good title to the disputed land if it is situated in either Victoria, Tasmania or Western Australia.

Patrick's claim to the disputed land depends upon whether his possession of the land has had the effect of dispossessing Clive (and his successors). Patrick's acts and his *animus possidendi* in relation to the disputed land may, arguably, be held to amount to adverse possession since about 1980. If there is no extension to the limitation period due to Clive's heart attack, or if any extension is itself exhausted by lapse of time, Patrick may now have the best (possessory) title to the land.

Alternatively, if the properties were subject to the Torrens system of title registration, then it is crucial (in New South Wales particularly) that the disputed 500-metre strip does not constitute a 'whole parcel'. Conversely, in Victoria, this fact would make no difference to Patrick's claim. The Torrens statutes of the states vary significantly in how the claims of adverse possessors can be dealt with.

Examiner's Comments

10-29 While the concept of adverse possession is almost universal throughout Australia (the exception being the Australian Capital Territory), the sample answer correctly notes that there are significant differences in the details and the applications of the law of adverse possession from state to state. For expository reasons, this sample answer attempts to cover the field in a way in which a student's tutorial or examination answer would not be expected to. In so doing, some attention to detail is lost, but reference may be made to Question 4 above for this. It will be noted that in respect of the Torrens system alternative, the answer attempts to traverse all jurisdictions, while in relation to the rules concerning the extensions to the limitations periods for disabilities the answer only attempts to consider two states, New South Wales and Victoria. Again, there is some degree of artificiality here for expository reasons.

The legislation regarding the extension of the limitation period for persons suffering a disability (other than New South Wales and Victoria), is to be found in: s 29 Limitation of Actions Act 1974 (Qld); s 45 Limitation of Actions Act 1936 (SA); ss 26–28 Limitation Act 1974 (Tas); ss 16, 40 and 41 Limitation Act 1935 (WA). Also, in relation to the extension of the limitation period for persons suffering a disability, note that in New South Wales there is, nevertheless, an 'ultimate' bar. In normal circumstances, no action to recover land may be commenced more than 30 years after the right of action first arose: s 51 Limitation Act 1969 (NSW). However, even this 'ultimate' bar can be extended. In extremely abnormal situations, it may be possible to extend the period beyond 30 years under the provisions in Pt 3 Div 3 Subdiv 3 of the Act. Other states' 'ultimate' bars are to be found in: s 29(2)(b) Limitation of Actions Act 1974 (Qld); s 45(3) Limitation of Actions Act 1936 (SA); s 26(4) Limitation Act 1974 (Tas); s 23(1)(c) Limitation of Actions Act 1958 (Vic); and ss 18 and 19 Limitation Act 1935 (WA).

The Torrens systems of the states vary in many respects, not the least in so far as they deal with the rules of adverse possession. It should be noted that the position in Tasmania is not entirely identical to the positions in Victoria and Western Australia. In the latter two states there is, within the Torrens statutes, an explicit recognition of the rights of adverse possessors. In Tasmania, the legislation is expressed in terms of a 'trust' which binds the registered proprietor in favour of the adverse possessor. Nonetheless, the 'effective' position is probably accurately stated. It should also be noted that the caveat procedure (noticed in relation to South Australia) also applies in Queensland, although without the apparently strict requirement upon the registrar to determine the claim in the favour of the caveat-lodging registered proprietor. The answer provides a good summary of the various legislative regimes, without losing focus on the facts of the problem.

 # Keep in Mind

10-30 Students should keep in mind the following:

- Unless otherwise stated in a question, you should assume that the relevant law (for your answer) is that of your own state. This does not mean that, in the appropriate circumstances, some references to the nuances or subtleties of other jurisdictions might not still be relevant and interesting.

- The answer states: 'The effect of the extension of the limitation period, if the land is in New South Wales, and if Clive was 'disabled' in the sense designated by the legislation, and (of course) if Patrick in fact dispossessed Clive not later than in 1980, is that Patrick's estate in the 500-metre strip was complete in 1998 (notwithstanding the inheritance of Clive's son and the conveyance to Clarke Properties Pty Ltd).' Although probably correct, this answer is elliptical. Beware the 'three-year' extension and note that it applies if the limitation would *otherwise* expire within three years after the documentary owner ceases to be under the disability: then the period is extended to allow the owner a full three years after the disability ceases.

- The section (s 52 Limitation Act 1969 (NSW)) states (with emphasis added):

(1) Subject to subsections (2) and (3) and subject to section 53, where:
    (a) a person has a cause of action;
    (b) the limitation period fixed by this Act for the cause of action has commenced to run; and
    (c) the person is under a disability, in that case:
    (d) the running of the limitation period is suspended for the duration of the disability; and
    (e) *if, but for this paragraph, the limitation period would expire before the lapse of three years after:*
        (i) *the date on which the person last (before the expiration of the limitation period) ceases to be under a disability; or*
        (ii) *the date of the person's death,*
    (whichever date is the earlier), the limitation period is extended so as to expire three years after the earlier of those dates.

(2) This section applies whenever a person is under a disability, whether or not the person is under the same or another disability at any time during the limitation period.

(3) This section does not apply to a cause of action to recover a penalty or forfeiture or sum by way of penalty or forfeiture, except where the person having the cause of action is an aggrieved party.

In other words, (in New South Wales) in no circumstance does the legislation operate to render the limitation period of a person under a disability to a total of less than 12 years.

Chapter 11

The Doctrine of Fixtures

Key Issues

11-1   The doctrine of fixtures deals with the law regarding the distinction between real property (land), and items or things which are in some way attached or connected to real property. The doctrine can provide answers to questions such as 'what items connected with land can be considered part of the land?' and 'when will items connected to the land be classed as part of the land and when will they still be viewed as chattels?' The doctrine of fixtures exhibits marked inconsistencies and can fairly be described as disjointed. Many of the cases appear to disagree and even after application of the tests, the conclusion can often, at best, be termed likely rather than definitive. It is important to recognise apparent inconsistencies in this area of law, rather than try and avoid them.

It is important to apply the legal tests to each item in question individually, and to pay attention to the different criteria that can be assessed to reach a conclusion. As this area of law generally does not provide clear precedents that can be applied in a straightforward or direct way, each case turns on its individual merits which must therefore be properly examined before any final determination.

11-2   Before attempting the following questions, please ensure familiarity with the following:

✓	the distinction between realty and personalty;
✓	the common law of fixtures, together with legislative modifications of the common law;
✓	*ANZ Building Group (NZ) Ltd v Haines House Haulage Co Ltd* (1993) 2 NZ ConvC 191;
✓	*Australian Provincial Assurance Co Ltd v Coroneo* (1938) 38 SR (NSW) 700;
✓	*Belgrave Nominees Pty Ltd v Barlin-Scott Airconditioning (Aust) Pty Ltd* [1984] VR 947;
✓	*Brand v Chris Building Society Pty Ltd* [1957] VR 625;
✓	*Farley v Hawkins* [1997] 2 Qd R 361;
✓	*Grigor v International Harvester* [1942] St R Qld 238;

✓ *Hobson v Gorringe* [1897] 1 Ch 182;

✓ *Holland v Hodgson* (1872) LR 7 CP 328;

✓ *Johnston v International Harvester* [1925] NZLR 529;

✓ *Leigh v Taylor* [1902] AC 157;

✓ *McMahon's (Transport) Pty Ltd v Ebbage* [1995] 1 Qd R 185;

✓ *National Provincial Bank v Ainsworth* [1965] AC 1175;

✓ *Norton v Dashwood* [1896] 2 Ch 497;

✓ *Palumberi v Palumberi* (1986) NSW ConvR 55-287;

✓ *Reid v Smith* (1905) 3 CLR 656;

✓ *Standard Portland Cement Co Pty Ltd v Good* (1982) 47 ALR 107;

✓ *Vesco Nominees Pty Ltd v Stefan Hair Fashions Pty Ltd* [2001] Q ConvR 54-555;

✓ *Vopak Terminal Darwin Pty Ltd v Natural Fuels Darwin Pty Ltd* [2009] FCA 742.

Question 1

11-3 Tom and Katie Jones decide to buy David Malloy's mansion in Sydney. David is a famous football player, and the mansion is a scaled-down replica of the Sydney Opera House. The contract contains the standard clause: 'All fixtures included as seen on inspection'. The replica Opera House roof sails of the main building have been designed as water slides, leading into a pool on the lower section of the main building. The pool has tiled pictures of David on the floor of the pool and on the tiles around the pool. The back garden is a football pitch, the goalposts at one end have been signed by all of David's Sydney football team mates, and the other goalposts are signed by his old Brisbane team mates. There is a modern 10-foot-high freestanding bronze statue of Victoria Malloy, David's wife, in the mansion's garden. A fountain cemented into the ground in the front garden has water leaping through a series of goalposts. Each bedroom in the house is themed around a famous soccer player with a tapestry of the player nailed to the wall with special tapestry nails, and themed curtains and quilt sets enhancing the theme for each room. All the door handles in the house are shaped and painted like soccer balls and all the door frames are made from goalposts.

None of these items is specifically mentioned in the contract. Tom and Katie have just adopted a young Brazilian boy who is hailed as a future soccer star, and they chose the house specifically to make Pedro feel more part of the family.

The gardener, Joseph, lives in a cottage on the grounds. Joseph is entitled to take limes and oranges for his own use as one of the perks of his job.

Katie inspected the house the day before settlement and found the statue, fountain and all the tapestries and soft furnishings from the bedrooms had been removed. She also discovered the following missing items:

Door handles and door frames: All the soccer door handles and goalpost door frames had been replaced with normal wooden ones.

Goal posts: The goal posts had been dug up and new turf laid in their place.

Limes in the orchard: Katie found all the oranges still in place on the trees but no limes. When she went to inspect the gardener's cottage she found a little shed piled high with limes and a schedule on the door listing deliveries of limes to all the local bars and pubs.

Are Tom and Katie entitled to any of the missing items?

Time allowed: 45 mins

 ## Answer Plan

11-4 This is a problem fixtures question which requires students to sift through the information and identify which of the missing items is a chattel and which has become a fixture. Students should:

- identify each missing item;
- apply the fixture tests to each separately;
- reach a conclusion;
- identify the remedy available.

 ## Answer

11-5 Tom and Katie (as the land purchasers) would be entitled to any missing items that are expressly conferred by the contract (*Standard Portland Cement Co Pty Ltd v Good* (1982) 47 ALR 107), or have become fixtures (*Holland v Hodgson* (1872) LR 7 CP 328).

Since the contract is silent on the items, the common law doctrine of fixtures is applicable. To determine whether an item is a fixture one must apply the fixture tests from *Holland v Hodgson* (1872) LR 7 CP 328 and *Hobson v Gorringe* [1897] 1 Ch 182 to each item in turn.

Holland v Hodgson is a prima facie test determining the degree and purpose of annexation, while *Hobson v Gorringe* looks to the intention of the fixer at the time of fixing, and allows consideration of various factors.

Statue: This item is free-standing. Under *Holland v Hodgson* the item is not attached by more than its own weight so it is prima facie a chattel. This places the onus of rebuttal on the fixture advocates, Tom and Katie. Under *Hobson v Gorringe* the fact that the item is not fixed does not necessarily point to the fixer's intention, as a 10-foot bronze statue is unlikely to need any fixing. The item is easy to remove and unlikely to leave much damage other than a crushed area in the grass: *Farley v Hawkins* [1997] 2 Qd R 361. Tom and Katie could use the 'part of the scheme of decoration' argument which was successfully raised in *Norton v Dashwood* [1896] 2 Ch 497 and *Leigh v Taylor* [1902] AC 157. Contrasted with that must be the personal nature of the item: it is a statue of David's wife, and therefore it is unlikely the original affixer (probably either David or Victoria) ever intended it to be left behind as a fixture. Ultimately this item is probably a chattel. Tom and Katie have no remedy to demand the statue's return, but David and Victoria have a duty to make good any damage left behind upon removal of the statue.

Fountain: This is cemented into the ground therefore definitely attached by more than its own weight and thus prima facie a fixture under *Holland v Hodgson*. As regards the intention of the fixer at the time of fixing under *Hobson v Gorringe*, this item will be difficult to remove and will cause a great deal of damage (*Hawkins v Farley*), and it could be said it is also integral to the theme: *Leigh v Taylor*. Both tests conclude this item is most likely a fixture, and Tom and Katie would be entitled to it. Their best remedy would be specific performance, forcing David and Victoria to return and reinstall the fountain.

Soft furnishings: A fixture is an item, once a chattel, which has become, in law, a fixture through having been attached to and become part of the land: *National Provincial Bank v Ainsworth* [1965] AC 1175. It is unlikely these items could ever be regarded as anything other than personal chattels as they have never become fixed in any way, temporarily or permanently.

Tapestries: Under *Holland v Hodgson* the tapestries are prima facie fixtures, as they are attached by tapestry nails. There are competing judgments to bring to bear here under the *Hobson v Gorringe* test.

Under *Leigh v Taylor* they could be determined chattels because they are removable without substantial damage as they were put up with tapestry nails designed to minimise damage. Further, the only way to effectively display tapestries as chattels is to put them up with some kind of fixing, therefore the nailing is more likely to reflect the nature of the item than the intention of the fixer. Alternatively, under *Norton v Dashwood* they may well be determined fixtures because they are difficult to remove without some disfiguring of the wall, as the nails will leave holes requiring repair, and they are an integral part of the decor and theme of each room; comparatively, the tapestries would be of little use or value as individual chattels. This is a discussion that could go either way, but if they are determined to be fixtures, Victoria and David would have to return and replace them, probably under a specific performance order, whereas if they are determined chattels, Tom and Katie would have no recourse.

Door handles and door frames: Under *Holland v Hodgson* these items are attached by more than their own weight and therefore are prima facie fixtures. Under *Hobson v Gorringe* the door handles are clearly easily removable whilst the door frames are an integral part of the house's structure. However, both need to be attached to function which does not help determine the fixer's intention. Regardless, one could always fall back on the argument that both items are integral to the theme of the house: *Norton v Dashwood*. The door frames are likely to be determined as fixtures as being almost structural, but the door handles could go either way.

Goalposts: These items are attached by more than their own weight and are there to better enjoy the land and not the goalposts themselves; therefore, they are prima facie fixtures: *Holland v Hodgson*. Given their personal value (the signatures), it could be argued the fixer always intended them to be temporary. They do have to be attached in order to be used and they do not leave that much damage behind after removal (*Hobson v Gorringe*), but they are also clearly part of the decor and theme: *Norton v Dashwood*. These could also go either way.

Limes: The limes that should have been on the trees would have been viewed as part of the land when in situ, not fixtures, and thus included automatically in the sale. Any limes taken off the tree to which Joseph was entitled would have become chattels once removed from the tree, and Tom and Katie would not have been entitled to them anyway. The gardener is entitled to take limes for his own use, either under a *profit a prendre* agreement linked to residency in the cottage, or as part of his employment contract — how he is entitled to this right is not clear in the question. The issue is whether the right to take for his own use includes all the limes, and whether that entitles him then to sell them and make money. For his own use clearly does not intend for him to take them all and sell them. However, once removed from the tree they became chattels and Tom and Katie are unlikely to want all the loose limes returned. This would be better addressed as a damages claim as the gardener would be in breach of his entitlement.

Tom and Katie's remedies: Specific performance to demand the return and restoration of the items which have become fixtures, or to repair any damage caused by removal of chattels and damages.

Damages for the lost limes.

Examiner's Comments

11-6 To answer this question students should: develop a systematic and structured approach to fixtures without skipping any steps; use the same cases to argue both sides — 'fixture arguments' and 'chattel arguments'; use the same facts to argue both sides. Students should appreciate that there are no clear-cut answers as none of the existing authorities can be conclusive.

Students should cite *Holland v Hodgson* for the initial prima facie tests, that is degree and purpose of annexation, and *Hobson v Gorringe* for the second test, which should consider factors such as ease of removal; damage caused by removal; and reasons why the item may/may not have been fixed aside from the fixer's intentions. Students must be clear the test is an objective person's view of the fixer's intention at the time of fixing, not the actual intention of the fixer. Other factors such as ease of removal, damage caused by removal, and other reasons for the method of fixing can be brought to bear to determine the fixer's intention, as can other cases such as *Norton v Dashwood*.

This answer is fairly thorough and systematically addresses all the arguments for each item. Many of the issues are grey and it is important both perspectives are discussed for each item. There are still opportunities here where chattel and fixture advocate arguments could have been taken further. It is important to do as this answer has, and address each test in full for each item. Overall this sample answer is a good example of how to address the various tests for a doctrine of fixtures question.

Keep in Mind

11-7 Students should keep in mind the following:

- Do not be tempted to lump tests or items together. Each item should have both tests applied in detail, separately. Lumping items or tests together is likely to cause you to miss steps or opportunities to apply cases.
- Try and keep a simple, clear structure to your answer. Item by item with each test applied is easiest. Otherwise there is the danger of losing track of issues and getting lost in argument.
- There is nothing wrong with saying, openly and honestly, that the law is confused or that authorities appear to conflict. They do. If students can justify their opinions or correctly point out the inconsistencies, they can make it clear a decisive conclusion is not always possible in these matters, as is frequently the case.

Question 2

11-8 What issues can you identify in the doctrine of fixtures?

Time allowed: 45 mins

Answer Plan

11-9 This question calls for a broad-based and comparatively free-ranging assessment of the doctrine of fixtures. It requires some definition of the doctrine of fixtures accompanied by an explanation of the historical roots of the doctrine, and should examine the inconsistencies created by how it has been applied and an analysis of how useful the doctrine is in practice. The historical analysis needs to be contextualised with reference to the effect of relevant social and economic influences upon judicial decisions. Some consideration should also be devoted to relevant legislative intervention, especially in relation to tenants' fixtures.

Issues which invite discussion, and cases which (may) exemplify some of these issues, include:

- the 'facts and circumstances' of individual cases may often be determinative of a judicial outcome: *Hobson v Gorringe* [1897] 1 Ch 182;
- the treatment of houses as part of the freehold: *Brand v Chris Building Society Pty Ltd* [1957] VR 625 and *Reid v Smith* (1905) 3 CLR 656;
- the annexation principle: *Holland v Hodgson* (1872) LR 7 CP 328;
- the purpose of annexation: *Hobson v Gorringe* [1897] 1 Ch 182; *Love v Bloomfield* [1906] VLR 723; and *Geelong City Building Co v Bennett* [1928] VLR 214;
- the anomalies which appear to disrupt the smooth application of theories to facts: *Johnston v International Harvester* [1925] NZLR 529; *Grigor v International Harvester* [1942] St R Qld 238;
- the Australian position: *Australian Provincial Assurance Co Ltd v Coroneo* (1938) 38 SR (NSW) 700; and *Reid v Smith* (1905) 3 CLR 656.

A reasonable conclusion could be that the doctrine of fixtures is outdated, and that decisions based upon an application of the doctrine often appear to be subjective. The decisions frequently seem to turn upon facts and circumstances individual to each case, rather than providing broad principle for application later. Perhaps legislative intervention reflects the weaknesses of the doctrine.

Answer

11-10 The doctrine of fixtures has long been established in common law. The basic premise of a permanent fixture is that an object which is affixed to the soil becomes part of the soil. The conceptual origin of 'fixtures' has its roots in agrarian society, but has been shaped over time by social and economic factors as well as changing fashions and habits, which have been recognised by the common law courts: *Leigh v Taylor* [1902] AC 157. However, legislatures have felt the necessity to clarify and drastically alter the conclusions arrived at by courts. There can be some exceptions as to what is considered as a fixture, as was held in *Hobson v Gorringe* [1897] 1 Ch 182. The *Hobson v Gorringe* principle of exception anchors the doctrine as one decided on the 'facts and circumstances' of individual cases, with the rules applied in an objective fashion. To properly understand the doctrine it is necessary to follow its development. The origins of the doctrine are lost in late feudal times, but it appears that rules about what constituted land arose at a time when land tenure was held in relatively few hands, and therefore it may be possible to link the rise of legal rules about fixtures with the long struggle for tenants' rights.

It is probably true to say the doctrine's original underpinning was a judgment to determine the extent of the fixing of a chattel according to the 'degree of annexation'. Social and economic changes during the Industrial Revolution, including the increased mobility of business and trade ventures, the growth of leases for business purposes and the growth of new forms of finance for large-scale commercial chattels, were new social facts which could not be ignored by the courts. The days when something so large that it sank into the soil could be assumed to have been intended to remain there, passed with the advent of industrial machinery and fluid business arrangements. These changes in physical realities led to the realisation that the 'purpose of annexation' was critically important: *Palumberi v Palumberi* (1986) NSW ConvR 55-287. In *Holland v Hodgson* (1872) LR 7 CP 328, the court noted that an anchor holding down a ship is still a chattel, whereas that part of the cable of a suspension bridge which 'anchors' the bridge to the bank becomes part of the soil.

Dwelling houses have generally been treated by the courts as ceasing to be chattels and becoming part of the freehold (eg, *Brand v Chris Building Society Pty Ltd* [1957] VR 625), even when they are not truly 'fixed' to the soil. In *Reid v Smith* [1905] 3 CLR 656, a weatherboard house sat on piers, separated from the piers by white ant guards. Griffith CJ, in *Reid v Smith*, did point out that in some cases a house may remain a chattel, for example, in temporary mining leases, and that the court's determination may in fact depend on the 'purpose' of annexation, objectively assessed. This point was recently re-examined by the House of Lords (*Elitestone v Morris* [1997] 2 All ER 513) where the *Reid v Smith* approach was approved. In *ANZ Building Group (NZ) Ltd v Haines House Haulage Co Ltd* (1993) 2 NZ ConvC 191, the New Zealand courts recognised a relocatable house as a chattel when the owner removed it prior to the mortgagor taking possession.

The purpose of annexation has been held by courts to be an objective test, and not necessarily assessed according to written documentation (if any). For example, in *Hobson v Gorringe* [1897] 1 Ch 182, it was asserted that a 'hire and purchase' document was not good proof of an intention that the machinery should remain a chattel. In so doing, the court decided that the machines bolted to concrete blocks (and probably detachable without damage to the freehold) were part of the freehold and therefore available to the mortgagee in possession. Similarly, in *Love v Bloomfield* [1906] VLR 723, the machinery, much of which was sunk into the ground, and the remainder attached to a shed which was also sunken into the ground, was held to be 'affixed'. The court in *Geelong City Building Co v Bennett* [1928] VLR 214, likewise, felt that the existence of a lease referring to a cafe's fittings as fixtures was not sufficient evidence of an intention to affix, and looked elsewhere to decide that the fittings were not chattels, and therefore not available to the liquidator of the cafe. This approach can lead to apparent anomalies.

In *Johnston v International Harvester* [1925] NZLR 529, farm dairy machinery was held to be a chattel, being merely attached to the floor of the farm shed 'for better enjoyment of the chattel'. In contrast, in *Grigor v International Harvester* [1942] St R Qld 238, the milking machinery, bolted and attached in the milking shed, was held to be a 'fixture', for the better enjoyment of the freehold.

A key case in Australia was *Australian Provincial Assurance Co Ltd v Coroneo* (1938) 38 SR (NSW) 700, where a decision had to be made about various items in a movie theatre. Sir Frederick Jordan applied both 'tests': the 'degree of annexation' test and the 'purpose of annexation' test. The degree test was mainly used in order to establish the onus of proof. Thus, if a chattel is affixed to the freehold, however slightly, the rebuttable presumption is that it is a fixture and the onus rests on the chattel advocate (those asserting it is not a fixture), to prove it. Similarly, if a chattel is resting on its own weight, the rebuttable presumption is that it remains a chattel and the onus rests on the party asserting it is not, the fixture advocate. Generally, the greater the degree of annexation, the greater the presumption that it is a fixture. However, this conclusion is tested further in light of the 'purpose of annexation' test. For example, very heavy printing machinery bolted into concrete supports in a basement has been held to be a chattel (*Attorney-General (Cth) v RT Co Pty Ltd (No 2)* (1957) 97 CLR 146), and easily removable air-conditioners on the roof of an office building have been held to be part of the freehold, air-conditioning being an essential element for 'enjoyment' of modern office buildings and thus placed there for the enjoyment of the building, and not the air-conditioning unit: *Belgrave Nominees Pty Ltd v Barlin-Scott Airconditioning (Aust) Pty Ltd* [1984] VR 947. The key determinant is generally whether the item can be concluded to be fixed to better enjoy it, or the land. An air-conditioner may be essential in Australia, not necessarily in London. This reflects a certain degree of flexibility in the *Coroneo* rules, and additionally, a judicial recognition of the effect of changing fashions and tastes.

Nonetheless, legislative intervention has necessarily reflected modern needs and trends. For example, the overturning of the old common law presumption that agricultural machinery of tenants became part of the freehold has revealed legislative acceptance of the increasingly commercial nature of farming in more modern times. While judges in the nineteenth century realised tenants would never improve their property if they were to be automatically deprived of the improvements on termination of the lease, somehow this approach never extended to agricultural leases. Residential tenancies, while providing for reversion of tenants' fixtures to landlords on termination, allow for fair compensation. The recent House of Lords decision in *Elitestone v Morris* canvasses the confusing situation of chattels, 'trade fixtures' and actual parts of the freehold, and suggests that this threefold division is desirable.

The doctrine of fixtures is undoubtedly archaic, reflecting the values of earlier eras and, in spite of the claimed 'objectivity' of its test, is very much subject to judicial whim. Based on 'facts and circumstances', a tenuous case could be made that the doctrine conforms to a conservation of resources approach, by discouraging the removal of 'things' so attached to the land they may damage the land or themselves. But this is a thin argument, based upon only one strand of the test — the least judicially used one at that. As such, the doctrine of fixtures probably could be linked with another ancient doctrine — that of 'waste' — as both are concerned with the rights and duties of landlords and tenants. Legislative intervention has probably reflected the innate weaknesses and conservatism of these doctrines.

 ## Examiner's Comments

11-11   This answer is quite thoughtful, and one of its strengths is that it attempts (with some considerable success) a fairly broad historical contextualisation of the doctrine of fixtures. The answer traverses many of the social factors, such as the doctrine's roots in an agrarian society, and the profound social changes over the last two centuries which have shaped the development of the law of fixtures. As an answer to an exam or tutorial problem it achieves just about the right level of analysis in these terms. Naturally, further and deeper research would be expected if this question was posed as the topic for a research-oriented essay. The answer is to be highly commended for its attempt to integrate these historical and sociological factors into more traditional forms of legal analysis, such as case analyses.

In terms of orthodox legal analysis, case studies and the like, it would have been pleasing to have seen a more critical approach (see 'Keep in Mind' below). The commentary concerning legislative interventions is not the strongest element of the answer — it lacks specificity and is apt to confuse the reader. Likewise, some of the concluding statements, particularly with regard to the aims or objectives of the doctrine of fixtures, are not really supported by reference to the preceding observations.

 ## Keep in Mind

11-12   Students should keep in mind the following:

- Do not shy away from the confused state of the case law itself. The doctrine of fixtures is legendary in property law for its inconsistencies. Do not always attempt to see order where, perhaps, there is none.

- However, do not let disorder in the object of your investigation flow into your own thinking about it. Make an extra effort to think clearly about it. The argument put in the sample answer above needs better construction in order to overcome the inherent disorder of the subject matter: that (after all) is one of the objectives of the question.

- There is nothing wrong with saying, openly and honestly, that the law is confused, if that is the view of the student and that view can be supported with reference to the cases.

Question 3

> **11-13**   Susan Sorrento sells her tenanted cottage to Graham Gage. The contract refers simply to the sale of 'Certificate of Title 5423 folio 271'. Nancy, the cottage tenant, was a friend of Susan's, and when she heard the cottage was sold she ended her lease, taking some items with her. Nancy had removed the washing machine and dryer which she had originally bought, and which were attached by the usual electrical and plumbing connections. Their removal did leave some unsightly scratches on the floor and wall. The fridge Nancy bought had been fitted into the kitchen cupboards during a refurbishment, slotting into an alcove behind a door with a wooden surface matching the other cupboards, and its internet connection was physically joined to the cottage's hardwired broadband network. In order to remove the fridge, Nancy had taken off the wooden door, which she left leaning against the cupboards, and she left the wiring hanging loose out the wall. The wires had short-circuited and shut down the whole cottage's network. The floor had not been tiled under the fridge either. Nancy had also taken a set of venetian blinds that she had asked Susan to put in instead of curtains, which were attached to the window frames with screws and metal clips.
>
> What is Graham Gage's entitlement to the missing items?
>
> **Time allowed: 45 mins**

Answer Plan

11-14   Introduce the answer by stating the general rules which apply to disputes about chattels and fixtures between vendors and purchasers and between landlords and tenants. Note:

- *Standard Portland Cement Co Pty Ltd v Good* (1982) 57 ALJR 151;
- *Australian Provincial Assurance Co Ltd v Coroneo* (1938) 38 SR (NSW) 700.

Apply the basic tests, and relevant presumptions, to each of the items in the question, and if an item is concluded to be a fixture, test whether the tenant's fixtures exception can apply. Bear in mind this exception does not apply if an item is concluded to be a chattel!

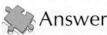 Answer

11-15 It is customary for parties to a contract for the sale of land to expressly agree on what items are to be included as 'fixtures'. The standard form contract for the sale of land permits the parties to specify particular items as 'included' in the property, and therefore part of the purchase. If a fixture is excepted by contract from a sale of land, it remains the property of the vendor: *Standard Portland Cement Co Pty Ltd v Good* (1982) 57 ALJR 151. In the absence of an agreement such as this, whether the specified items are part of the property ('being Certificate of Title vol 5423 folio 271') must be determined by reference to the doctrine of fixtures.

The first step is to determine whether the missing items are chattels or fixtures, using the *Holland v Hodgson* and *Hobson v Gorringe* tests.

Washing machine and dryer: Nancy may remove these items if they remain chattels, or fall within the tenant's fixture exception. The degree of annexation test (*Holland v Hodgson*), which focuses upon the tangible connection of the washing machine and dryer, would appear to raise an evidentiary presumption that they are fixtures: *Australian Provincial Assurance Co Ltd v Coroneo* (1938) 38 SR (NSW) 700. This would be the prima facie presumption, rebuttable by the chattel advocate.

In order to rebut this presumption, Nancy must show that the washing machine and dryer were not affixed with the intention of enjoying the premises but were instead affixed for the better enjoyment of the items themselves, as chattels. Once again, the nature of the premises and their typical use could be highly relevant to the court's assessment of the intention of the fixer at the time of fixing. Were it the case that the premises were an ordinary dwelling house, then it might be inferred that the washing machine and dryer were affixed with the intention of equipping the house with the usual facilities of a residential dwelling, in other words, that the affixation was done with the intention of better enjoying the property as a dwelling (rather than enjoying the items as chattels). If this is the case, then Nancy is obliged to return and reconnect the washing machine and dryer. On the other hand, it could also be considered that the electrical and plumbing connections are merely connections that make the items usable, and not fixings as such, which would make the items chattels. If this is the case, Nancy is under no obligation to return them.

If the items are determined to be chattels, then the rules concerning tenants' fixtures are not applicable. However, if they are deemed fixtures and if Nancy is confirmed as the purchaser and supplier of the items, and if she attached them, then they will be removable as tenant's fixtures (either under the common law or under one of the statutory regimes), and Nancy is under no duty to reinstate them.

Fridge: This is likely to remain a fixture due to its difficulty of removal and strong attachment to the specifically designed wall unit (akin to *Hawkins v Farley*, where the dishwasher was built-in to match the kitchen benches and cupboards and left a great deal of damage when removed). Again, the onus is on Nancy to rebut the fixtures presumption by raising 'chattel arguments', especially the limited (or non-permanent) duration of attachment, as Nancy is a tenant rather than landowner.

The issues focus on the degree of annexation and the ease of removal: it is heavy and has left considerable damage.

Fixture arguments:

- A fridge is generally considered essential for modern household living, particularly in Australia's temperatures: this is an argument of necessity, akin to that raised about the air-conditioner in *Belgrave Nominees*. A tenant must have one, so the mere installation of the fridge does not make it a fixture.
- The dishwasher in *Hawkins v Farley* was held to be a fixture because the plumbing connections showed strong affixation; it was not easily removable without damage; the kitchen benches and cupboards were constructed to incorporate the dishwasher which was 'intended as an integrated whole'; the area of floor on which the dishwasher stood was untiled; the removal left 'a glaring and unsightly gap in the kitchen'.

It seems there are similar albeit weaker fixture arguments here and Nancy would have to rely on the tenants' fixtures exception, specifically that she bought it, installed it and it is an item for domestic use. Given the tendency of the fixtures doctrine to be so circumstance-specific, it is an open question as to whether she would win.

If Nancy can't rebut the fixture presumption with chattels arguments for any of these items, then she may raise the tenant's fixture exception to justify her removal of the washing machine, dryer and fridge.

Tenants' fixtures

Under *Vopak Terminal Darwin Pty Ltd v Natural Fuels Darwin Pty Ltd*, tenants' fixtures are subject to the tenants' right to remove them during the term of the lease, or within a reasonable time thereafter, and so convert them back into chattels as long as:

- the item was attached for 'trade, domestic or ornamental purposes' (*Holland v Hodgson*) on a tenant's behalf and at the tenant's cost (*Vesco Nominees Pty Ltd v Stefan Hair Fashions Pty Ltd*); and
- the item is removable without causing substantial damage, or the tenant has repaired any damage caused; and

- the tenant has exercised the right of removal during the tenancy or within a reasonable time after expiry of tenancy (*McMahon's (Transport Pty Ltd v Ebbage)*.

The exception is likely to apply in Nancy's favour as she installed the washing machine, dryer and fridge at her own cost and for domestic purposes (*Holland v Hodgson; Vesco Nominees v Stefan Hair Fashions*). She may show that the washing machine and dryer were not intended to be permanent additions to the cottage. The only difficulty with the fridge is that she worked with the landlord to have the fridge built into and incorporated into the design of the refurbished kitchen, which could argue against her intending it to remain a temporary addition to the cottage.

It should also be noted Nancy removed these items upon her ending of the lease and presumably without causing any really substantial damage (*McMahon's Transport v Ebbage*), although she will clearly have to make good the scratches on the wall and floor, and may even have to tile the area covered by the fridge.

Venetian blinds attached to the window frames with screws and metal clips: The degree of annexation test, which focuses upon the physical attachment of the blinds, would appear to raise an evidentiary presumption that the venetians are fixtures: *APA v Coroneo* (1938) 38 SR (NSW) 700. In order to rebut this presumption, Nancy must show that the blinds were not affixed with the intention of enjoying the premises per se, but were merely affixed for the better enjoyment of the venetian blinds as chattels. Perhaps if it could be shown by Nancy that the blinds had some special quality (like the oak panelling in *Spyer v Phillipson* [1931] 2 Ch 183), a quality indicating that they were attached for the better enjoyment of the items as blinds, then it might be held that they were not attached for the enjoyment of the premises. However, in the absence of any such particular circumstances, it appears that the venetians were attached with the ordinary intentions of shading sunlight and providing privacy, and thus were attached for the better enjoyment of the property. Accordingly, they are likely to be held to be fixtures and the purchaser may demand their return.

Prima facie, if the venetians were installed by Nancy, and if it can be established that they were fitted for bona fide trade, ornamental or domestic purposes, then at common law she may remove and retain them. However, these blinds were paid for and installed by the landlord, Susan, so the fixture presumption will stand.

It should be noted that statute has modified the tenants' fixture rule in numerous specific areas. For example, in relation to agricultural fixtures and in relation to fixtures under retail leases there are detailed legislative provisions. If the tenancy is one to which residential tenancies legislation applies, there may be further (statutory) rules to consider. In New South Wales, s 67 of the Residential Tenancies Act 1987 (NSW) provides for a right for the tenant to remove his or her validly affixed fixtures. This must be done with the consent of the landlord, but if that consent is unreasonably withheld, the tenant may claim compensation from the landlord. In Victoria, under s 64 of the Residential Tenancies Act 1980 (Vic), the tenant is *obliged* to remove all his or her fixtures and restore the residential premises to the condition it was in prior to affixation, or otherwise compensate the landlord. As such, it is highly relevant that it can be determined who attached the items, what the nature of the tenancy was (ie whether it is to the common law or some statute one must look), and under what jurisdiction the tenancy was. For example, if the fridge was attached by Nancy, and if the tenancy was a residential tenancy in New South Wales (and if she obtained the consent of the landlord), then she may remove and keep the fridge. In contrast, as the blinds were installed by the landlord, they are not tenants' fixtures, and the rules of tenants' fixtures are irrelevant.

Examiner's Comments

11-16 The sample answer adopts a direct and commonsense approach to tackle the problem. Where an answer is in several parts, and especially where it is necessary to explore both alternative views, an almost bullet- point approach, although it can be repetitive, is often appropriate and the safest way for a student to ensure they do not miss any points.

The question does not call for a detailed dissection of the doctrine of fixtures: it calls for a practical answer about the disputed items. Some further reference to other classic cases such as *Holland v Hodgson* (1872) LR 7 CP 328 and *Hobson v Gorringe* [1897] 1 Ch 182, may have given a more polished result, but generally most of the relevant ground was covered here.

Also, in relation to parties to contracts for the sale of land excepting specified fixtures from the sale, while it was correct to cite *Standard Portland Cement Co Pty Ltd v Good* (1982) 57 ALJR 151, the answer left this case without thorough explanation. One might be induced to conclude that it is the intention of the parties which is determinative of the identification of what is a fixture. This would be contrary to what is expressed in cases such as *Melluish v BMI (No 3) Ltd* [1996] AC 454. It should have been made clearer that what *Standard Portland Cement Co Pty Ltd v Good* stands for is that the parties may agree that a vendor may remove what — according to the doctrine of fixtures — is the property of the purchaser.

On the question of venetian blinds as tenants' fixtures there has been a judgment of the Full Court of the Supreme Court of South Australia which may be worth considering: *Wincat Pty Ltd v South Australia* [1997] SASC 6287.

The sample answer lacks a concluding paragraph. This may not be critical, especially in a problem such as this which requires a comparatively routine application of the law, but it is always good to summarise the position reached as a conclusion. In excluding a concluding paragraph, the answer also fails to provide remedies, a common occurrence when conclusions are missed.

Keep in Mind

11-17   Students should keep in mind the following:

- Do not launch straight into a discussion of the 'object of annexation' test. Even if only briefly, establish the results of the 'degree of annexation' test, and state the guiding presumption (who is likely to bear the onus of proving or disproving that the item is or is not a fixture). From this point, discuss how this onus may be borne with reference to the more sophisticated 'object' test: see *Palumberi v Palumberi* [1986] ANZ Conv R 592.
- Do not rely too heavily on one case for a basic proposition. If the matter is 'well settled' it should be possible to cite a number of instances where the courts have adopted the same position.
- Nothing affixed to the property at the commencement of a lease becomes a tenant's fixture simply by virtue of the fact that the property is now leased. A tenant's fixture is something affixed by the present tenant which, while it becomes part of the freehold during the currency of the lease, may be lawfully severed by its fixer when his or her lease expires.
- Never forget that many forms of tenancies are now heavily regulated by statute. See the Agricultural Tenancies Act 1990 (NSW); Retail Leases Act 1994 (NSW); Residential Tenancies Act 1987 (NSW); Landlord and Tenant Act 1958 (Vic); Residential Tenancies Act 1980 (Vic); Residential Tenancies and Rooming Accommodation Act 2008 (Qld) and so on. Always check to see whether specific legislation provides rules which override the common law.
- Do not forget conclusions and remedies. Regardless of how straightforward a question seems, a conclusion should always be used to neatly summarise the items in dispute, the conclusion reached, and the remedies available to enforce those conclusions. Students who leave out conclusions are likely to fall into the trap of forgetting remedies, as occurred here.

Question 4

11-18   Mrs May Cork lives in an old Queenslander cottage. When she moved in, in the early 1960s, the whole area was a remote backwater. Since then, with the effects of urban sprawl and improved highways, the area has become desirable as a commuter suburb. Land in the area has skyrocketed in value in recent years, and a number of residential zones have been developed.

The cottage, of substantial weight, is constructed from galvanised iron and rests on top of concrete piers. It is not otherwise attached to the piers or to the ground. The cottage has stood in its present position since 1942, and while it was originally designed as a 'demountable', it is unlikely that it could be moved now without falling apart.

Farrar Developments Pty Ltd has recently purchased the freehold of the land upon which Mrs Cork's cottage stands. The company has also acquired most of the land in the surrounding area for the purposes of constructing and selling a new housing estate. Mrs Cork has a 60-year lease of her land, entered into in 1965, by the terms of which Farrar Developments Pty Ltd are obliged to abide. However, in the lease, which she didn't read very carefully, Mrs Cork acknowledged:

> The cottage presently on the lot is a chattel, and may be removed by the owner or his assigns at will.

Farrar Developments Pty Ltd wishes to remove the cottage, because they say that it detracts from the 'look' of the overall development plans for the entire area. Mrs Cork argues that the cottage has become part of the land, that is a fixture, and that her lease of the land gives her the right to retain and use any and all fixtures, including the cottage.

Advise Mrs Cork.

Time allowed: 45 mins

Answer Plan

11-19   The answer should be set out as follows:

* Introduction

   The question posits facts which are similar to the facts of both *Reid v Smith* (1905) 3 CLR 656 and *Elitestone Ltd v Morris* [1997] 2 All ER 513. Give a brief summary of the area of the law (fixtures). Concentrate upon the 'purpose of annexation' test, with reference to the issue of the adverse term in the lease. Proceed to a consideration of the two principal authorities.

* The standard tests and presumptions of the doctrine of fixtures:
   * the 'degree of annexation' test;
   * the 'purpose of annexation' test;
   * *Holland v Hodgson* (1872) LR 7 CPP 328; *Belgrave Nominees Pty Ltd v Barlin-Scott Airconditioning (Aust) Pty Ltd* [1984] VR 947; *Melluish v BMI (No 3) Ltd* [1996] AC 454; *Australian Provincial Assurance Co Ltd v Coroneo* (1938) 38 SR (NSW) 700.

- Two authorities dealing specifically with this type of situation:
  - ◆ *Reid v Smith* (1905) 3 CLR 656;
  - ◆ *Elitestone Ltd v Morris* [1997] 2 All ER 513.
- Conclusion:

  Advise that the law of fixtures permits dwelling houses which are not designed to be mobile to be considered part of the land upon which they rest. The objective determination of the 'purpose of annexation' will, most likely, be that the cottage is a fixture. This finding may be made without reference to the lease.

Answer

11-20 Mrs Cork is advised that there is little chance that her cottage can be removed by Farrar Developments Pty Ltd. On the basis of a well-established legal rule, she may argue that her cottage is properly considered as forming part of the land, and thus is not available for removal as a chattel. Mrs Cork is also advised that there is a possibility (which, although unlikely, cannot be entirely discounted) that a court could hold that the cottage remains a chattel. The legal rules which relate to Mrs Cork's cottage are grouped together under the doctrine of fixtures, and it is this area of the law which will be initially considered below. From this point, Mrs Cork's case can be compared with two important decisions (*Reid v Smith* (1905) 3 CLR 656; *Elitestone Ltd v Morris* [1997] 2 All ER 513), and it will be shown that, on the basis of these cases, her legal position is strong.

A fixture is a chattel attached to land so as to become part of the land. The effect of the doctrine is to extinguish the chattel owner's legal title to the chattel. The landowner is consequently entitled to the fixture by virtue of his or her ownership of the land. The rules determining when a chattel becomes a fixture are simple to state, but difficult to apply. Generally, the standard tests used are the 'degree of annexation' test and the 'purpose of annexation' test. Presumptions are also relied upon in some circumstances.

The 'degree of annexation' may be determined by reference to the physical conditions of the chattel in its attachment to the land. Thus, a chattel may be a fixture if very securely attached and hard to remove (without causing damage to the land or the chattel). If a thing merely rests upon its own weight, then there is no 'annexation' and thus, under this test, it may be presumed that the thing remains a chattel. Mrs Cork's cottage would fail the 'degree of annexation' test; however, it has been held that this test may be reversed by reference to the 'purpose' or 'object' (of annexation) test.

The purpose for which a chattel has been attached to the land is regarded as the better test of fixation. Under this test, whether a chattel can be determined to be a fixture is usually ascertained by looking at whether the attachment is for the permanent and substantial improvement of the building, or merely for a temporary purpose and the more complete enjoyment of it as a chattel. Blackburn J, in *Holland v Hodgson* (1872) LR 7 CPP 328, said:

Thus blocks of stone placed one on the top of another without any mortar or cement for the purpose of forming a dry stone wall would become part of the land, though the same stones, if deposited in a builder's yard and for convenience sake stacked on the top of each other in the form of a wall, would remain chattels.

The relevant intention is that of the person fixing the chattel, at the time of the installation. Both of these matters are to be objectively ascertained, from the circumstances of the installation, without reference to external factors which might point to the actual fixer's intention at the time of affixation. In determining the purpose for which the chattel was attached, the courts take into account such factors as the nature of the chattel and the relationship of the parties. Thus in *Belgrave Nominees Pty Ltd v Barlin-Scott Airconditioning (Aust) Pty Ltd* [1984] VR 947, Kaye J held that an air-conditioner standing on its own weight was a fixture. It had been installed on the roof of an office building in such a way that it stood on pads between its legs. This was to avoid substantial noise by vibrations. When installed, however, it formed an essential part of the building as modern office premises. Kaye J stated:

> The test ... is whether [the chattel] has been fixed with the intention that it shall remain in position permanently or for an indefinite or substantial period, or whether it has been fixed with the intent that it shall remain in position only for some temporary purpose. The intention of the person fixing it must be gathered from the purpose for which, and at the time during which, use in the fixed position is contemplated.

Written or verbal expressions of the purpose of the attachment between the fixer and another person are immaterial to this 'objective' assessment. This last point has been endorsed by the House of Lords in *Melluish v BMI (No 3) Ltd* [1996] AC 454. In that case, Lord Browne-Wilkinson held:

> The terms expressly or implicitly agreed between the fixer of the chattel and the owner of the land cannot affect the determination of the question whether, in law, the chattel has become a fixture and therefore in law belongs to the owner of the soil. The terms of such agreement will regulate the contractual rights to sever the chattel from the land as between the parties to that contract and, where an equitable right is conferred by the contract, as against certain third parties. But such agreement cannot prevent the chattel, once fixed, becoming in law part of the land and as such owned by the owner of the land so long as it remains fixed.

It is to be acknowledged that this test may be much easier to formulate in abstract terms than to apply, with consistency, to many cases. Three common guiding presumptions have been used by the courts to determine whether a chattel has become a fixture, such presumptions being rebuttable by evidence of intention to the contrary.

The first is that a chattel is presumed not to have become a fixture if it is resting by no more than its own weight on the land. The burden of proving otherwise is on the party who asserts to the contrary: the fixture advocate. On the other hand, where a chattel is attached to land, as for instance chattels buried in the soil or bolted to the ground, the presumption is that these have become fixtures. It matters not that the attachment is slight; it is sufficient to cast the burden on the party asserting to the contrary to prove that it is not a fixture. The third presumption is that, where a chattel has been so securely fixed to the land that it cannot be detached without substantial injury to either the thing itself or that to which it is attached, there is strong evidence that it was meant to be permanently fixed. It is this last presumption, drawn from *Australian Provincial Assurance Co Ltd v Coroneo* (1938) 38 SR (NSW) 700, which may place the onus of proof upon Mrs Cork.

There are two powerful authorities which will assist Mrs Cork in discharging this evidential burden. In *Reid v Smith* (1905) 3 CLR 656, the Supreme Court of Queensland held that an ordinary dwelling house, unattached to the land, remained a chattel. The High Court reversed this decision. The house in this case was made of wood, and rested by its own weight on brick piers. The house was not attached to the brick piers in any way. It was designed to be demountable, but was not, properly speaking, a 'mobile home'. It was separated from the piers by metal overlays, situated on top of the piers, to combat white ants. It was held that the absence of any attachment did not prevent the house forming part of the realty.

The approach of the High Court has been expressly endorsed by the House of Lords. In *Elitestone Ltd v Morris,* a bungalow resting on its own weight, in circumstances similar to both the situation in *Reid v Smith* and the instant case of Mrs Cork, was held to be affixed, and thus part of the land. In *Elitestone Ltd v Morris,* Lord Lloyd stated:

> The nature of the structure is such that it could not be taken down and re-erected elsewhere. It could only be removed by a process of demolition … If a structure can only be enjoyed in situ, and is such that it cannot be removed in whole or in sections to another site, there is at least a strong inference that the purpose of placing the structure on the original site was that it should form part of the realty at that site, and therefore cease to be a chattel.

Mrs Cork is advised that despite the fact that her cottage rests on its own weight (and is prima facie to be considered a chattel), that the law of fixtures permits dwelling houses which are not truly designed to be mobile, and which can only be moved by creating major structural damage, to be considered part of the land upon which they rest. The rule enunciated by the High Court of Australia in *Reid v Smith* (and recently adopted by the House of Lords in *Elitestone Ltd v Morris),* appears to cover Mrs Cork's cottage. It may be argued by Farrar Developments Pty Ltd that Mrs Cork has conceded, by the terms of her lease, that the cottage is a chattel. The company may argue that, accordingly, Mrs Cork is estopped from asserting that the cottage is a fixture. However, it is clear, on the basis of *Melluish v BMI*, that the objective determination of the 'purpose of annexation' will be made without reference to the written or oral representations of the parties concerned. Mrs Cork is advised to oppose any attempt on the part of Farrar Developments Pty Ltd to remove the cottage.

Examiner's Comments

11-21 On the question of written and oral representations, and their incapacity to be determinative of the resolution of the chattel/fixture dispute, some reference might have also been made to *Love v Bloomfield* [1906] VLR 723 where machinery, much of which was embedded into the ground, and the remainder annexed to a cottage which was also sunken into the ground, was held to be 'affixed'. On the whole, however, the discussion of this point is quite well accomplished.

There have been a number of cases with similar facts to those set forth in the hypothetical. The answer, quite correctly, refers to *Reid v Smith* and *Elitestone*. It appears that this type of situation is fairly common: see also *Webb v Frank Bevis Ltd* [1940] 1 All ER 247. One wonders whether there might be room for legislation on the matter, particularly in times when more and more people seem to reside permanently in dwellings which (to greater and lesser degrees) could be described as 'mobile' or 'demountable'. See the Residential Parks Act 1998 (NSW) for an attempt to come to terms with this trend. Reference could also be made to the persuasive ruling of *ANZ Co Pty Ltd v Haines House Haulage Co Ltd*, where a relocatable house was held to be a chattel when the owner removed the house prior to the mortgagor taking possession.

Keep in Mind

Students should keep in mind the following:

11-22 Be sparing and strategic with quotes from decided cases. In researched essays and the like it is common to see enormous slabs of quotations, and this often reveals more about a student's 'cut and paste' word-processing abilities than any understanding of the law. However, do not quote so selectively that the real sense of the decision is misrepresented. Advocates have a duty to the court not to distort the authorities upon which they rely.

Index

References are to paragraph numbers

Index